PRIVATE LAW AND INTELLIGENT MACHINES

This book analyses the extent to which the common law can accommodate the new issues arising from the AI revolution, and where legislation may instead be necessary.

In doing so, the book takes into account not only doctrinal principles but also conceptual and theoretical foundations of common law.

Over the next few decades, the use of AI in commercial and other transactions is likely to be one of the most disruptive influences ever to affect private law. Its impact will be wide and deep, affecting not simply the traditional areas of contract and tort but also agency, trusts, fiduciary relations and a great deal besides.

The common law is known to be extremely flexible, and to some extent rules can be organically stretched and manipulated to respond to disruption of this kind. However, there is equally no doubt that such organic development is not enough on its own, and will have to be supplemented by legislative alterations and at times serious changes of thinking.

The book therefore discusses how established legal doctrines and principles in private law need to be reconsidered in view of the increasing pervasiveness of intelligent machines capable of taking decisions.

The analysis contained in this book provides a key contribution to ongoing debates regarding potential law reform, not only in England and Wales but also in other common law jurisdictions.

Private Law and Intelligent Machines

Continuity and Reform

Barış Soyer
and
Andrew Tettenborn

•HART•
OXFORD • LONDON • NEW YORK • NEW DELHI • SYDNEY

HART PUBLISHING

Bloomsbury Publishing Plc

Kemp House, Chawley Park, Cumnor Hill, Oxford, OX2 9PH, UK

1385 Broadway, New York, NY 10018, USA

Bloomsbury Publishing Ireland Limited, 29 Earlsfort Terrace, Dublin 2, D02 AY28, Ireland

HART PUBLISHING, the Hart/Stag logo, BLOOMSBURY and the Diana logo are trademarks of Bloomsbury Publishing Plc

First published in Great Britain 2026

A catalogue record for this book is available from the British Library.

A catalogue record for this book is available from the Library of Congress.

Library of Congress Control Number: 2026936643

ISBN: HB: 978-1-50999-058-0
ePDF: 978-1-50999-056-6
ePub: 978-1-50999-057-3

Typeset by Compuscript Ltd, Shannon

For product safety related questions contact productsafety@bloomsbury.com

To find out more about our authors and books visit www.hartpublishing.co.uk. Here you will find extracts, author information, details of forthcoming events and the option to sign up for our newsletters.

This book is dedicated to the memory of Caroline Tettenborn (1959–2022), beloved wife of Andrew Tettenborn and dear friend of Barış Soyer

PREFACE

This book, in good academic tradition, builds on earlier work. Its origins lie in our experimental article, '*Artificial Intelligence and Civil Liability – Do We Need a New Regime?*', published in the *International Journal of Law and Information Technology* in 2022. There, we began to explore how far existing doctrines in tort law could accommodate new challenges arising from the use of intelligent systems. However, what started as an inquiry limited to tort quickly revealed an expansive set of questions about the wider capacity of the common law system as a whole to respond to the transformative pressures of AI. It became clear that what was at stake was not simply a series of discrete doctrinal problems, but a fundamental test of the adaptability of private law in an age of vastly increased autonomous decision-making.

Over the past few years, the pace and scope of AI's development have greatly exceeded expectations. Its integration into commercial life and everyday experience has been both rapid and profound. Even the humble Google search now has an AI mode that surprisingly often yields rather helpful results: meanwhile we see AI systems not only performing analytical and administrative tasks but increasingly exercising forms of judgement that once belonged exclusively to human agents. Our view is that these developments compel a reconsideration of foundational legal concepts – agency, intention, negligence, reliance, consent, and causation among them. They also force us to ask whether the common law's characteristic flexibility will continue to suffice, or whether the sheer novelty and pervasiveness of AI will demand more radical intervention through legislative design.

One need only look at the world around us to see how far-reaching the legal implications already are. In 2025, a new service known as Grapple Law was launched in the United Kingdom: an entirely AI-powered platform offering advice and representation in employment and insurance disputes. It operates without any human lawyers, providing users who pay a modest subscription fee with tailored legal letters, responses, and procedural guidance. Although not a regulated law firm, Grapple Law has rapidly gained attention for the quality and accessibility of its outputs, offering a glimpse of what AI-driven dispute resolution might look like in practice. For the first time, you can pursue an employment claim or an insurance grievance through an artificial agent capable of analysing the situation, drafting correspondence, and managing the procedural flow of a case – all without direct human involvement. This is not an isolated example. Financial institutions too increasingly rely as a matter of course on AI platforms (a straightforward example being Kensho) to analyse market data and news in real time to make or recommend trades autonomously. And the same goes for many other professionals, from doctors and surveyors to insurance brokers.

Such examples reveal both the promise and the challenge of the AI revolution. On the one hand, there is potential for extraordinary gains in efficiency and access to justice. On the other, there are profound questions about responsibility, trust, and regulation. If an AI system misstates a legal position, mishandles a claim, or otherwise makes a mistake, who bears liability – the developer, the platform operator, or the end user? Can a system that learns and evolves through interaction be meaningfully supervised under doctrines built around human agency? And if a dispute arises out of an AI-generated act, how should courts identify intention, negligence, or reliance when the 'actor' itself is non-human? Grapple Law may be only one instance among many, but it crystallises the issues this book seeks to address: whether, and how far, the common law can absorb these new realities without fundamental re-engineering.

As we developed this project, we had the privilege of presenting our ideas at numerous academic events, conferences, and workshops across different jurisdictions. The insights and questions raised by colleagues, practitioners, policymakers, and technologists have profoundly shaped our thinking. These discussions confirmed that the challenges posed by AI are not confined to any single field or jurisdiction: on the contrary, they cut across the boundaries of contract, tort, agency, and equity, and they demand comparative reflection among all common law systems. We are deeply grateful for the opportunities we have had to test and refine our arguments in these forums. The conversations that followed reinforced our conviction that any meaningful reform must engage not only with doctrinal detail but also with the conceptual architecture of the common law itself.

Hence, this book is not simply a discussion of doctrinal issues and how far they can be stretched to accommodate the AI revolution. We have taken into account the conceptual issues, and our primary aim has been to make recommendations that will work without disturbing the coherence of law, while nevertheless remaining practical and appropriate in a commercial setting.

The chapters that follow examine, from both doctrinal and theoretical perspectives, the extent to which traditional legal concepts can accommodate the realities of intelligent machines making autonomous decisions. We begin by identifying the conceptual tensions that arise when legal categories built for human actors are applied to non-human agents (Part I). From there, we analyse the doctrinal tools – contractual interpretation, tortious duty, fiduciary obligation, and the law of agency – that might be adapted or reinterpreted to meet these challenges (Part II). Throughout, we seek to balance two complementary instincts: the common law's capacity for incremental, organic development and the need for deliberate legislative intervention when that flexibility reaches its limits.

Our central argument is that, while the common law has historically demonstrated remarkable resilience and creativity in adapting to technological and social change, the advent of AI presents a disruption of an entirely different order. The speed, autonomy, and opacity of AI systems strain traditional doctrines in ways that cannot be resolved by analogy or incrementalism alone. Legislative frameworks will be required, but these must be informed by an appreciation of the common law's internal logic and values, lest reform inadvertently undermine the coherence of private law itself.

This book is therefore both an exploration and an invitation. It explores how the conceptual foundations of private law – culpability, consent, causation, and control – must evolve in light of intelligent automation. It invites readers, whether judges, practitioners, scholars, or policymakers, to reflect on what kind of legal order we wish to build as we enter this new era. We hope that the analysis offered here will contribute meaningfully to ongoing debates about law reform, not only in England and Wales but across all common law jurisdictions grappling with similar questions. The task before us is not simply to fit AI into existing categories, but to ask, with intellectual honesty and institutional imagination, what those categories themselves must become.

We have been working on several projects over the past two decades and have been immensely supported by our Law School. One of us was granted a research sabbatical to ensure the completion of this book. We are also indebted to all our colleagues at the Institute of International Shipping and Trade Law (Swansea University) for discussing various concepts with us in internal workshops and providing valuable feedback. Last but not least, we would like to express our gratitude to Hart Publishing, and especially Roberta Bassi and Verity Stuart, for their assistance and support throughout the publication process. Hart has published a number of prestigious works examining the impact of AI across different fields – including public law, intellectual property, and the rule of law – and we hope this book will complement that series by offering a critical analysis of AI's potential impact on private law.

The law is stated, as far as possible, as of October 2025. Where web sources are cited, these were accessed, unless the contrary is stated, in December 2025.

BS & AT
Swansea, October 2025

CONTENTS

TABLE OF CASES

TABLE OF LEGISLATION

UK Statutes

UK Secondary Legislation

EU Legislation (Including Retained Legislation)

Other Legislation

Australia

PART I

Identifying the Scope of the Work

1

Setting the Scene

I. Preliminary

This book is about intelligent machines. More specifically, we are concerned with machines equipped with artificial intelligence – devices which, for want of a better term, we will refer to in this book as artificial intelligence enabled machines (AIEMs).[1] Our aim in writing this work is to deal with the relationship between AIEMs and the law, especially private law.

Not being computer scientists, we do not aim to provide any substantial coverage of how AIEMs work. Instead, we take as given their distinguishing features and work forward from there. These distinguishing features, as will appear below, we see as consisting in their ability not only to process input data according to a fixed algorithm, but in addition to mimic human behaviour in the limited sense of being able to learn from experience and recursively refashion the way they deal with data or make decisions in the future.

AIEMs, while not human, are thus equipped with something that in some ways can resemble human intelligence. When they feature in the course of commerce or other interactions, this immediately has the potential to cause difficulties with existing legal rules. It is these difficulties, and what ought to be done about them, that form the subject of this book.

The primary focus of this book is, therefore, existing legal rules concerning private law and how they are likely to be affected by the use of intelligent machines by human and corporate actors. In particular, it is not concerned with deeper questions of 'law as code', and how far law as we traditionally know it can be replaced by some kind of normative, or even directly controlling machine code. Such matters raise their own complexities and speculations, and the reader is referred to works specifically on that subject.[2]

[1] Throughout this book we shall use these terms – ie intelligent machines and AIEMs – interchangeably.

[2] See eg R Brownsword, *Law 3.0: Rules, Regulation, and Technology* (Oxford, Routledge, 2020); M Hildebrandt, 'Law as Information in the Era of Data-Driven Agency' (2016) 79 *Modern Law Review* 1; and the more radical W Lucy, 'The Death of Law: Another Obituary' (2022) 18(1) *Cambridge Law Journal* 109.

II. Artificial Intelligence and Intelligent Machines – What Are They and How Do They Function?

A. AI Systems

There is no consensus on a standard definition of artificial intelligence (AI) systems, but a useful one, which we will use for our purposes, has been provided by the Organisation for Economic Cooperation and Development:[3]

> An AI system is a machine-based system that, for explicit or implicit objectives, infers, from the input it receives, how to generate outputs such as predictions, content, recommendations, or decisions that can influence physical or virtual environments. Different AI systems vary in their levels of autonomy and adaptiveness after deployment.[4]

Although the definition does not explicitly mention this, a vital point about such systems is that they are designed, at least to some extent, to think and act rationally in the same manner that human beings would. And of course, the computational power they possess means that that potentially they could, in certain ways, function even more efficiently than humans. It is, in fact, this attribute of such systems that makes them so attractive to businesses and governmental organisations.

Systems of this kind typically work by means of their ability to analyse large sets of data to which they are given access. Such datasets are commonly referred to as 'big data' and essentially take the form of 'structured' or 'unstructured' digital information. An AI system relies on algorithms capable of recognising patterns in this data and making and testing predictions against new data sets, a process known as 'machine learning' (ML). There are various machine learning methods that can be applied depending on the task that needs to be performed. For example, supervised learning is a method where the algorithm is provided with a new raw data set and a target and is expected under supervision to find the relationships between the feature set and the label set. Unsupervised learning is rather different, in the sense that the algorithm is provided with raw data, but no target is set, and the algorithm is expected to identify patterns in the data provided with no supervision. It is often used for clustering together related data and finding associations among features of it.[5]

[3] This is from an updated version of the *Explanatory Memorandum on the Updated OECD Definition of An AI System* (OECD Artificial Intelligence Papers, No 8, March 2024) 4.

[4] A similar definition has been provided by the Independent High Level Expert Group on Artificial Intelligence established by European Commission, *Ethics Guidelines for Trustworthy AI* (2019) 34: 'Artificial intelligence (AI) systems are software (and possibly also hardware) systems designed by humans that, given a complex goal, act in the physical or digital dimension by perceiving their environment through data acquisition, interpreting the collected structured or unstructured data, reasoning on the knowledge, or processing the information, derived from this data and deciding the best action(s) to take to achieve the given goal.'

[5] For more technical information on the subject, see MW Berry et al (eds), *Supervised and Unsupervised Learning for Data Science* (Cham, Springer, 2020).

Whichever method is adopted, the ultimate aim of any ML algorithm is to detect patterns in data and use the results to improve the algorithm automatically and without explicit further instructions from the original programmer. For the ML model to be able to achieve its goals, it is necessary to train it in a fashion that is appropriate to the task in hand. An AI program developer uses various methods in the process of such training. It is useful, even for lawyers, to have a basic understanding of some of the more widely used training methods. One such means, a neural network, is a method that teaches algorithms to process data in a way that is inspired by the human brain. It uses interconnected nodes or neurons in a layered structure that resembles the human brain and is very effective in analysing complex data.[6] Another method is 'random forest', which combines the output of multiple decision trees to reach a single result. It is usually developed using supervised learning and is well suited to decision problems (eg for clinical diagnosis).[7] Again, probabilistic graphical models offer a rich framework for encoding probability distributions over complex domains;[8] their use can be either supervised or unsupervised.[9]

B. Law and AI Systems

In the broadest sense, this book deals with a number of private law issues emerging from the use of AI systems deployed in various commercial settings. Such systems in business practice are commonly known as 'intelligent machines' or (as we refer them in this book) AIEMs. They are programmed to achieve certain goals (eg making investment or underwriting decisions, or diagnosing illnesses) by making sense of data as they perceive it and, on some occasions, to solve problems by making inferences and optimising possible outcomes. Put differently, such machines are designed to process natural language and data sets and reason in an automated fashion functioning appropriately and with foresight in the environment after processing the data available to them.

To mark the boundaries of our inquiry, we shall highlight the areas of business and other practice where such machines are deployed, as well as special

[6] For more technical information on such systems, see MA Nielsen, *Neural Networks and Deep Learning* (San Francisco, Determination Press, 2015). There are many variants of this method, for example, convolutional neural networks and deep natural networks. The former is a specialised type of deep learning algorithm mainly designed for tasks that necessitate object recognition, including image classification, detection, and segmentation. The latter is a type of artificial neural network with multiple layers between the input and output layers. These networks are inspired by the structure and function of the human brain, and they are used to solve a variety of problems in machine learning, including image recognition, natural language processing, and speech recognition.

[7] For more information on this method, see KR Gray et al, 'Random Forest-Based Similarity Measures for Multi-Modal Classification of Alzheimer's Disease' (2013) 65 *Neuro Image* 167.

[8] There are several types of probabilistic graphical models, including Bayesian networks and Markov networks.

[9] For more information, see D Lowd and A Rooshenas, 'Learning Markov Networks with Arithmetic Circuits' (2013) 21 *Artificial Intelligence & Statistics* 406.

characteristics they pose, in the following section. We then aim to clarify the scope of what we cover in this book, as well as what aspects of the debate emerging from the use of such machines in commercial practice will not be deliberated as part of this book.

III. Uses and Fundamental Characteristics of Intelligent Machines

A. Commercial and Professional Uses of Intelligent Machines

Intelligent machines are pervasive in our everyday lives, and most (if not all) organisations and businesses have utilised such machines as part of their day-to-day operations. It will be a useful starting point to remind readers of various functions that such machines are deployed to perform, especially in contemporary business practice.[10]

i. Role of Intelligent Machines in Increasing Productivity

Processes that require significant human labour can benefit from the use of intelligent machines by enabling organisations to operate faster, more accurately and more productively than any human could. Software agents (bots) can, for example, be trained to prioritise tasks, manage routine interactions with other colleagues (and other bots), and plan schedules.[11]

Again, the agricultural sector has recently started making use of intelligent machines on a large scale. Improvements in computer vision (eg 3D), kinematics for harvesting and weeding robots,[12] Internet of Things (IoT) augmentation (enabling real-time data coupled with eye-in-the-sky drones) and data changes are enabling optimisation of harvest quality and yields. For example, 3D scanning technology delivers precise insights into soil health, crop conditions and livestock welfare, helping farmers make data-driven decisions that optimise resources and boost yields.[13]

Health care is another sector that benefits immensely from the use of intelligent machines. Such machines are used to analyse the vast troves of data collected over

[10] This is not an exhaustive list. The aim here is to illustrate the wide-reaching use of intelligent machines in different sectors.

[11] For example, Google's Smart Reply has been developed to draft messages to respondents based on previous responses to similar messages.

[12] Real-Time Kinematics (RTK) is a specific technology that uses GNSS (Global Navigation Satellite System) data to achieve high-precision positioning.

[13] For more detailed analysis on the subject, see S Kaushal and S Kumar, 'Artificial Intelligence in Agriculture' (2023) *International Journal of Science and Research* 1682.

decades to uncover patterns and insights that humans are unable to find on their own. The data used often comes from a range of detections, eg wearables, medical scans and measurements, digital health records, patient monitoring systems, genome sequencing systems etc. Algorithms in diagnostic tools are helping clinicians to make more accurate diagnoses earlier in a disease's progression. Other intelligent machines are used to help clinicians to develop more individualised treatment plans designed for maximum efficiency.[14]

ii. Role of Intelligent Machines in Making Efficient Use of Resources

Possibly this is another area where intelligent machines could potentially yield significant gains for businesses. It is widely known that firms like Ocado and Amazon use intelligent machines to optimise their storage and distribution networks, plan the most efficient delivery schedules, and make best use of their warehousing capacity. Similarly, large retail companies use such devices to forecast what products will be needed and the optimal time to move supplies.

Intelligent machines also play a significant role in the financial sector. Financial institutions use such machines in wealth management, stock picking, loan approvals, and trading decisions.[15] Perhaps an even more common use of intelligent machines in the financial sector is as an aid to fraud detection. This involves analysing patterns in transactions to point out unusual cases, thus enabling humans or bots to investigate further where suspicions are raised. Similarly, in the insurance sector many underwriters are increasingly using machine learning with a focus on detecting suggestive anomalies when claims are submitted by assureds.[16]

iii. Role of Intelligent Machines in Developing or Expanding Lines of Business

Businesses are expanding the range of services they offer with the aid of intelligent machines. Notably they use such devices to understand actual and potential users and their buying patterns, so that they can create targeted marketing campaigns with a higher success rate. Some organisations are also combining AI technologies such as facial recognition and geospatial analytics to identify in-store customers and promote products and services that are likely to match their personal preferences.

[14] For more detailed illustrations on the subject, see J Bajwa et al, 'Artificial Intelligence in Healthcare: Transforming the Practice of Medicine' (2021) 8(2) *Future Healthcare Journal* 188.

[15] AI developments such as robo-advice have made it possible to develop customised investment solutions for mass market consumers in ways that would, until recently, only have been available to high-net-worth clients. For more detailed discussion on how AI is assisting in the financial sector, see World Economic Forum, *Artificial Intelligence in Financial Services* (White Paper, 2025).

[16] For a fascinating illustration on the role of AI in fraud detection in the insurance sector, see F Aslam et al, 'Insurance Fraud Detection: Evidence from Artificial Intelligence and Machine Learning' (2022) 62 *Research in International Business & Finance* 101744.

We see the use of similar technology in the insurance sector as well. For example, telematics, which is often plugged into the on-board diagnostic port of a vehicle,[17] can collect information on numerous aspects of an insured's driving behaviour, including geographical position, speed, acceleration and braking severity, vibration, and impact events, and forward it to the relevant insurers. The data thus obtained can be used to enable those insurers not only to offer dynamic insurance products (pay as you go), but also to assess risks more accurately at the renewal stage. Likewise, home and contents insurers provide some customers with the opportunity (and sometimes incentives in the form of discounts) to use home telematics, which are often connected to smoke alarms, carbon monoxide detectors, smart locks and doors and windows. In addition, such devices can notify insurers (not to mention insureds) instantly in case of irregularity. Similarly, some life and health insurers provide wearables that can gather and transmit real-time data about blood pressure, blood sugar and heart rate.[18] Such wearables can also be used to monitor various aspects of an individual's lifestyle and wellbeing, including diet, weight, sleep, and exercise, and could enable insurers to offer insurance products at a rate that more accurately reflects the risk that an individual poses.

iv. Role of Intelligent Machines in Enhancing Safety

Entities working in outside localities or open geographical areas (eg farms and construction companies), or those operating in dangerous locations (eg mines and quarries), regularly gather data from endpoint devices such as cameras, drones, thermometers, motion detectors and weather sensors. Such data can then be fed into intelligent systems for any number of purposes. For example, they may be used to identify problematic behaviours or dangerous conditions with a view to taking preventive or corrective measures; they could also be used to identify business opportunities and make recommendations. Nor is this limited to physical safety. Intelligent machines have recently gained an important role in the cybersecurity context as well. Various AI systems are used to monitor the enterprise IT environment to detect anomalies that could indicate a cyber threat.[19]

B. Intelligent Machines and Emerging Issues

i. A Moving Target

The technology used in developing intelligent machines is moving fast and is undeniably still evolving rapidly. This fluidity certainly creates a challenge for

[17] The same outcome can be achieved by installing an on-board diagnostic device (commonly known as a 'black box') that is equipped with a SIM card to transmit data over the mobile network.

[18] Wearable personal technology is sometimes referred to as 'fit tech'.

[19] For an interesting analysis on the subject, see World Economic Forum, *Artificial Intelligence and Cyber Security: Balancing Risks and Awards* (White Paper, 2025).

lawmakers, as well as for academics trying to make recommendations on the manner in which the legal rules need to respond to the challenge.[20] That said, the fundamentals of how such systems operate (ie the role of data management, machine learning and various AI training methods) are likely to stabilise over time, and we will endeavour to base our analysis on our understanding of the most recently available technology. We make no claim to be experts in data and computer science, but with the benefit of various texts studied as part of writing this book, we have acquired a general understanding of how such systems function through the combination of data, algorithms and machine learning models, and this knowledge will guide the legal analysis carried out throughout the book.

ii. The Nature of the Technology under Scrutiny

It is critical to understand the intended functions of intelligent machines that are currently in use or likely to be deployed in the near future (ie the next decade or so). Advanced versions of such machines have the capability to assess data, learn from such data, and make decisions in order to perform a particular task (eg financial or underwriting decision) or provide domain-specific expertise (eg safety warnings). In the literature, this is referred to as 'narrow (or weak) AI',[21] and throughout this book when we evaluate the suitability of the legal framework and the need to reform legal doctrines and principles in the context of private law, we shall assume that we are dealing with machines that possess this kind of technical ability.

At some point in the future, improvements in technology and computing might allow machines to achieve general intelligence. This benchmark would be possible through a closer replication of the workings of the human brain and a better simulation of human cognitive functions. Such systems could potentially exhibit intelligence comparable to a human and would likely outperform humans across a range of contexts.[22] There are indeed suggestions that if computer science technology reaches that level, these machines might develop autonomy as well as a kind of 'consciousness' and pose existential risks for human beings.[23] Inevitably, this development would result in profound changes in the way we think about ourselves and the world and how we interact with systems that have that kind of

[20] In *Technology, Humans, and Discontent with Law* (Oxford, Routledge, 2024), Roger Brownsword, at 140, described the process of governance of new technologies as one that is 'largely driven by the interaction of pragmatic accommodation of pluralistic interest and contested ethical principles'.

[21] For more technical information on narrow AI see VS Babu and K Banana, 'A Study on Narrow Artificial Intelligence' (2024) 24 *International Journal of Engineering Science & Advanced Technology* 210 and R Marrone et al, 'How Does Narrow AI Impact Human Creativity' (2024) *Creativity Research Journal* 1.

[22] See M Shanahan, *The Technological Singularity* (Cambridge, MA, MIT Press, 2015) 85–109.

[23] See E Yudkowsky, 'Artificial Intelligence as A Positive and Negative Factor in Global Risk' in N Bostrom and MM Ćirković (eds), *Global Catastrophic Risks* (Oxford, Oxford University Press, 2008) and T Ord, *The Precipice: Existential Risk and the Future of Humanity* (New York, Hachette, 2020).

intellectual capacity. Naturally, the manner in which we attempt to deal with the legal landscape emerging would be rather different and we certainly would need to reconsider the viability of legal rules and doctrines that we discuss throughout this book (and possibly rewrite it). However, the technology is not at this level yet, and many authorities believe that it is highly unlikely that in the foreseeable future AI will have developed to the point of strong autonomy, let alone decide to harm human beings in the near future.[24]

iii. Limits on the Capacities of Technology

Machines seem set fair in the not-too-distant future to rival (or surpass) humans in the power of logical reasoning, making sense of otherwise impenetrable data, and taking action based on these criteria. But this is only part of the story. There are any number of other aspects and institutions of human society which are outside the parameters of what remains in essence high-powered data processing. There are also a number of important practical issues.

a. Limits on the Abilities of Technology: Practical Issues

One factor that can complicate analysis of AI, especially in the legal sphere, is that while intelligent machines equipped with ML can probably outperform humans in the process of dealing with, and finding patterns in, huge datasets, this is no guarantee that they will get it right. One serious difficulty is that when it comes to machine learning there is always the prospect of error or algorithmic bias creeping in. Bias could arise as a result of the data used to train algorithms being skewed or in some way unrepresentative of the real world, or even because of the predilections of the humans involved in training the system (and setting it up to train itself in future).[25] This is a factor that one needs to bear in mind in assessing the consequences of the decisions taken by the system. Another difficulty with machine learning systems lies in the converse fact that users often suffer from automation bias – they tend to trust the system's outputs without questioning them, even though they might be aware of the fact that machine learning systems produce outputs with some probability of error; hence there is always an intrinsic uncertainty regarding such outputs.[26]

Another factor, of particular importance as regards a human institution such as law, is that machines, and especially AIEMs, create their own difficulties when it comes to interactions between themselves and the outside world. For example, it is very often crucial to identify whether a given person's act has caused or contributed to a particular outcome. As soon as an AIEM is interposed, however,

[24] 'Artificial Intelligence and Life in 2030: One Hundred Year of Study on Artificial Intelligence', Standford's 2015 Study Panel (September 2016).
[25] S Barocas and AD Selbst, 'Big Data's Disparate Impact' (2016) 104 *California Law Review* 671, 680.
[26] See Nielsen (n 6).

machine learning makes it very difficult to determine why an AI system has acted in the way it has or what caused it to do so. This is particularly the case when the model is based on deep learning neural networks. In those models, the hidden layers are connected to other layers through weights and activation functions resulting in nonlinear and complex relationships.[27] This complexity makes the system 'opaque' to humans and creates a problem commonly referred to as a 'black box' problem. In terms of legal analysis, failing to explain why a system has reached a particular conclusion would make it difficult to apply various legal rules to intelligent machines, so throughout the study we shall elaborate on the effect of such difficulties.

Gradually we are witnessing the black box problem being addressed, with programmers developing additional systems designed to understand and express, in terms comprehensive to humans, the essential features of the logic in 'black box' systems. These additional systems are called Explicable AI. They do not intend to replace the black box system but rather investigate its operations and features and the key variables controlling a particular output. Naturally, such systems could provide some assistance to lawyers engaged in a forensic investigation as to why the system has acted in a particular way.

b. Limits on the Abilities of Technology: Human and Algorithmic Attributes

Even more important than the 'black box' problem just mentioned is the fact that there remain, and always will be, vital differences between the thought processes of humans and intelligent machines, and in the way we look at each. Even if we do not believe in ideas like intent, recklessness or knowledge as aspects of some discrete aspect of human beings such as 'mind',[28] rather than as aspects of the behaviour of humans as a whole in their capacity as rational agents,[29] they are inescapably features of human beings in their overall capacity as rational and moral actors.[30]

[27] For a stimulating analysis on this matter see S Wachter et al, 'Counterfactual Explanations without Opening the Black-box: Automated Decisions and the GDPR' (2017) 1 *Harvard Journal of Law & Technology* 841 and J Pearly and D Mackenzie, *The Book of Why: The New Science of Cause and Effect* (New York, Basic Books, 2018).

[28] An idea somewhat discredited: compare, for example, G Ryle, *The Concept of Mind* (London, Hutchinson & Co, 1949), insisting that there is no such thing, and HLA Hart, *Punishment and Responsibility – Essays in the Philosophy of Law* (New York, Oxford University Press, 1968) 101. Here we are merely discussing the way humans talk of knowledge, which is a vital feature of their factual approach to both morality and law.

[29] Compare M Moore, 'Nothing but a Pack of Neurons: The Moral Responsibility of the Human Machine' in B Donnelly-Lazarov (ed), *Neurolaw and Responsibility for Action* (Cambridge, Cambridge University Press, 2018).

[30] Compare F McAuley, 'Mens Rea in the Brain: New Frontier or Dead End?' (2025) 141 *Law Quarterly Review* 437, which, while espousing the idea that such matters are aspects of human behaviour as a whole, admits that we are here talking of human behaviour. Behaviour by a mere machine, even a smart one, is in our view qualitatively different. This is an article on criminal law, but many of its insights are equally relevant in private law.

For example, think of the ideas of desire and intention. In human terms these are (except on a fairly low level) matters not entirely of logic or reasoning, but instead comport a large element of free-standing emotion. Furthermore, they are not only tied to our ability to reason; more importantly, they have a distinct moral aspect. However smart a machine or AIEM, it is hard to think of its having desires or intentions in this sense. Conversely, were a human being to show tendencies to govern their life solely by reference to the iterative processing of data available to them, we would think them to that extent defective and lacking the characteristics of humanity.

Again, consider concepts such as beneficence or malice, once more potentially important in aspects of private law. While there may be an element of ratiocination behind them, there is a great deal more than logic in their make-up. More importantly, they seem essentially limited to living beings. You can say entirely coherently of a person that they have acted out of ill-will or spite towards another: it is difficult to say the same thing about an algorithm or the machine it controls while still maintaining a straight face. Of course, an AIEM may decide from its manipulation of the data available to it that it must now act in some way so as to interfere with the interests of a person, but that is not the same thing. With people you can distinguish between the soldier who shoots an enemy despite bearing no malice against them, and his companion who kills an enemy out of hatred. With machines, we take the view that this distinction makes no sense.

The third difficulty comes with knowledge. With humans, if we say that someone knows something we are saying something about that person's consciousness. We are normally implying that there is an item of information that is not only available to them, but in some way consciously present in their mind. Suppose that someone has been made aware of something but cannot or does not call it to recollection now, even though they may later recall it, thus showing that it is somewhere present, physically, in their brain. There is no difficulty in saying that at this point in time they do not know this fact. True, it may be that they ought to know it, or even that they are blameworthy for not being conscious of it, but that is something different. Yet no such distinction would seem to apply to a machine. You can say that a given item of data is present in the storage of a machine, or retrievable by it given suitable code and programming: further than this you cannot go.

The difficulty is that all the human attributes just mentioned – intent, malice, knowledge, and so on – are vital to private law. If a given rule of private law requires a person to have had actual knowledge of something, to have acted out of ill-will or to have deliberately sought a particular outcome, this immediately raises the question: what if the immediate actor, or decision-maker, was an AIEM incapable of such conduct? As will appear in the following chapters, it is issues such as these which lie behind a good many of the problems likely to be encountered in adapting our system of private law to the ever-more intensive use of AI in legal relationships.

IV. Defining the Scope of the Inquiry

This book is about private law rather than public law regulation. Nevertheless, all this will take place against a background of increased regulatory supervision, and it is worth taking a quick look at this. Every product that is the outcome of a revolutionary new process and functions differently than the exiting alternatives potentially creates a governance problem. When cars first hit the roads in the late 1800s, there were no traffic rules in place. However, within a few decades, when cars began to be manufactured at mass scale, detailed traffic laws became necessary.[31] The increasing number of road accidents led to the introduction of compulsory motor insurance in the UK in 1930.[32] In the 1960s and 1970s, with the aim to protect consumers and the environment, various safety measures were mandated for car manufacturers (eg seat belts, padded dashboards and airbags), and emission standards were also introduced by regulators. More recently, the Automated Vehicles Act 2024 has set up a framework for self-driving vehicles.

It is inevitable that we shall see a similar pattern with intelligent machines. There is a growing literature deliberating how regulators and lawmakers need to address the governance challenge posed by the development of intelligent machines (and more generally AI).[33] In broad terms, the pending governance challenge would require policymakers to focus on three areas (see Table 1 below):

(a) Regulation might be needed to specify minimum production standards. For example, it could be made compulsory for a self-driving car to encompass a certain type of cyber security system. Similarly, regulators could dictate that when intelligent machines are used to make financial decisions, such systems must also be accompanied by another program aiming to explain why the machine has made a particular decision.
(b) Regulation could also be introduced to safeguard human dignity and other values. For example, regulators might require that algorithms that are designed to make underwriting decisions are programmed in such a way as to disregard applicants' genetic characteristics. Or public authorities might be banned from using intelligent machines for social scoring purposes.
(c) Regulators could also introduce rules to ensure that risk allocation is conducted in a fair and proportionate manner between parties entering private arrangements or when a party suffers a loss as a result of the deployment of an intelligent machine. For example, legislators could introduce rules

[31] In the UK the Motor Car Act 1903 introduced the need to register vehicles and for drivers to be licensed and set the speed limit to 20 mph.

[32] See the Road Traffic Act 1930 (now, in much amended form, the Road Traffic Act 1988).

[33] See, in particular, R Brownsword, *Rethinking Law, Regulation and Technology* (Cheltenham, Edward Elgar, 2022); S Wiesmuller, *The Relational Governance of Artificial Intelligence* (Cham, Springer, 2023); P Burgess, *AI and the Rule of Law- The Necessary Evolution of A Concept* (Oxford, Hart Publishing, 2024) and S Himmelreich et al (eds), *The Oxford Handbook of AI Governance* (Oxford, Oxford University Press, 2024).

enabling rectification of a smart contract that has already been executed. Or statutory rules could be adopted making those who deploy intelligent machines responsible for personal injury suffered as a result.

Table 1 Governance Challenge for Intelligent Machines

Areas that need regulatory attention	Ideal means of regulation	Time frame for intervention
Determining technical standards required of such machines to be able to function in a safe manner	Facilitating the development of industry standards and/or statutory/legislative intervention	High priority
Protecting humans, human dignity and fundamental human values against harmful consequences that might emerge	Statutory/legislative intervention	High priority
Addressing risk allocation issues (liabilities) that might emerge	Contractual devices and/or statutory/legislative intervention	Priority as far as it concerns consumers

Even though the UK has so far adopted a non-interventionist approach in an attempt to encourage the development of the AI sector,[34] a rather different approach has been adopted in the EU. Regulation (EU) 2024/1689, known as the AI Act, which entered into force on 1 August 2024,[35] aims to lay down harmonised rules on artificial intelligence.[36] In a nutshell, this Regulation classifies AI systems based on the potential risk that they pose to humans and divides such systems into different categories.[37] Under the regime set by the AI Act, some AI systems (such as emotion recognition software used in education or the workplace or real-time biometric identification used for law enforcement) are deemed to pose unacceptable risks and their use is prohibited.[38] Some AI systems, on the other hand, are classified as 'high risk' (eg systems used in evaluation of candidates

[34] See the policy paper published under the previous Conservative government on 3 August 2023 'A Pro-Innovation Approach to AI Regulation'. There was an expectation that this position would have changed under the new Labour government. The 'AI Opportunities Action Plan' presented to Parliament on 13 January 2025 by the Secretary of State for Science, Innovation and Technology sets out steps that the UK aims to take, with the goal of boosting economic efficiency and growth, and refers to the need to consider development of well-designed regulation to enable safe and trusted AI development and adoption; no tangible steps have yet been taken in this regard.

[35] The AI Act will be fully applicable on 2 August 2026, but some of its provisions are already in force: for instance, prohibitions and AI literacy obligations entered into application from 2 February 2025, and the governance rules and obligations for general-purpose AI models on 2 August 2025.

[36] Chapter I, Art 3(1) of the AI Act defines an AI system as 'a machine-based system that is designed to operate with varying levels of autonomy and that may exhibit adaptiveness after deployment, and that, for explicit or implicit objectives, infers, from the input it receives, how to generate outputs such as predictions, content, recommendations, or decisions that can influence physical or virtual environments'.

[37] It is worth noting that this Act is extra-territorial in that it applies to non-EU entities offering their AI products and systems in the EU.

[38] Chapter II, Art 5 of the AI Act.

seeking employment and those conducting credit assessment). Those systems need to comply with certain requirements – including around risk management, data quality, transparency, human oversight, and accuracy – and the businesses providing or deploying such technology face obligations around registration, quality management, monitoring, record-keeping, and incident reporting. They also need to satisfy a conformity assessment, obtain certificates, and complete a registration process carried out by designated authorities.[39] Some AI systems are deemed to pose low risks (eg generative AI systems generating or manipulating content such as images, audio or video), and for those cases some transparency obligations have been imposed.[40]

One objective of this Regulation is to impose minimum compliance requirements for some types of AI systems and also to ban the use of some types that are deemed to create harmful results from a human dignity perspective. By doing so, the EU has engaged in regulatory practices described above under (a) and (b). It is not our intention to elaborate such matters and their implications (ie in protecting the fundamental rights of individuals) in this book.[41] It is possible that the UK might follow the lead of the EU and introduce its own regulation to ensure AI systems satisfy certain requirements before they are put to public use, and it is not unthinkable to imagine certain restrictions being imposed on the use of some AI systems, but those issues are part of the governance challenge that are not within the remit of this book.

Instead, we aim to elaborate on the nature and scope of statutory intervention needed in different areas of private law (eg contract, tort, agency, and insurance) so that unexpected and novel risks emerging from the deployment of intelligent machines are allocated in a fair and reasonable manner. Put differently, our objective is to deliberate the issues identified under (c) above. The Law Commission has provided analysis on some of the legal issues that might arise (especially on smart contracts, digital assets, and conflict of laws issues),[42] but as no academic analysis has been carried out on the effect of AI and intelligent machines on traditional doctrines and principles of private law, this book intends to fill the void.

For the sake of completeness, we should mention that the EU is in the process of dealing with some of these issues (eg the impact of AI on matters concerning private law). Most notably, the Revised Product Liability Directive) (RPLD),[43]

[39] See Chapter III, Arts 8–49, and Annex III.

[40] See Chapter IV, Art 50.

[41] Those matters have been admirably dealt with by other authors, such as C Reed, *AI Fairness and Beyond – Law, Regulation and Technology* (Oxford, Hart Publishing, 2024); P Burgess, *AI and the Rule of Law – The Necessary Evolution of A Concept* (Oxford, Hart Publishing, 2024) and R Brownsword, *Rethinking Law, Regulation and Technology* (Cheltenham, Edward Elgar, 2022).

[42] The Law Commission published an advice to Government on Smart Legal Contracts (Law Com No 401) in 2021 and a scoping paper in July 2024 on Decentralised Autonomous Organisations.

[43] Directive (EU) 2024/2853 on liability for defective products and repealing Council Directive 85/374/EEC.

which came into force on 9 December 2024,[44] brings AI systems into the EU liability regime for consumer products, with software included as a product[45] and the meaning of 'defect' extended to include the 'effect on the product of its ability to continue to learn or acquire new features after it has been placed on the market or put into service'.[46] Similarly, the term 'damage' now includes the loss or corruption of data and medically recognised psychological harm. This amendment in the Directive effectively opens the door for consumers to bring an action against the manufacturer (or, if the manufacturer of the product is not based in the EU, the importer) for death or personal injury, damage to property, or destruction or corruption of data caused by the AI software system. The RPLD also shifts the burden when a claimant has presented facts and evidence to support the 'plausibility of the claim for compensation'. In such case, the manufacturer of the AI system must disclose information that is relevant to the claim.[47] The RPLD also imposes a presumption of defectiveness in severe circumstances, including when the AI system does not comply with mandatory safety requirements. The RPLD also makes life easy for the claimant by imposing a presumption to the effect that where a defect is established and the damage to the claimant is typically consistent with that defect, a causal link between the two will be presumed.[48]

The direction that common law should take on similar issues (not limited to tort liability) emerging from the deployment of intelligent machines will be the essence of this book. More precisely, our aim is to offer a comprehensive legal and theoretical debate on the impact of intelligent machines on various aspects of private law (eg contract, tort, agency, and property). We particularly aim to debate to what extent existing common law doctrines and principles will respond to the changing scene. It is also our intention to deliberate on the direction that law should take in order to protect the interests of contracting parties and those who are ancillary to the contracting process (eg agents) and those who might suffer losses as a result of the use of artificial intelligence in commercial settings such as insurance and finance.

It is undeniable that common law enables judges to be creative, so one might naturally assume that when novel legal problems emerge as a result of the deployment of intelligent machines, the starting point is to consider how the precedents and historical principles of law could be construed and adapted (perhaps even be manipulated) by judges to offer a sensible solution. This outcome is achievable to a certain extent, but one must also bear in mind that judges often exercise restraint and they would be mindful of being accused of assuming an unauthorised

[44] Member States must implement this Directive into their national laws by 9 December 2026.

[45] See Art 4(1).

[46] See Art 7(2)(c).

[47] Art 9.

[48] Also, the EU institutions are currently debating an EU Liability Directive which aims to address non-contractual fault-based claims for damage caused by AI systems.

legislative role.[49] What we have observed when writing this book is that it is not realistic to expect common law judges to fill all the gaps in law that emerge as a result of the deployment of intelligent machines in an attempt to preserve the coherence of common law.

Apart from creating uncertainty which might hinder the development and adoption of these new technologies,[50] there are two other fundamental reasons why we could not simply rely on judges to facilitate rapid adoption of new technologies in business and commercial environments. First, common law principles in the realm of private law are very often predicated on the idea of human misconduct (eg negligence, wilfulness etc). It might be rather difficult (if not impossible) to apply such concepts to the workings of AIEMs. Secondly, most legal rules are designed to take into account the actions and omissions of natural persons. Stretching those rules when dealing with machines that are capable of making decisions themselves might at best create artificial results, at worst absurdity. Therefore, our intention throughout the book is, after identifying those areas of law that would not respond to the challenges posed by intelligent machines, to make suggestions on how common law and statutory rules need to be amended, or in some cases devised, to ensure a seamless transition to the new era of intelligent machines.

Lastly, we need to say a few words as to where we stand on the relationship between law and ethics when dealing with the implications of intelligent machines on private law. There are scholars who firmly believe that law and ethics should remain separate.[51] Whilst we are of the opinion that it is not the ultimate goal of law to achieve moral ends, it is undeniable that moral considerations to a certain extent have influenced some of our proposals and recommendations. It is our view that this dimension is inevitable, especially when the task in hand is to offer legal solutions to novel issues. In this respect, we find ourselves concurring with Jeremy Waldron, who said:

> if a question is intractable, it will be so, whether it is legal or not, but if it is tractable, there seems to be no reason why one should not at least first see whether moral theory cannot contribute to its resolution before rejecting it, particularly considering that many of the techniques used in legal or moral analysis are similar.[52]

[49] See the observations of R Brownsword on this point in *Technology, Humans, and Discontent with Law – The Quest for Better Governance* (Oxford, Routledge, 2024) at 22.

[50] Uncertainty in liability regimes is likely to increase the cost of insurance not only for the manufacturers but also for those who will be liable for the consequences of deploying such systems.

[51] HLA Hart, 'Positivism and the Separation of Law and Morals' (1958) 71 *Harvard Law Review* 593 and RA Posner, *The Problematics of Moral and Legal Theory* (Cambridge, MA, Belknap Press, 2002) 227–64.

[52] J Waldron, 'Ego-Bloated Hovel' (2000) 94 *Northwestern University Law Review* 587, 618–19. See also L Green, 'Positivism and the Inseparability of Law and Morals' (2008) 83 *New York University Law Review* 1035.

2

Private Law in the Era of Intelligent Machines

The main purpose of this chapter is to give an overview of some of the legal concepts that might need to be dealt with and possibly reconsidered when addressing challenges that intelligent machines pose on traditional doctrines and principles of private law. However, before embarking on an analysis of that nature it is necessary to comment on how we expect private law reform[1] to be shaped in the near future when rising to this challenge. Understanding the possible direction it may go will be extremely helpful when following our analysis on different aspects of private law that appears in the subsequent chapters.

I. Intelligent Machines – The Direction of Private Law

When new technologies appear, the instinct of any lawyer (whether practising or academic) is to question how they can be fitted within the existing legal framework. Given a legal culture which strongly promotes the anchoring of legal reasoning to existing doctrine, their instinct is to protect the integrity and internal consistency of the legal structure in the face of the potential disruptive influence of the emerging technologies.[2] True, judges might be forced to stretch principles of law to deal with unique situations and challenges, but an accommodation can normally, even if at a pinch, be found.[3] However this approach has limitations, not least because judges are very chary (and rightly so) of anything that might be seen as assuming an unauthorised legislative role.

We are not dismissing entirely the prospect of judges developing their own solutions when addressing uncertainty caused by new technologies.[4] However,

[1] Traditionally, private law encompasses contract, agency, bailment, tort, unjust enrichment and restitution, property, trusts and succession (see Law Commission, *Smart Legal Contracts: Advice to Government* (Law Com No 401, 2021) at para. 1.13). For the purposes of this book, we shall adopt a similar approach.

[2] See R Brownsword, *Technology, Humans and Discontent with Law* (Oxford, Routledge, 2024) 22.

[3] See, for example, *Ruscoe v Cryptopia Ltd (in liquidation)* [2020] NZHC 728, [2020] 2 NZLR 809, where the New Zealand High Court held that cryptocurrencies, as digital assets, are a form of property that are capable of being held on trust.

[4] We witnessed this recently when the Supreme Court was asked to clarify the scope of business interruption policies in *Financial Conduct Authority v Arch Insurance (UK) Ltd* [2021] UKSC 1, [2021]

ad hoc judgments of this kind are likely to create a dangerous degree of uncertainty and ambiguity in law, not to mention being potentially unsystematic, possibly quietly value-laden, and designed to deliver justice in a particular instance rather than coherence in the law as a whole.[5] In turn, this could have serious adverse economic implications (especially in terms of potential increases in liability insurance due to legal uncertainties) and also hinder the pace of innovation.

We therefore start with something of a bias in favour of legislation to deal with any serious potential problems arising from the use of intelligent machines. The focus of such reform should be not only to preserve legal coherence but also properly to balance the legitimate interests of those using them and those who are affected from their use, in the light of the views of stakeholders and others. We hope that the recommendations we make will contribute to this development and reform.

We do not see any reason why the existing values and principles of private law should need altering wholesale to deal with intelligent machines. For example, imagine that an algorithmic error in the design or supervision of an AIEM deployed to make investment decisions leads to a financial loss for the relevant investor. The primary purpose of the law remains compensation for the party suffering loss. This would be exactly the same exercise if the loss had emanated from the error of a human professional adviser; the determination of liability would be as close as possible to the rules of contract and tort already applying as we can get, and the measurement of compensation would be identical. Again, we do not see any difference in terms of values that need protection where injury emanates from the malfunctioning of an intelligent machine, or alternatively from the fault of a person driving a car.

The position is not different in the context of contract law. The fundamental function of contract law is to ensure that we maintain the general structure of what counts as an agreement; that the legitimate interests of contracting parties are protected; and, if necessary, terms are implied to supplement any express terms and on occasion to deal with such matters as constraining otherwise unlimited discretion or imposing limitations on opportunism. These values need to be protected equally when a contract is concluded by, or through the intermediacy of, an AIEM or as a result of negotiations between humans.

AC 649. The construction adopted by the Supreme Court has been often criticised for disregarding the wording of the policies to protect the interest of some 370,000 affected business interruption insurance policyholders following the lockdowns and restrictions imposed by the government during the early days of the COVID-19 pandemic. See, in particular, O Gurses, 'The Supreme Court on Business Interruption Insurance and COVID-19: *Financial Conduct Authority v. Arch Insurance (UK) Ltd*' (2021) 32 *King's Law Journal* 71 and G Meggitt, 'Business Not as Usual – *The Financial Conduct Authority v. Arch and Others*' (2022) 4 *Journal of Business Law* 257.

[5] In his seminal text, D Goddard, *Making Laws That Work* (Oxford, Hart Publishing, 2022), stipulates that '[c]ourts are not generally well placed to determine policy issues'. See also R Dworkin, *Taking Rights Seriously* (London, Duckworth, 1978) 84.

That said, we are not suggesting that the introduction of intelligent machines will never introduce new problems or unintended vulnerabilities. On the contrary: they will. As we shall discuss at various points throughout the book, AIEMs will throw up emerging issues of fundamental values and principles. For example, third-party victims who are unusually vulnerable or otherwise particularly at risk from the use of intelligent machines ought to be fairly compensated. Similarly, when determining the suitable liability regime, we need to pay attention to the interests we are seeking to protect, and where necessary recognise that different kinds of harm may deserve different treatment.[6]

In the field of contract law, there might be different vulnerabilities that need to be protected, such as the prospect of a mistake emerging as a result of the manner in which an algorithm operates. In a recent Commonwealth case,[7] the judiciary was able to provide a solution to a problem (ie an allegation of a unilateral mistake invalidating the contract) emerging as a result of the functioning of a deterministic algorithm[8] within the confines of existing common law; but we suspect that resolving a similar problem could be more challenging when dealing with algorithms that are planned to continually learn from data input and modify their decision-making process. More comprehensive discussion on these issues and the values that need protection will be carried out in the relevant chapters of this book.

II. Key Concepts of Private Law in Need of Reconsideration

All existing principles and doctrines of private law currently assume a decision-making process by humans. They are invariably framed in a language that is capable of being applied to humans. However, some pose significant difficulties in relation to intelligent machines. In this book, we aim to deliberate how such concepts should be modified to address the legal challenges posed by intelligent machines. It would be a useful starting point to highlight these key concepts at the outset, and this is the primary objective of this section.

[6] In the law of tort as a whole, we regularly distinguish personal injury, dignitary interests, property damage and pure financial loss. For example, nuisance only protects a person in their enjoyment of land; the law of libel does not compensate personal injury; and strict product liability ignores damage to profits or business property. There is no reason to treat liability for intelligent machines differently.

[7] *Quoine Ltd v B2C2 Ltd* [2020] SGCA (I) 2, [2020] 2 SLR 20 (Singapore Court of Appeal). Legal implications of this authority will be deliberated further in Chapter 3.

[8] An algorithm without ML that follows a predictable sequence of steps to arrive at a definitive result.

A. Fault

Although there are plenty of examples of strict liability,[9] in a great deal of private law fault is an essential ingredient (particularly in the context of tort law, but it should be remembered that in practice a great deal of contract law, not to mention parts of equity, also deal with duties to take care). Under the present law, the notion of 'fault' presupposes a human act or omission coupled with a human mental state failing to measure up a particular standard (or at least its negative, blameworthy inadvertence). When an AIEM fails to act as it should and causes personal injury or financial loss, the claimant will still have to show fault in a person connected with the operation of the machine – unless of course, either we can develop some idea of a negligent algorithm, or ascribe legal personality to the machine in question.

As regards the latter idea, in the literature at one point it was seriously discussed whether some kind of legal personality should be ascribed to AIEMs;[10] even the European Parliament toyed with the idea.[11] Our view, however, is that this solution is over-complex and makes little sense. This opinion is not given on the basis that a machine cannot be a moral agent (itself a very controversial proposition, but in any case, largely irrelevant since even if it is true,[12] there is precious little of personal morality in negligence law). Rather it is for a more practical reason. A legal duty to compensate, and ownership of the money to do it with, or the ability to contract for insurance cover, have been in practice vested in either a human or a legal person acting through a human.[13] Without this connection with humankind the notion of fault liability becomes unworkable.[14]

If we do not go down the personality route, the fact remains that finding fault in a person responsible for the failure of an intelligent machine (eg programmer, developer, or operator) will be extremely difficult owing to the special characteristics of AI systems. For an intelligent machine to function, multiple integrated

[9] For example, product liability under Part I of the Consumer Protection Act 1987, the liability of sellers under the Sale of Goods Act 1979 and the Consumer Rights Act 2015, liability under the rule in *Rylands v Fletcher* (1868) LR 3 HL 330, and animal keepers' liability under the Animals Act 1971.

[10] See, in particular, C Novelli et al, 'A Conceptual Framework for Legal Personhood and Its Application to AI' (2022) 13 *Jurisprudence* 194; J Doomen, 'Artificial Intelligence Entity as A Legal Person' (2023) 32 *Info & Communications Technology Law* 277; and KB Forrest, 'The Ethics and Challenges of Legal Personhood for AI' (2023) 133 *Yale Law Journal* 1175.

[11] See the European Parliament Resolution with Recommendations to the Commission on Civil Law Rules on Robotics (2015/2103(INL)) (European Parliament, 16 February 2017) para 59(f).

[12] A view towards which we incline.

[13] True, one could say a corporation is just as artificial a seat of personality as an intelligent machine. But the property-holding powers of a corporation make limited sense except in the context of detailed rules as to capitalisation, agency, and powers of disbursement. All these are matters somehow incongruous in regard to an algorithm. A similar point was made by S Chesterman, 'Artificial Intelligence and the Limits of Legal Personality' (2020) 69 *International & Comparative Law Quarterly* 822, 822–27.

[14] See also B Brozek and M Jakubiec, 'On the Legal Responsibility of Autonomous Machines' (2017) 25 *Artificial Intelligence and Law* 293, and RD Brown, 'Property Ownership and the Legal Personhood of Artificial Intelligence' (2021) 30 *Information & Communications Technology Law* 208.

systems will be running concurrently. The interdependence of software, hardware, algorithms and data input in the operation of a system would make it rather difficult to identify the main source of harm and individuals behind it.

Even if the source of harm is identified, another complex problem arises. Given that most AI systems are opaque and present a difficulty in explaining why they functioned in the way they did,[15] any claimant will face an uphill task in presenting to a court a detailed explanation linking breach of duty by the defendant to the harm suffered. The task of the client is made more difficult due to the fact that most developers of AI products treat the algorithms used and other aspects of their design as trade secrets.[16] Unless they are required by law to provide such details in case of a litigation, any claimant will find themselves in a very precarious position.

B. Causation

In private law causation plays a vital role in justifying the imposition of some burden upon a particular individual for the benefit of another. For example, when bringing a claim for compensation, the claimant must prove a causal connection between the legally relevant aspect of the defendant's conduct or the conduct of some entity for which the defendant is responsible,[17] and its loss. In similar vein, when seeking to establish recession of a transaction on grounds of vitiating factors, such as misrepresentation or non-disclosure in commercial insurance contracts, the right-holder must show how that vitiating factor was a cause of entry into the transaction.

Causation raises many issues. A good number of them, while complex, are not likely to be affected by the interposition of intelligent machines: examples include multiple causes,[18] intervening events,[19] and complexities in the factual setting such as arise in the context of industrial diseases.[20] However, on a practical level the simple proof of causation may raise awkward issues with AIEMs. Given the opacity associated with the autonomous non-human decision-making process that

[15] We should not forget the fact that these machines often employ algorithms that are designed to learn as they work, which might complicate the inquiry further.

[16] For an informative article on this point, see JG Sprankling, 'Trade Secrets in the Artificial Intelligence Era' (2024) 76 *South Carolina Law Review* 181.

[17] The latter applies in cases where vicarious liability arises.

[18] See, for example, *Baker v Willoughby* [1970] AC 467; *Jobling v Associated Dairies Ltd* [1982] AC 794; *Wilsher v Essex AHA* [1988] 1 AC 1074 and *Fitzgerald v Lane* [1989] 1 AC 328.

[19] See, for example, *Baker v TE Hopkins & Son Ltd* [1959] 1 WLR 966 and *Home Office v Dorset Yacht Co Ltd* [1970] AC 1004.

[20] This has been particularly the case in litigation concerning asbestos and mesothelioma, where it has proven impossible to establish scientifically which among several wrongful risk exposures caused a person's cancer (*Fairchild v Glenhaven Funeral Services Ltd* [2002] UKHL 22, [2003] 1 AC 32). See also *Bonnington Castings Ltd v Wardlaw* [1956] AC 613 and *Barker v Corus UK Ltd* [2006] UKHL 20, [2006] 2 AC 572.

these machines rely on, it is not going to be an exaggeration to say that proving a causal effect between their actions (or some cases inactivity) and any allegedly resulting loss or damage will be rather challenging. The difficulties with burden of proof are likely to grow further with increasing levels of autonomy and complexity of the algorithms used.[21] There have been suggestions that such problems could be resolved by requiring AI systems to collect or retain such information when reasonable to do so,[22] but the practicality of this remedy is doubtful and it is questionable whether it is functionally possible due to the complexity of machine learning systems.

It should also be borne in mind that addressing the causation challenge could be more difficult in cases where there has been an interaction between a human agent and the intelligent machine. Imagine, for example, that essential regular updates of an intelligent machine have not been conducted, leaving the product prone to a cyber-attack. In such instance, it is possible that the intervening agency of others could preclude the liability of those responsible for the defective AI product in respect of a harm.

C. Remoteness

To determine which types of losses caused by a breach of a legal duty are compensable, a test known as 'remoteness of damages (foreseeability)' is often employed.[23] The test of foreseeability is in most cases expressed in terms of what consequence a reasonable person (defendant) would be expecting to arise from their act or omission.[24] Although the test seems to be an objective one, it is still rooted in human experience and human perceptions of cause and effect and risk materialisation.

It is a genuine concern whether this test is conceptually capable of being applied in predicting the kind of consequences that would be reasonably expected when a non-human AI decision-making process is in operation. It is a realistic possibility that the result of the AI's decision or conduct may not have been in any way foreseeable by the AI's creator or user, considering that the AI may reach a counter-intuitive solution, or find an obscure pattern hidden deep in the data sets evaluated, or make decisions based on higher-dimensional relationships between variables that no human can visualise.[25] This difficulty

[21] See R Calo, 'Robotics and the Lessons of Cyber Law' (2015) 103 *California Law Review* 513, 543.

[22] See S Watcher et al, 'Counterfactual Explanations without Opening the Black Box: Automated Decisions and the GDPR' (2018) 31 *Harvard Journal of Law & Technology* 841.

[23] In a few torts, such as deceit, this does not apply. There is also authority that intended consequences are never too remote (eg *Reeves v Metropolitan Police Commr* [2000] 1 AC 360, 394 (Lord Hobhouse)).

[24] This was laid down authoritatively in tort by the Privy Council in *Overseas Tankship (UK) Ltd v Morts Docks Engineering Co Ltd (The Wagon Mound)* [1961] AC 388, having been established in contract a bit over a century earlier in *Hadley v Baxendale* (1854) 9 Ex 341.

[25] See Y Bathaee, 'The Artificial Black Box and the Failure of Intent and Causation' (2018) 31 *Harvard Journal of Law & Technology* 889, 924.

has led some scholars to argue that the concept of reasonable foreseeability will need to be applied differently in cases where harm results from the operation of an AI system. As the argument goes, in those instances, rather than being applied with regard to the particular manner in which risk materialised in the given case, reasonable foreseeability must be understood as considering predictability and the emergence of known risks that potentially give rise to unknown ones.[26]

We do not necessarily subscribe to this view. If a lower threshold for liability is set for defendants responsible for intelligent machines than defendants in other tort cases, this discrepancy might not only discourage adequate risk assessment and maintenance of best practices in the field, but also hinder the pace of innovation.[27] The case law points to the conclusion that the causal mechanism by which the act might cause harm does not need to be reasonably foreseeable with much granularity even if there is a somewhat unusual mechanism (eg machine learning) by which the harm occurs.[28] So long as that harm is reasonably describable as the materialisation of a foreseeable risk of the activity that is pursued by the intelligent machine, the foreseeability requirement could be satisfied. Put differently, the law as it currently stands allows a risk to be described broadly for the purposes of the foreseeability rules,[29] which should allow us to reach the conclusion that if there is a breach of a duty of care (eg in the design of an intelligent machine). The fact that the particular risk that has materialised was not reasonably foreseeable should not be a barrier to liability. That said, the issue could be more complicated in practice, and we shall revert to the ramifications of the foreseeability test with regard to loss emerging from various types of intelligent machines throughout the book.

In contract law, the remoteness principle is also relevant in determining which consequential losses emerging as a result of breach of the contract would be allowed. The test here is formulated in a way so as to limit recovery to those consequences of a breach that might have been reasonably foreseen at the time of contracting. The test requires courts to determine whether the loss arose according to the usual course of things from breach of contract, or may reasonably be supposed to have been contemplated, by both parties at the time

[26] K Thomasen, 'AI and Tort Law' in F Martin-Bariteau and T Scassa (eds), *Artificial Intelligence and the Law in Canada* (Toronto, LexisNexis, 2022) 117.

[27] It is worth referring to European Parliament Resolution of 20 October 2020 (2020/2014 (ING)) which states: '… 7- Citizens should be entitled to the same level of protection and rights, irrespective of whether the harm is caused by an AI-system or not, or if it takes place physically or virtually, so that their confidence in the new technology is strengthened.'

[28] *Hughes v Lord Advocate* [1963] AC 837; *Jolley v Sutton London Borough Council* [2000] 1 WLR 1082.

[29] It has been stressed that if the risk of harm is more than 'far fetched', it may be reasonable. In *Bolton v Stone* [1951] AC 850 (HL), Lord Reid, 864–65, said: '… generally speaking if injury to another person from the defendants' acts is reasonably foreseeable the chance that injury will result is substantial and it does not matter in which way the duty is stated … I do find at least a tendency to base duty rather on the likelihood of damage to others than on its foreseeability alone.'

they made the contract, as a probable result of the breach of it.[30] The second part of the test[31] clearly requires an elaboration of whether the loss emerging was within the contemplation of the parties,; which would inevitably mean that the courts would need to assess whether the parties had any special knowledge of certain types of losses at the time of contracting. This issue will create some difficulties when it comes to contracts entered into through intelligent machines. It may well be that the test of remoteness will have to be reformulated according to what would have been foreseeable to a reasonable human in the position of the contracting parties, had that person had knowledge of the breach caused by the activities of the AIEM.

D. Agency and Representation

In contract claims, issues often arise as to the authority of a human or corporate agent to bind their principal to a given agreement or liability. Where a natural or juridical person acts through an AIEM, however, there are strong doubts as to whether the existing law relating to agency can be carried across to deal with this situation, and there may be a need for considerable reforms.

So too with tort claims. An interesting and difficult question relates to the relationship between an intelligent machine and the human agents that use the machine, in terms of determining who will be liable if a harm arises as a result. Imagine, for example, that a surgeon using a semi-autonomous surgical robot as an assistant makes a decision about appropriate placement of the autonomous portions of the robot, and something goes wrong during the operation, resulting in a personal injury to the person operated on. At first sight, one might consider vicarious liability principles being applicable here, and the intelligent machine (or its developers) being held vicariously liable in the same manner an employer is vicariously liable for certain actions of their employees.[32]

The relationship between an intelligent machine and its developers mirrors in some way that of an employee and employer. It is the developer that identifies the need to use AI, researches the skills and capabilities needed from the AI, chooses a specific model, and trains it to perform the necessary tasks whilst providing an oversight. There is, however, one major difference between AI and employees,

[30] See *Hadley v Baxendale* (1854) 9 Ex 341 and *Victoria Laundry (Windsor) Ltd v Newman Industries Ltd* [1949] 2 KB 528.

[31] We are of the view that the rule laid down in this area is a composite one under which the defendant is liable for any loss which was or may be regarded as having been in the parties' contemplation, in the light of any special knowledge they may or may not have had when contracting. This view has also been expressed in various judgments: see, for example, *Koufos v C Czarnikow Ltd* [1969] 1 AC 350, 384 (per Lord Reid); *Jackson v Royal Bank of Scotland plc* [2005] UKHL 3, [2005] 1 WLR 377, [49] (per Lord Walker) and *Transfield Shipping Inc v Mercator Shipping Inc (The Achilleas)* [2006] EWHC 3030 (Comm), [2007] 1 Lloyd's Rep 19, [49] (per Christopher Clarke J).

[32] See, for example, *Lister v Hesley Hall Ltd* [2001] UKHL 22, [2002] 1 AC 215 and more recently *Adams v Law Society* [2012] EWHC 980 (QB).

which is the fact that human employees have the capacity for autonomous decision-making independent of – and perhaps in direct contradiction with – the guidance provided by the employer. However, there are, as in contract, strong doubts whether the existing rules on vicarious liability can deal with this situation. These cases are dealt with in detail in Chapter 7 below.

E. Fraud

In several areas of private law, it is relevant that a person has acted dishonestly, or that they did not believe that a representation made by them was correct or knew in some other way that they were deceiving someone. The tort of deceit is a straightforward example;[33] another, the rule that a person cannot sue under a letter of credit[34] or other abstract payment undertaking[35] if they know at the time of presentation that the underlying claim is fraudulent; and yet a third the rule that a contracting party cannot exclude liability arising from their personal fraud in inducing or performing the contract.[36] Also, proving fraud might in some instances provide the representee with additional remedies. For example, in commercial insurance law, when an assured fails to present the risk in an honest fashion, the insurer, apart from having the right to avoid the insurance contract,[37] could potentially seek damages either under the tort of deceit[38] or the Misrepresentation Act 1967.[39] In those instances, the damages would be awarded to compensate the representee for all the loss which can properly be said to have been caused by his reliance on the fraudulent misrepresentation,[40] subject always to the representee's duty to mitigate their loss after discovering the fraud.

There is a distinct difficulty here in the case of the activities of AIEMs. Clearly, the general rule will apply if fraud can be shown in the person behind the intelligent machine: but if this is impossible, it seems very doubtful whether the laws against fraud, which is a human-oriented and often highly moral concept, can be applied to AIEMs as such. Imagine, for example, an intelligent machine

[33] See generally A Tettenborn (ed), *Clerk & Lindsell on Torts*, 23rd edn (London, Sweet & Maxwell, 2023) Ch 17.

[34] M Brindle and R Cox, *Law of Bank Payments*, 5th edn (London, Sweet & Maxwell, 2017) para 7-099 ff.

[35] See eg *Kvaerner John Brown Ltd v Midland Bank Ltd* [1998] CLC 446.

[36] *S Pearson & Sons Ltd v Dublin Corpn* [1907] AC 351; *Boyd & Forres v Glasgow & South Western Railway Co* 1915 SC (HL) 20 and more recently *HIH Casualty and General Insurance Ltd & Others v Chase Manhattan Bank & Others* [2003] UKHL 6, [2003] 2 Lloyd's Rep 61, [16] (per Lord Bingham). As stressed by the House of Lords in the *HIH* case, this is limited to personal fraud. There is no objection on public policy grounds to excluding liability for the fraud of agents or even employees: see eg *Frans Maas (UK) Ltd v Samsung Electronics (UK) Ltd* [2004] EWHC 1502 (Comm), [2004] 2 Lloyd's Rep 251.

[37] See Insurance Act 2015, s 8 and Schedule 1.

[38] *Derry v Peek* (1889) 14 App Cas 337.

[39] See s 2 of the Act.

[40] *Smith New Court Securities Ltd v Scrimgeour Vickers (Asset Management) Ltd* [1997] AC 254.

that is entrusted in making investment decisions based on market intelligence, fluctuations in the market, reports on companies, and any other data obtained from various networks. Leaving the opacity problem aside, it would be very difficult to prove that the designer of the relevant algorithm intended that the machine operate in a particular manner to the detriment of the investors that entrusted the system to them and put it into operation on their behalf. There have been instances where the courts have inferred fraud on the basis of existing evidence,[41] but we shall consider in subsequent parts of this book whether such an inference could be relevant in the context of intelligent machines, and what kind of legal principles could be developed to deal with potential lack of evidence due to the opacity issue that affects intelligent machines.

F. Knowledge

Often, in contract law, it is essential to determine whether one of the parties can be fixed with information or knowledge so as to make that party responsible for the legal consequences that follow. For example, a unilateral mistake as to the terms of the contract, if known by the other party, could potentially invalidate a contract.[42] When intelligent machines are involved in contract formation, it could be a rather challenging task to identify whether knowledge of certain issues could be attributed to one of the contracting parties. The Singapore Court of Appeal dealt with this difficulty in *Quoine v B2C2 Ltd*,[43] where automated trading algorithms resulted in trades being conducted at 250 times the market rate. In assessing the state of knowledge attributable to the parties, the Court of Appeal held that in case of deterministic algorithms, 'the relevant inquiry cannot be directed at the parties themselves, who had no knowledge of or direct personal involvement in the formation of contract'.[44] It was held that the relevant inquiry should be the knowledge of the developer or deployer of the program, which must be assessed from the time of programming until the formation of the contract. Accordingly, the Court concluded that no case of a unilateral mistake was made (either at common law or equity) given that the trading price was the result of deterministic algorithms and they functioned exactly as they had been programmed to function. We believe a different outcome could have followed if the algorithm in question was designed to continually learn from data input and modify its decision-making process. This example illustrates that further discussion on how and which type of knowledge would be attributed to a contracting party is required when that party uses an intelligent machine to run its affairs.

[41] See, for example, *Connolly Ltd v Bellway Homes Ltd* [2007] EWHC 895 (Ch).
[42] *Hartog v Colin and Shields* [1939] 3 All ER 566.
[43] [2020] SGCA (I) 2.
[44] Ibid, [98].

Similar issues might arise in commercial contracts where knowledge or lack of it could be vital for the validity of the contract. This is particularly the case in insurance contracts. It is an interesting question whether the insurer could be deemed to know information which an AI system entrusted to take underwriting decisions could find out by trawling through various databases and sources by making full use of big data analytics. If that is the case, the assured is not expected to disclose such information to the insurer – or, put differently, the insurer will not be able to argue breach of the pre-contractual duty of good faith of the assured for failing to disclose such material information. The relevant sections of the Insurance Act 2015[45] presuppose that underwriting decisions are taken by human agents, and the language adopted in those provisions does not provide a conclusive answer to this inquiry. This matter will be deliberated extensively in the relevant part of the book (Chapter 8), but essentially we shall argue that some adjustments in the relevant sections of the Act would be needed, especially given that underwriting will be more and more delegated to intelligent machines in the near future.

[45] See Insurance Act 2015, ss 3(5)(b)–(d) and 5.

PART II

Private Law in Action: Domains Influenced by Intelligent Systems

3

Intelligent Machines, AI and Contract Law

I. Introduction

The use of AI in business and professional life is increasing at an exponential rate. It follows that the workings of the commercial law of contract are going to be heavily affected by input from AI, whether in the process of forming contracts or performing them once formed.[1] The effect of this process is in our view likely to be threefold.

First, there will be increased instances of entirely automated contracting. This notably comprises so-called 'smart contracts', by which we will understand a process under which agreements are not only concluded automatically between AIEMs but actually performed without human intervention.[2] But these are likely for the foreseeable future to remain a fairly marginal kind of arrangement, at least for the moment limited to a few specialised businesses. Examples are the automatic ordering and dispatch of inventory and supplies; automated dealings in securities or currencies; insurance arranged without human intervention; and so on. Such contracts, while there is no reason to see them as anything other than valid,[3] nevertheless raise a number of specific issues which would not arise in the case of human interaction.

Secondly, and rather more importantly, the use of AIEMs, and the issues they throw up, will slowly but surely increase in connection with ordinary contracts where there is also a human input. Even at the time this book was being written, for example, the negotiation of any online purchase was increasingly likely to be

[1] There will also, of course, be indirect input, with AI being used, for example, as an aid to help a party determine whether to contract in the first place. But this raises few issues, save in extreme cases (such as where the other party interferes with the AI to gain an advantage), and this chapter will not concentrate on such matters.

[2] 'A smart contract is a self-executing contract with the terms of the agreement between buyer and seller being directly written into lines of code': L Procopie, 'Are Smart Contracts Actually Contracts? How Smart Contracts Can Work Globally' (2021) 36 *Journal of International Banking & Regulation* 25, fn 1.

[3] See the Law Commission's 2021 paper *Smart Legal Contracts: Advice to Government* (Law Com CP 563), especially Ch 3; also M Durovic and A Janssen, 'Formation of Smart Contracts under Contract Law' in LA DiMatteo et al (eds), *The Cambridge Handbook of Smart Contracts, Blockchain Technology and Digital Platforms* (Cambridge: Cambridge University Press, 2019) 61–79. In the light of this it seems we must see as heterodox the suggestion in L Scholz, 'Algorithmic Contracts' (2017) 20 *Stanford Tech Law Review* 128, 151–57, that contracts concluded through a 'black box' algorithm are probably not enforceable under ordinary contract doctrine.

conducted by an AIEM on at least one side; and, at least in urban areas, unmanned supermarkets automatically tallying goods as they were taken out were a growing presence on high streets.

Thirdly, during the currency of a contract, performance will increasingly be monitored by AI, which may also take decisions as to whether and when payments may be triggered – a feature increasingly seen in, for example, the construction industry.[4] And more directly, performance itself (for example in the case of financial or legal advice, maintenance and repair of buildings and equipment, and even technical matters such as delicate surgery) will to a much increased extent be taken over wholly or partly by AI or an AIEM.

Apart from all this, AI is also increasingly likely to be used in the background as an aid to negotiations. It is likely to be used both in providing information to a counterparty, and also in taking decisions whether to do business with that counterparty, and if so on what terms. While this is unlikely to affect the basic structure of contract law, it is likely to raise a number of specific issues.

With these preliminary matters out of the way, we now turn to a number of areas within traditional contract law where in our view it is likely that the use of AI will raise particular issues.

II. Formal Requirements

A. Formal Requirements Generally

The starting point here is that there is no distinction in principle between contracts made by AI and other human agreements. English law, like nearly all European legal systems,[5] recognises 'freedom of form': in other words – absent a specific rule to the contrary – it has no formal requirements for a valid contract beyond agreement to create a legal obligation.[6] By and large this principle will carry over fairly seamlessly to AI contracts, especially human-to-AI ones. It will not, it is suggested, be very difficult for a court to look at the circumstances of an interaction between a human and an AIEM and determine whether, however formal or informal, it bears the outward appearance of an agreement which is the mark of a valid contract. If it does, it will be valid and the parties bound by it.[7]

[4] Notably, in an increasing number of construction contracts, AI in the shape of the IoT is being used in the process of determining whether a particular stage has been reached so as to trigger a stage payment (which payment itself may also be automated).

[5] Compare the EU's proposal for preliminary steps to harmonise private law contained in the *Draft Common Frame of Reference*, II – 1:106(1).

[6] H Beale, *Chitty on Contracts*, 36th edn (London, Sweet & Maxwell, 2025) para 8-001 (hereinafter referred to as *Chitty on Contracts*).

[7] See *Smith v Hughes* (1870–71) LR 6 QB 597, 607 and *MWB Business Exchange Ltd v Rock Advertising Ltd* [2018] UKSC 24, [2019] AC 119, [7] (per Lord Sumption). This point is seemingly regarded as obvious by the Law Commission (*Advice*, para.3.76): the Commission concentrated on such things as requirements of writing.

A little complexity may, however, arise in the case of pure AI-to-AI contracts, where 'agreement' consists entirely in exchanges of code under a specialised protocol introduced between two machines. In the absence of some guidance here, it may be difficult for a court using ordinary evidence to determine whether there is agreement *in abstracto* without further guidance as to what is to count as agreement and what is not.[8] If this causes difficulty, it may be necessary in future for legislation to intervene to clarify the matter. We suggest that the best way to do this could be by imposing a limited formal requirement specific to contracts of this sort. It might provide, for example, that agreement exists if, and only if, either: (a) the facts satisfy any definition previously agreed between the AIM controllers; or (b) the exchange between the two AIMs contains particular specified code apt to indicate agreement which would be apparent to a reasonable expert in the relevant protocols.

B. Specific Formal Requirements

In a few cases, English law recognises formal requirements: notably, contracts that have to be in writing (or evidenced in writing), and agreements that are required to be by deed.

i. Writing

A contract for the sale or lease of real estate must be in writing and signed under section 2 of the Law of Property (Miscellaneous Provisions) Act 1989 for contracts for the sale of real estate);[9] there are a few similar requirements in other specialised cases.[10] In addition, there must be a signed memorandum for a contract of guarantee to be enforceable against the guarantor (under the Statute of Frauds 1677).[11]

Under the present law, any requirement of writing is fairly clearly satisfied by computer output or material on a hard disk or other storage medium. Hitherto, most argument has concerned computer output resulting from fairly direct human entry, but provided there is some more or less permanent record accessible to

[8] Compare P Księżak and S Wojtczak, *Toward a Conceptual Network for the Private Law of Artificial Intelligence* (Cham, Springer, 2023) para 9.2.2.

[9] Other instances are consumer credit contracts (Consumer Credit Act 1974, s 61(1), requiring a signed document): and representations as to credit (Statute of Frauds Amendment Act 1828, s 6).

[10] For example, negotiable instruments must be in writing under the Bills of Exchange Act 1882 (though now the Electronic Trade Documents Act 2023 allows them to be in electronic form). A consumer credit agreement must be in writing and signed by the consumer: see Consumer Credit Act 1974, s 61. An employee has a right to a written copy of his employment agreement (Employment Rights Act 1996, s 1), as does a seafarer (Merchant Shipping (Maritime Labour Convention) (Minimum Requirements for Seafarers etc) Regulations 2014, SI 2014/1613, reg 12).

[11] There are technical requirements for contracts executed by companies in ss 43 and 44 of the Companies Act 2006. These are dealt with at p 35 below.

someone, it is submitted the same will apply to action by a machine or AIEM set up by a person[12] to make contracts in their name.[13]

ii. Writing: Two Special Cases

Two things may, however, cause difficulties: signatures and deeds.

a. Signatures

There is, it seems, little doubt today that where a signature is required, a mechanically placed identification of a contractor on an electronic communication, other than one appearing merely as a matter of form in a header or similar section,[14] will do,[15] at least if provided as part of a readily readable document.[16] This, indeed, is provided explicitly by legislation in the case of an individual, though not of a company.[17] On the other hand, where a contract is made without human intervention, this rule seems difficult to apply. The test is whether the name on the communication seems to have been placed there with a view to authentication rather than automatically and as a matter of course: but where the contract is caused to be made by an inanimate AIEM which cannot have any intention or indeed views on the matter, this is a little hard to apply. There may be a necessity for legislation to deal with this lacuna too. The best idea, it is suggested, would be a provision stating that for a valid signature in such a case there must in the code produced under the agreement be an explicit reference to 'signature' or 'authentication', or something which would be understood as such by a reasonable expert coder.

[12] Including a corporation.

[13] The Interpretation Act 1978, Sch 1, defines 'writing' to include 'typing, printing, lithography, photography and other modes of representing or reproducing words in a visible form'. This would seem to include electronic media, presumably on the basis that the words are visible, albeit only through intermediacy of a computer screen: see eg *Golden Ocean Group Ltd v Salgaocar Mining Industries Pvt Ltd* [2012] EWCA Civ 265, [2012] 1 WLR 3674 ('writing' for Statute of Frauds includes emails). This view is adopted by the Law Commission: Law Com No 386 (2019), *Electronic Execution of Documents*, para 3.6 and Statement of the Law, para 1; and see too its advice on *Smart Contracts*. See generally R Hewitson, 'Electronic Signatures and Contracts for the Sale of Land' (2021) *Conveyancer* 120, 123.

[14] This is clear from *Pereira Fernandes SA v Mehta* [2006] EWHC 813 (Ch), [2006] 1 WLR 1543.

[15] See *Neocleous v Rees* [2019] EWHC 2462 (Ch), [2020] 2 P & CR 4. Suggestions apparently to the contrary from the Court of Appeal in *Firstpost Homes Ltd v Johnson* [1995] 1 WLR 1567 are, it seems, obiter and now discredited: *Chitty on Contracts*, 36th edn, paras 8-045–8-047; *cf Goodman v J Eban Ltd* [1954] 1 QB 550 (stamp); and see generally Hewitson (n 13).

[16] It is suggested that the mere fact that, buried deep in computer code, there appears what can be translated as a mention of the name of the person supposedly contracting, will not suffice: this seems to follow from *Pereira Fernandes SA v Mehta* [2006] EWHC 813 (Ch), [2006] 1 WLR 1543.

[17] See the EU Eidas Regulation, 910/2014, Art 3(9), 3(10), and Art 25, as amended (effective post-Brexit); and s 7 of the Electronic Communications Act 2000.

b. Deeds

These may also cause difficulties, both as regards individuals and companies.[18] Take individuals first. In order to take effect as a deed by X, not only must a document appear on its face to be such, but it must be signed by X and attested by a witness then physically present.[19] This may cause problems in the case of documents produced by an AIEM. Although there is no reason why computer output should not count as the signature to a written document (see above), the better view seems to be that the witness (who must presumably be human) must be present at the signing.[20] If so, it would seem to follow that the witness would have to be present when and where the signature takes place on the relevant server, which in most cases is likely to defeat the object of the exercise. It is hard to avoid the conclusion that, unless we are happy to say that an individual cannot make a deed through computer output (which may be seen as an acceptable risk of doing business through AI), statutory intervention may be necessary laying down that a signature by AI can be witnessed remotely and providing a procedure for doing this.

With companies, an analogous difficulty applies. A company can execute a deed in three ways: by affixing its common seal;[21] by signature by two authorised signatories (or by one director, if in the presence of an attesting witness);[22] or through an agent appointed by deed who then executes the document as a deed.[23] In practice this means that companies cannot enter into deeds through AIEMs. An AIEM cannot affix a company's physical seal,[24] even assuming it has one at all (it is not compulsory for it to possess one); and in so far as the deed is signed, either by two signatories or a director, or by a human agent authorised by deed, the same problems arise: the document must still be witnessed,[25] and this effectively rules out contracting using this method. The same comment applies as for deeds executed by individuals. Unless we regard the executing of deeds by companies as

[18] It must be admitted, however, that in most cases this will not matter. Although a properly-executed deed is required to contract a valid obligation without consideration, where there is consideration a would-be deed can normally be given effect as a parol contract: see eg *Signature Living Hotel Ltd v Sulyok* [2020] EWHC 257 (Ch), [2020] Bus LR 588. On electronics and deeds, see generally K Potts, 'A (T)test for the Traditional Deed? Examining the Scope of Electronic and Smart Deeds: Part 1' (2025) *Conveyancer* 69.

[19] Law of Property (Miscellaneous Provisions) Act 1989, s 1(3)(ii).

[20] Law Commission No 386, para 5.35, and *cf* the unreported FTT decision in *Yuen v Wong* (8 January 2020) (available at https://www.falcon-chambers.com/images/uploads/news/Yuen-v-Wong-2019.pdf) (doubtful if deed could be validly witnessed over Skype).

[21] Companies Act 2006, s 44(1)(a).

[22] ibid s 44(1)(b), (2), (3).

[23] See PG Watts and FMB Reynolds, *Bowstead & Reynolds on Agency*, 23rd edn (London, Sweet & Maxwell, 2025) para 2-040 (hereinafter referred to as *Bowstead & Reynolds on Agency*).

[24] That a seal must be physical is made clear by the Companies Act 2006, s 45(1), requiring the company name to be 'engraved'.

[25] Law of Property (Miscellaneous Provisions) Act 1989, s 1(4A).

so uncommon that there is no need to allow its being done by an AIEM (which is possibly a plausible approach), there will be a need for legislation.

III. Substantive Requirements: Agreement, Consideration, Certainty, etc

Aside from agreement, which is dealt with below, there is no reason to think that the cardinal substantive requirements for the creation of valid contractual obligations, such as consideration or certainty, will create any serious need for change as regards contracts entered into by or through AIEMs. Whatever the source of the contract, it will normally remain possible to ascertain whether, objectively, there exists a quid pro quo for one party's undertaking to the other,[26] and whether, using the means of interpretation that will be referred to below, the agreement is certain enough for a court to know what it is being asked to enforce. The technical form, in other words, is irrelevant.

IV. The Process of Contracting: Offer, Acceptance and Agreement

A. Agreement, Offer and Acceptance: The Objective Theory

Consideration and certainty are, as mentioned above, likely to be straightforward when it comes to contracts entered into by AIEMs. The same cannot, by contrast, be said about agreement – at least at first sight. The idea of 'agreement' normally implies an intent to agree, and an indication of a psychological state in someone amounting to a belief that agreement has been reached: in other words, an essentially human process.[27] But an AIEM without consciousness cannot in any real sense be thought of as deliberately agreeing to anything. And *a fortiori*, there is something instinctively incongruous about the idea of a meeting of mechanised minds. Nor can this be entirely got over by invoking the objective theory of contract under which, whatever the parties actually think or believe, something can be regarded as an agreement if it would look like one to a

[26] Subject to one small qualification. It has been said (*Arrale v Costain Civil Engineering Ltd* [1976] 1 Lloyd's Rep 98, 106) that it is no consideration to refrain from doing what one never intended to do in the first place. Although this might theoretically cause problems with computers that are unable to form intents, its practical significance seems infinitesimal.

[27] The humans need not necessarily, it should be noted, be the actual parties to the contract. Where a contract is entered into by human agents, as is always the case with contracts between corporations, the issue is as to the intent of those agents. But that is by-the-by: some agreement between humans is normally assumed.

reasonable bystander.[28] The difficulty here is a logical one: if there cannot in the nature of things be a meeting of minds between two computers, there equally cannot in logic be something that a reasonable person would see as being one.

Furthermore, offer and acceptance, normally seen as components of agreement, also present analogous difficulties of principle. An offer, it will be remembered, is traditionally described as a statement that would reasonably be understood by the addressee as indicating an intent in the offeror to be bound if the addressee assents.[29] But what if machines cannot sensibly be said to be able to grasp the idea of an intent to be bound? A person faced with an 'offer' from a machine cannot reasonably think that the machine intends to be bound if the machine itself cannot form such an intent: conversely a machine to which an offer is made by a person cannot believe in the latter's intent to be bound if it has no such conception. And *a fortiori* where offers are made by machine to machine: the logical difficulties multiply.

It might possibly be that a bit of judicial ingenuity could get over these points. It could be argued, for example, that in deciding whether something looked to a hypothetical reasonable third party[30] like an agreement on particular terms, in order to make sense of the objective principle the fact that one or other of the negotiators was an AIEM should simply be disregarded. It seems clear that this solution would in most cases[31] do little violence to the real parties' position.[32] So too with offer and acceptance: given the rule that having made what looks like an offer or an acceptance, a person cannot generally argue that they had some different intention, or no intention at all,[33] could be applied without getting too worried about the machine's technical capabilities.

Nevertheless, uncertainty would remain. It is our view that this should be avoided if possible. We suggest legislation, possibly providing that where the circumstances would indicate a binding agreement entered into directly between natural or legal persons, the validity of that agreement should not be denied on the ground only that it was concluded on one or both sides by or through an AIEM.

[28] This seems to us to be the most convincing position, perhaps subject to exceptions in a few cases: see M Howarth, 'The Meaning of Objectivity in Contract' (1984) 100 *Law Quarterly Review* 265; M Howarth, 'A Note on the Objective of Objectivity in Contract' (1987) 103 *Law Quarterly Review* 527. (Compare, however, the scepticism in N Sage, 'Reconciling Contract Law's Objective and Subjective Standards' (2023) 86 *Modern Law Review* 1422.)

[29] See *Chitty on Contracts*, 36th edn, para 4-003 ('Under the objective test of agreement, an apparent intention to be bound may suffice, ie the alleged offeror (A) may be bound if their words or conduct are such as to induce a reasonable offeree to believe that he intends to be bound, even though in fact he has no such intention' (footnotes omitted)).

[30] We presumably have to hypothesise a third party who, where necessary, is equipped with the ability to read and interpret non-human-readable computer code: but this does not seem too much of a stretch.

[31] Though not all: see below.

[32] *VTB Capital plc v Nutritek International Corpn* [2013] UKSC 5, [2013] 1 All ER 1296, [140]; *Chitty on Contracts*, 36th edn, para 4-002 and cases cited there.

[33] For the authorities, see *Chitty on Contracts*, 36th edn, paras 4-003 and 4-004.

B. The Relevance of Psychological Agreement

Despite the general acceptance of the objective theory of contract, in the case of agreements between humans there are cases where the law will discount the appearance and instead look to the parties' actual intent. Thus, it seems, a court will hold: (a) that actual psychological agreement can create a contract even if the parties' outward expressions indicate otherwise, for example because they are irreconcilably ambiguous;[34] and (b) that even where outwardly parties entered into a written agreement on terms *x*, if in fact they both shared, and each understood the other to share, an intent to agree on terms *y*, then the contract can be rectified to reflect that intent.[35]

In theory these could cause difficulties as regards contracts concluded wholly or partly through AI. In our view, however, the difficulty is more theoretical than practical. This is because, however much artificial intelligence a machine has, it will be near impossible to go behind its output in order to ascribe to it any inner intent to contract on particular terms. If so, it seems that to all intents and purposes an outward manifestation of agreement (or non-agreement, as the case may be) is likely to be conclusive.

A further possible difficulty arises from the so-called 'snapping-up' rule. This refers to the principle exemplified in cases like *Hartog v Colin & Shields*,[36] under which a person who knows that a counterparty's apparent agreement arises from an unintended statement cannot enforce the contract on those terms.[37] Now, often this should not be too difficult to apply to contracts concluded by an AIEM. A neat analogy would be a human internet shopper attempting a 'snap up' an offer on an AIEM-powered sales website, knowing that the goods were being offered for a tenth of their proper price owing to a computer decimal point glitch. But will this reasoning work as well the other way round, where it is the human and not the machine that is 'mistaken?' It is suggested that under the present law the point is difficult. A machine, however sophisticated its AI, cannot realistically be said to have had a belief as to the real intention of a human counterparty. This

[34] For an instance of this, assume that on the facts of *Raffles v Wichelhaus* (1864) 2 H & C 906 both parties had in fact been thinking of the same cargo. It seems inconceivable, as David McLauchlan suggests (see D McLaughlan, 'A Better Way of Making Sense of Contracts?' (2016) 132 *Law Quarterly Review* 577, 582–83), that a court would hold there was no contract merely because of the existence of a theoretical ambiguity which might have put the parties at cross-purposes but did not.

[35] This is the result of the decision in *FSHC Group Holdings Ltd v GLAS Trust Corpn Ltd* [2019] EWCA Civ 1361, [2020] Ch 365.

[36] [1939] 3 All ER 566. There, a seller mistakenly offered goods at a third of their usual price owing to an obvious slip of the pen: the buyer, knowing of the slip, unsuccessfully tried to hold the seller to the offer. See too the similar *O'Grady v B15 Group Ltd* [2022] EWHC 67 (QB), concerning an obvious keyboard error in an offer to settle. But the other party must know of the error: *cf OT Africa Line v Vickers* [1996] 1 Lloyd's Rep 700 (offer to settle claim mistakenly made in terms of pounds not dollars: accepted in good faith by claimant: valid contract).

[37] Indeed there is authority that the rule goes further, and that if the contract was in writing it may be rectified and enforced on the terms the mistaken party thought it was agreeing: *Roberts & Co Ltd v Leicestershire CC* [1961] Ch 555.

could be a potential source of uncertainty. Rather than leave the matter to the vagaries of litigation, in our view the best solution here is a statutory extension of the 'objective meaning' test, with inquiry limited in cases like this to the question of whether a reasonable person with a basic knowledge of AI would have seen an agreement here.

V. Interpretation and Implication

A. The Background Rules of Interpretation

The general rules of contractual interpretation applying to contracts concluded between human negotiators are well-known.[38] First, in principle, in seeking to determine the common intention of the parties, the court is required to:

> consider the language used and ascertain what a reasonable person, that is a person who has all the background knowledge which would reasonably have been available to the parties in the situation in which they were at the time of the contract, would have understood the parties to have meant.[39]

Secondly, words used must be understood as a whole and in the light of the purpose of the contract, and to this end may, if necessary, be read non-literally or even contrary to their dictionary sense.[40] Thirdly, truly unambiguous provisions must be given effect, although the result may be unfair and perhaps even unexpected.[41] Lastly, the 'factual matrix' against which the contract was concluded – that is, the general knowledge available to the parties – must be taken into account,[42] although as a general rule the parties' prior negotiations cannot be regarded.[43]

[38] See, for a useful summary, Lord Neuberger in *Arnold v Britton* [2015] UKSC 36, [2015] AC 1619, [16]–[23]; *Chitty on Contracts*, 35th edn, para 16-047 ff.

[39] *Rainy Sky SA v Kookmin Bank* [2011] UKSC 50, [2011] 1 WLR 2900, [21] (per Lord Clarke); *Chartbrook Ltd v Persimmon Homes Ltd* [2009] UKHL 38, [2009] AC 1101, [14] (per Lord Hoffmann). See too *Investors Compensation Scheme v West Bromwich Building Society* [1998] 1 WLR 896. However, if the parties actually intended a different meaning, then this rule is qualified, and at the very least rectification may, it seems, be available: *FSHC Group Holdings Ltd v GLAS Trust Corpn Ltd* [2019] EWCA Civ 1361, [2020] Ch 365.

[40] See generally *Chartbrook Ltd v Persimmon Homes Ltd* [2009] UKHL 38, [2009] 1 AC 1101, [14] ff (per Lord Hoffmann); also *Wood v Capita Insurance Services Ltd* [2017] UKSC 24, [2017] AC 1173, [10]–[13] (per Lord Hodge).

[41] *Arnold v Britton* [2015] UKSC 36, [2015] AC 1619, [15]–[20], [23], [66], [76]–[77]; also *Rainy Sky SA v Kookmin Bank* [2011] UKSC 50, [2011] 1 WLR 2900, [23] (per Lord Clarke).

[42] *Investors Compensation Scheme Ltd v West Bromwich Building Society* [1998] 1 WLR 896, 912–13 (per Lord Hoffmann); also *Wood v Capita Insurance Services Ltd* [2017] UKSC 24, [2017] AC 1173, [10] (per Lord Hodge) and the much earlier *Prenn v Simmonds* [1971] 1 WLR 1381, 1383–85 (per Lord Wilberforce).

[43] *Chartbrook Ltd v Persimmon Homes Ltd* [2009] UKHL 38, [2009] 1 AC 1101, esp [28]–[42] and [69]–[70] (per Lords Hoffmann and Rodger); also *Prenn v Simmonds* [1971] 1 WLR 1381, 1384–85 (per Lord Wilberforce).

B. Interpretation and Machine-Made Contracts

The question is how far these principles can be transferred over and applied where one or both parties negotiating the contract are not persons but AIEMs.[44] We begin with the probable situation under the present law.

In some cases, there is no difficulty. In many situations, even if a contract is technically concluded through the use of an AIEM on one or both sides, the important terms will be contained in detailed boilerplate previously negotiated between, and drafted by, humans. Internet purchases, for example, will normally involve reference to the seller's standard terms and conditions, which will be agreed to either by tick-box or click-wrap.[45] Again, machine-driven currency trades or stock purchases are likely to be carried out against a background of a detailed umbrella agreement previously set up between the real parties; automatically-generated currency or interest swaps on the basis of something like the ISDA agreement; and so on. In all these cases, it is suggested that the interpretation exercise is simply a matter of applying the ordinary principles of interpretation. There being no AIEM involvement in the drafting of the boilerplate, as against the sealing of the deal, the rules for interpreting it must, in our view, be the same as for any other non-machine contract as described above. Hence the intention of the (human) parties who negotiated the underlying agreement has to be divined from the document's natural meaning in the light of its commercial purpose, the factual matrix as known to the parties, a healthy refusal to correct commercial imbalances if the words clearly point to them, and so on.

But other situations may be less tractable. It is perfectly possible for a contract to be concluded in a fairly skeletal form without reference to any underlying document, either between a legal person and an AI-enabled machine (for example, an internet purchase where, because of a glitch or for some other reason, there was no adequate reference to the seller's standard terms), or even conceivably between two AI-enabled machines.[46] How in that case should the resulting agreement be interpreted, given that there are difficulties in the idea of a common intention shared between a person and a machine (even an AI-equipped one), and also in the notion that such a machine might have contracted with reference to a factual matrix known to it?

Some rules, it has to be admitted, can be carried across quite neatly. For example, provided we postulate a hypothetical tech-savvy bystander familiar

[44] See generally S Green, 'Smart Contracts, Interpretation and Rectification' (2018) *Lloyd's Maritime & Commercial Law Quarterly* 234.

[45] Which are generally effective as means of conclusion of contracts and inclusion of terms, subject to the same exceptions as with signed documents: see *Ebury Partners Belgium SA/NV v Technical Touch BV* [2022] EWHC 2927 (Comm), [2023] 2 All ER (Comm) 314 and *Durber v PPB Entertainment Ltd* [2025] EWHC 498 (KB).

[46] An example might be where, in an automated raw material procurement situation, an order was placed and filled for a commodity which, owing to an oversight, was not mentioned in the underlying boilerplate.

with computer code, the rule that contracts are interpreted according to the view of a reasonable observer as to the meaning of any outward manifestations of assent is capable of applying to computer-generated just as much as to human agreements.[47] So too, we suggest, with the need to reconcile any words used with the commercial purpose of an agreement. Since the latter is in most cases a matter open to objective estimation without delving into any issues of actual party intent, there should be no difficulty in conducting a 'reality check' against it when interpreting any words (or code) used. And yet again, the same goes for the refusal to rewrite clear words which give a contract a particular meaning merely because they lead to a harsh or surprising result; indeed, it probably applies with even greater force to AIEM agreements than to traditional contracts.

This still leaves one major awkwardness, however: the factual matrix. All the rules just mentioned can be applied abstractly, without reference to anyone's actual beliefs, knowledge or intentions. The factual matrix rule cannot. It inescapably mandates a look into the relevant surrounding facts, not as seen by bystanders generally, or reasonable observers, but more particularly as those facts were known to both parties.[48] Now, with humans this makes perfect sense: people as a rule enter into agreements with one eye on the world as known to them. But with AIEMs? Even if it were possible for a court to deploy expert evidence to fathom whether particular data lurked somewhere, in some form, in the memory of a supercomputer, there would still, it is suggested, be difficulties as to whether this counted as 'knowledge', and an almost insuperable problem in determining how relevant it might have been to the supercomputer's thought processes. Nor does it improve matters if we go behind the AIEM to the contracting party (human or corporate) behind it and ask instead what was known to that party. The point of an AIEM negotiating a contract is that it, rather than the party it represents, takes the initiative and decides whether to agree, and if so on what terms. It follows that the connection between the factual matrix available to the actual party and the terms of the contract is correspondingly remote. It is hard to avoid the conclusion that a court would in such a situation simply avoid taking the factual matrix into account at all, and look instead to other means of interpretation of the agreement reached.

This might seem unfortunate. Nevertheless, in our view, however clear the mismatch between human and machine-made agreements, this is probably an unavoidable problem when it comes to AIEM-driven contracts. We suggest that in any case it is unlikely that it will cause a great deal of injustice and take the tentative view that the best practical solution to this issue is to let sleeping dogs lie.

[47] A point nicely made in Green (n 44) 244–45.

[48] Thus, Lord Hodge has referred explicitly to the factual background 'known to the parties': *Wood v Capita Insurance Services Ltd* [2017] UKSC 24, [2017] AC 1173, [10].

C. Implied Terms

Whether a term is to be implied into a contract is a somewhat complex affair in English law.[49] Despite suggestions at one time that implication and interpretation were essentially aspects of the same subject, since both were aimed at establishing the precise parameters of the obligations undertaken by the parties,[50] it now seems that the better view is that they are to be regarded as separate[51] (though obviously closely related).[52] The rules are essentially these.

First, a person alleging that a term should feature in a contract that does not appear from its actual words bears the burden of establishing this, and this burden can be heavy: a term will not be implied merely because it is reasonable, or will better balance the parties' obligations.[53] Secondly, a term can never be implied if contrary to an express term.[54] Thirdly, a number of terms are implied by usage as presumptively necessary incidents[55] of particular kinds of contracts, such as banking, tenancy or shipment arrangements:[56] in a few cases, notably sales of goods and the supply of services, these implications are now statutory.[57] Fourthly, a term may be implied by custom.[58] Fifthly, a term will be implied into a contract if the arrangement could not operate in a reasonably businesslike way without it being there.[59] And sixthly, where such a term would be regarded as

[49] See generally *Chitty on Contracts*, 36th edn, Ch 17.

[50] Notably as the result of remarks by Lord Hoffmann in *Att-Gen of Belize v Belize Telecom Ltd* [2009] UKPC 10, [2009] 1 WLR 1988, [17]–[27] (and defended later in L Hoffmann, 'Language and Lawyers' (2018) 134 *Law Quarterly Review* 553, 562 ff).

[51] See *Marks & Spencer plc v BNP Paribas Securities Services Trust Co (Jersey) Ltd* [2015] UKSC 72, [2016] AC 742, [31] (per Lord Neuberger); also *M/V Pacific Pearl Co Ltd v Osios David Shipping Inc* [2022] EWCA Civ 798, [2022] 2 Lloyd's Rep 448, [39].

[52] See *Tesco Stores Ltd v USDAW* [2024] UKSC 28, [2025] 2 All ER 565, [34] (per Lords Burrows and Simler), and also [98]–[101] (per Lord Leggatt).

[53] See eg *Barton v Morris* [2023] UKSC 3, [2023] AC 684, [22]. The result in *Marks & Spencer plc v BNP Paribas Securities Services Trust Co (Jersey) Ltd* [2015] UKSC 72, [2016] AC 742 provides a notable illustration of the effect of this principle.

[54] '[I]f there is an express term in the contract, which is inconsistent with the proposed implied term, the latter cannot, by definition, meet these tests, since the parties have demonstrated that it is not their agreement': Lord Hughes in *Ali v Petroleum Co of Trinidad & Tobago* [2017] UKPC 2, [2017] ICR 531, [5].

[55] *cf Société Générale, London Branch v Geys* [2012] UKSC 63, [2013] 1 AC 523, [56].

[56] See the reference by Lady Hale in *Société Générale, London Branch v Geys* [2012] UKSC 63, [2013] 1 AC 523, [55] to a 'class of contractual relationship, such as that between landlord and tenant or between employer and employee, where the parties may have left a good deal unsaid, but the courts have implied the term as a necessary incident of the relationship concerned, unless the parties have expressly excluded it'. The courts in such cases apply a fairly broad brush, not being limited to the actual relationship between these parties: eg *Scally v Southern Health & Social Services Board* [1992] 1 AC 294 and the earlier *Liverpool City Council v Irwin* [1977] AC 239.

[57] See the Sale of Goods Act 1979, esp ss 12–15; the Supply of Goods and Services Act 1982, Part I; and, in consumer cases, the provisions of the Consumer Rights Act 2015. In these instances the statutory implications derive from, but also build on, the implied terms that would have applied at common law.

[58] See eg *Cunliffe-Owen v Teather* [1967] 1 WLR 1421 (customs of the Stock Exchange).

[59] The classic example is *The Moorcock* (1889) 14 PD 64. A more modern one is *Duval v 11–13 Randolph Crescent Ltd* [2020] UKSC 18, [2020] AC 845.

obviously necessary were the parties to have thought of the matter, then it will generally be inserted.[60]

What of contracts concluded by or through AIEMs? Can these rules be carried over? It is our view that, subject to what we say above about the factual matrix, in most cases they probably can. The rules as to implied terms, while restrictive, are also very largely abstract and objective. They overwhelmingly look to the circumstances of the contract, and to the potential reaction of abstract reasonable contractors, rather than to the detailed process of concluding the agreement. Indeed, when it comes to the insertion of terms that would not otherwise appear in the contract as properly interpreted, the courts are as often as not at pains to minimise the relevance of the parties' actual intentions, beliefs and hopes.[61] We suggest that for this reason there is no need for statutory or other intervention in this area to take account of the possible effects of AI.

VI. Vitiating Factors

A. Mistake and Misrepresentation

The traditional rules as to how far a contract can be impugned for mistake or misrepresentation[62] are complex. We summarise them here as briefly and succinctly as possible.

First, a contract is ineffective if concluded as a result of both parties A and B sharing a fundamental mistake[63] of fact or law, or if both parties make a tacit but ill-founded assumption about a matter of fundamental importance.[64] Secondly, if one party A misunderstands the terms they are agreeing to and the other

[60] See in particular the 'of course' test of Scrutton LJ in *Reigate v Union Manufacturing Co (Ramsbottom) Ltd* [1918] 1 KB 592, 605 and McKinnon LJ in *Shirlaw v Southern Foundries Ltd* [1939] 2 KB 206, 227; *cf* too *Modahl v British Athletic Federation Ltd* [2001] EWCA Civ 1447, [2002] 1 WLR 1192, [119].

[61] '[O]ne is not strictly concerned with the hypothetical answer of the actual parties, but with that of notional reasonable people in the position of the parties at the time at which they were contracting': Lord Neuberger in *Marks & Spencer plc v BNP Paribas Securities Services Trust Co (Jersey) Ltd* [2015] UKSC 72, [2016] AC 742, [21].

[62] We here treat error and misrepresentation together, as civil lawyers do, despite the tradition in English law of separating the two topics. This is because both involve, fundamentally, error on the part of one party, and for the purposes of our discussion many of the same issues arise.

[63] A 'fundamental mistake' amounts to a fairly extreme requirement. The error must be one that makes the subject matter of the contract 'essentially and radically different': *Associated Japanese Bank (International) Ltd v Credit du Nord SA* [1989] 1 WLR 255, 268 (per Steyn J), citing the seminal decision in *Bell v Lever Brothers Ltd* [1932] AC 161. See too *Apvodedo NV v Collins* [2008] EWHC 775 (Ch), [43] and [46] (per Henderson J).

[64] Implicit in the decision in *Associated Japanese Bank (International) Ltd v Credit du Nord SA* [1989] 1 WLR 255.

party B is aware of the mistake,[65] B cannot enforce the contract against A.[66] Thirdly, if A is induced by B's misrepresentation of fact or law to contract with B, A can rescind the contract almost as a matter of course,[67] subject to a discretion in the court to disallow rescission and award damages in lieu[68] provided the misrepresentation was not fraudulent.[69]

The above matters go to the validity of the contract or the obligations contained in it, making it unenforceable by one or both parties and in certain cases allowing the undoing of performance already rendered. In addition, however, there is also a related right of rectification[70] available in respect of a written contract,[71] which leaves the contract valid but alters its apparent terms. This applies in two cases. First, where the supposedly authoritative written expression of the contract fails to reproduce an agreement that both parties intended, then (provided that the genuine agreement was not private to the parties but manifested externally in some way[72]) the written document can be rectified to make it correspond. And secondly, where Party A is mistaken as to what the written document contains and Party B knows of that mistake, the document can be rewritten at the application of A so as to make it embody A's understanding of its terms.[73]

How might these rules apply where AI is involved or a contract is concluded or mediated through an AIEM? Under the present law it is suggested that this will actually make a considerable difference. With one exception, it seems that data on or available to the AIEM, even if inaccurate and thus apparently amounting to an error, will have to be disregarded. The reason for this is technical. In the context of contract, relief for error depends in nearly all cases on questions of one or other party's beliefs, knowledge or assumptions. And, while an AIEM can hold data, it is difficult, as we suggest elsewhere,[74] to attribute a belief or an assumption to it. If so, then it seems to follow that material on the machine must be discounted, and the only error which a court can have regard to is error on the part of the humans behind it. A decision from Singapore illustrates this. In *Quoine Pte Ltd*

[65] B must be so aware: see *Riverlate Properties Ltd v Paul* [1975] Ch 133 and *OT Africa Line v Vickers* [1996] 1 Lloyd's Rep 700.

[66] *Hartog v Colin & Shields* [1939] 3 All ER 566; also, *Shogun Finance Ltd v Hudson* [2003] UKHL 62, [2004] 1 AC 919, [123] (per Lord Phillips) and *O'Grady v B15 Group Ltd* [2022] EWHC 67 (QB).

[67] See generally *Chitty on Contracts*, 35th edn, para 10-123 ff.

[68] Under s 2(2) of the Misrepresentation Act 1967.

[69] See the same section, requiring the misrepresentation to have been made 'other than fraudulently'. Note, however, that we suggest elsewhere (p 69) that a machine cannot itself act fraudulently, which means that this qualification is of limited significance in the AI context.

[70] See also p 84.

[71] Strictly speaking, rectification affects documents not contracts: hence the reference to 'written expression'. We suggest, however, that there will be no difficulty in showing that a written expression includes a copy of the contract in machine-readable form held in memory.

[72] This is essential: see *FSHC Group Holdings Ltd v Glas Trust Corpn Ltd* [2019] EWCA Civ 1361, [75]–[77]; also [80]–[87].

[73] As in *Roberts v Leicestershire CC* [1961] Ch 555, above. Also see more recently *Holaw (470) Ltd v Stockton Estates Ltd* (2000) 81 P & CR 29, [41].

[74] See p 101.

v B2C2 Ltd,[75] a case of automated trading in cryptocurrency, B2C2 sold Ether for something like 250 times its value because of a glitch in Quoine's software. Quoine failed to undo the trade on the basis of mistake, it being held that the only relevant error would have been an error on the part of Quoine itself (or some human representing it).

A similar limitation applies, we suggest, in the case of rectification. In *FSHC Group Holdings Ltd v Glas Trust Corpn Ltd*[76] the Court of Appeal analysed rectification, in the sense of making a written document reflect a prior agreement, as dependent on a showing of two things: first, actual intent (which had to be somehow manifested externally) to agree to something different; and secondly, a discrepancy between the prior manifestation of the parties' agreement, and its expression in written form. The latter raises no problems in the AI context: but the same cannot be said of the former. If we are right to suggest that a machine cannot meaningfully be said to have intended subjectively to agree anything, then it follows that a finding that it has participated in a prior meeting of minds would be incoherent. And a similar argument applies, though in a slightly different form, to the second form of rectification applying where one party knows of the mistake of a counterparty about what the latter is agreeing to.[77] If, as we argue, a machine cannot have a mistaken belief, it cannot logically have a conception of another contracting party being in that state. It follows that unless the law is changed, in AIEM-mediated contexts rectification is likely to be largely a dead letter.

So far, we have suggested that error, at least as normally understood in the law of contract, can only mean error by humans. Oddly enough, however, there may be one exception: namely, the case of misrepresentation and fraud.[78] There is existing authority that the duping of a machine as much as that of a human can give rise to a claim in deceit by the machine's operator,[79] and there is no reason to think that the position is any different in the case of a claim to impugn a contract on the same basis. This position may seem anomalous but arguably is defensible. This is on the basis that the reason why misrepresentation and fraud are vitiating factors lies not so much in the vitiation of the intention of the misled party, as in the idea that A should not be allowed to benefit from their own provision of false information to B that caused B to contract.[80] If so, then there is much to be said by

[75] [2020] SGCA(I) 2, [2020] 2 SLR 20.

[76] [2019] EWCA Civ 1361, [2020] Ch 365.

[77] That is, the rule in *Roberts v Leicestershire CC* [1961] Ch 555 referred to above.

[78] Fraud, of course, only in the case of a human misrepresentor deceiving a machine: we suggest elsewhere that a machine, being unable to hold a belief present to its mind, cannot be guilty of fraud.

[79] *Renault UK Ltd v Fleetpro Technical Services Ltd* [2007] EWHC 2541 (QB), [2008] Bus LR D17: and see also *IG Index plc v Colley* [2013] EWHC 478 (QB). There is, it seems, no parallel case about innocent misrepresentation, but the situation here is, it is suggested, the same.

[80] There is some support for this approach in the case law. Compare Jessel MR in the leading misrepresentation case of *Redgrave v Hurd* (1881) 20 ChD 1, 12–13: 'Even assuming that moral fraud must be shewn in order to set aside a contract, you have it where a man, having obtained a beneficial contract by a statement which he now knows to be false, insists upon keeping that contract. To do so is a moral delinquency: no man ought to seek to take advantage of his own false statements.'

analogy for allowing the usual remedies for fraud and misrepresentation by a party to a contract even though the false information has been made available not to the other party themselves but to a machine under their control.

Is the present position satisfactory, or do we need changes to accommodate AI? The matter is finely balanced, but in our view the case for change is not strong. Proof that a machine intended *x*, or knew *y*, in the way that a human does these things, is fraught with difficulty in any case, and this is a powerful argument against asking a court to try to decide whether this has been done. It will remain possible, where a contracting party contracts through the intermediacy of an AIEM, to prove that their own behaviour has been altered by the feeding to it of false information by the counterparty and, if it has, to have the appropriate remedy: in our view this is an adequate protection.

B. Undue Influence

In most cases the issue of undue influence is unlikely to be affected under the present law by the fact that one or other party has contracted through, or with the aid of, an AIEM. In so far as the exerting of undue influence involves the misuse by a party of personal ascendancy or emotional pressure,[81] it clearly cannot apply to the actions of an inanimate AIEM: the only issue is whether such pressure emanated from the person behind the machine. So too it is also hard to see how an AIEM, which is presumably not prone to human weaknesses, can be subjected to undue influence. If so, it follows that in most cases where relief from a contract concluded through or by AIEMs is sought on the basis of undue influence, the only issue will relate to the position of the humans behind the machines. There are, however, two possible cases where this is not so, and the use of AI may create difficulties: namely, cases where advisers are involved, and cases where the issue arises of knowledge or notice in third parties.

Take first the case of advisers. Where it is clear that, in the context of a contract between A and B, A relied implicitly on B to advise them or look after their interests, then any contract between them which arises out of that relationship is potentially vulnerable to attack by A on the basis of undue influence.[82]

Does this equally apply where the relationship is AIEM-mediated, for example where a firm of lawyers, brokers or financial advisers entrusts the giving of advice to a client to an AIEM which it has set up? In our view it does. This is because, although a machine obviously cannot be in a position of personal ascendancy over

[81] See eg cases like *Lloyds Bank Ltd v Bundy* [1975] QB 326 or *Crédit Lyonnais SA v Burch* [1997] 1 All ER 144.

[82] Eg *Tate v Williamson* (1866–67) LR 2 Ch App 55; *Goldsworthy v Brickell* [1987] 1 All ER 853 and *Bank of Credit & Commerce International SA v Aboody* [1990] 1 QB 923, esp 967. In certain relationships, such reliance is presumed in the absence of some independent justification for the transaction: see *Royal Bank of Scotland plc v Etridge (No 2)* [2001] UKHL 44, [2002] 2 AC 773, [16], [104] and [153] and cases such as *Wright v Carter* [1903] 1 Ch 27.

a human, the rule requiring the law to scrutinise contracts between a person and their adviser exists not on the basis of personal influence exerted by the latter, but on the likely vulnerability and susceptibility of the former. The principle is, it has been said, that 'once the … relationship has been shown to exist, no benefit can be retained from the transaction unless it has been positively established that the duty of fiduciary care has been entirely fulfilled':[83] in other words, the transaction cannot stand unless the other party has had the benefit of full information and concluded the transaction entirely voluntarily. It is entirely possible to apply this to the case of the AIEM.

Is this the right solution? We think it probably is. There is a clear logic in treating those dealing with a firm providing them with advice similarly, without regard to whether the advice is provided by human agency or wholly or partly through AI. If so, then it is right to apply the same criteria to decide whether their consent to the transaction is indeed voluntary and informed in the eyes of the law and hence whether any contract entered into in connection with it is open to attack.

So much for advisers. Now for the position of third parties. Whether or not the rules relating to the establishment of undue influence vary according to whether or not an AIEM is involved, the effect of any such influence that is brought to bear may also vary according to the level of knowledge or notice possessed by a third party seeking to enforce or take advantage of rights arising from the transaction. Typical is the situation where a lender, such as a bank, takes a guarantee from A (or security over A's property) in a case where there is a possibility that undue influence may have been exerted by B over A. The position in such cases where human contractors are involved is that the lender's rights may be affected, but only if either it has notice of such influence,[84] or it has notice of the fact that such influence may be present and fails to take steps to ensure the voluntariness of the transaction.[85]

What if the lender takes its lending decisions using AI? Unfortunately, a complication could arise here. As pointed out in connection with the doctrine of notice generally in equity,[86] an AIEM is not for legal purposes an agent; furthermore, there is no reason to think that the availability of data in the memory of, or in memory accessible by, an AIEM will as such be taken as equivalent to notice to its controller.[87] If this is right, then if the whole transaction was entrusted to an AIEM the whole basis for holding the lender affected by the undue influence in question arguably disappears. Only if knowledge, or blameworthy failure to make

[83] *Lloyds Bank Ltd v Bundy* [1975] QB 326, 346 (per Sir Eric Sachs); see generally *Chitty on Contracts*, 35th edn, para 11-116.

[84] See eg *Bainbridge v Browne* (1881) 18 Ch D 188; *Coldunell Ltd v Gallon* [1986] 1 All ER 429.

[85] The leading authorities being *Royal Bank of Scotland plc v Etridge (No 2)* [2001] UKHL 44, [2002] 2 AC 773 and *One Savings Bank plc v Waller-Edwards* [2025] UKSC 22, [2025] 2 WLR 1263. For a useful contemporary comment on the former see D O'Sullivan, 'Developing O'Brien' (2002) 118 *Law Quarterly Review* 33.

[86] See p 82.

[87] See p 82.

inquiries, can be brought home to the persons for whom the AIEM worked can the counterparty succeed in arguing that the lender was affected. In short, there is a worrying possibility that under the present law a fairly radical distinction may have to be drawn between third parties who conduct business through AIEMs and those who do not.

It seems to us that this is an unsatisfactory position, and that for obvious reasons of horizontal equity the treatment of all lenders ought to be approximated. In our view, it should be provided by legislation that for the limited purposes of the law of undue influence and other equitable vitiating factors affecting contracts, information available to an AIEM should be treated for all purposes as information available to its controller.

C. Unconscionable Bargains

In addition to undue influence and error, there is also a residuary jurisdiction in equity to set aside a contract as an unconscionable bargain: in particular, in so far as it is greatly unfair and results from a gross disparity in understanding of which unconscionable advantage has been taken by the advantaged party.[88] Typical cases involve sales of assets or other transactions where, first, there is a gross disparity between the performances on either side; secondly, advantage has been taken of that; and thirdly, it is clear that the capacity of one party to look after their interests is severely compromised.[89]

It is conceivable that this might be in issue in the AI context. Imagine, for instance, that a commercial buyer of real property uses an AIEM to carry on negotiations with a fairly uninformed and unsophisticated seller. Can the rules relating to unconscionability apply? There is a difficulty here, since it seems clear from the authorities that to trigger the application of these rules there is a requirement that the advantaged party be shown to have behaved unconscientiously;[90] that is, that they comported themselves 'in a morally reprehensible manner' which therefore 'affects his conscience'.[91] There is some doubt as to how far this could be applied to negotiations taking place through an AIEM where its controller is not aware of how the negotiations are being conducted. Can a machine behave in a morally reprehensible manner, or in such a way as to have its conscience affected?

[88] *Chitty on Contracts*, 36th edn, para 11-174, quoting Blair J in *Strydom v Vendside Ltd* [2009] EWHC 2130 (QB), [36]. This is sometimes known as the 'poor and ignorant' doctrine, after the words of Kay J in *Fry v Lane* (1888) 40 Ch D 312, 322. See generally D Capper, 'The Unconscionable Bargain in the Common Law World' (2010) 126 *Law Quarterly Review* 403.

[89] See eg *Clark v Malpas* (1862) 4 De G F & J 401 and *Boustany v Piggott* (1995) 69 P & CR 298. And *cf* the security case of *Crédit Lyonnais Bank Nederland NV v Burch* [1997] 1 All ER 144, esp 153.

[90] *Alec Lobb (Garages) Ltd v Total Oil (Great Britain) Ltd* [1985] 1 WLR 173, 182 (Dillon LJ).

[91] See *Boustany v Piggott* (1995) 69 P & CR 298, 303, quoting *Multiservice Bookbinding Ltd v Marden* [1979] Ch 84, 110 (per Browne-Wilkinson J); see generally *Chitty on Contracts*, 36th edn, para 11-177.

There are arguments both ways here. While it might seem obvious at first sight that it is a nonsense to ask whether an AIEM without a conscience has acted unconscientiously, there is a perfectly plausible counter-argument that a court could inquire whether the behaviour of AI would have been unconscientious if engaged in by a human, and then proceed to determine issues of unconscionability on the basis of the answer it reached. But the matter remains uncertain, and we see no good reason to leave it to the luck of litigation to sort it out. It is our view that legislation ought to provide that for the purpose of any jurisdiction to impugn a transaction as unconscionable on account of the relative position of the parties, account should be taken of both the actions of any AIEM and the state of mind of its controller, and a decision made as to whether the conscience of a reasonable person in the position of the latter would be affected had they known of the actions of the former.

D. Duress

This is a subject that is discussed at greater length in Chapter 6 on unjust enrichment, to which the reader is referred. But it is also of great significance as a potential means of impugning the validity of a contract.[92]

As we say elsewhere, cases of duress are on the whole likely to raise few specific issues as regards the use of AIEMs. This is certainly true of duress in its most elemental form of physical threats, if only because machines cannot exert such duress themselves, are unlikely in the nature of things to threaten it and conversely are even less likely to suffer it.

On the other hand, the issue of AIEMs may conceivably arise in connection with more subtle forms of duress, such as the threat of a wrong or breach of contract.[93] Both these could certainly be threatened by a computer, and equally a similar threat made to it might influence it in any decisions it took to contract, or to advise its controller to do so. However, it is suggested that there is no reason to think that the interposition of an AIEM will make much difference to the rules applicable here. Although at one level the thinking behind duress might be thought to embody the compromise of another's will or freedom of action (something that does indeed make little sense in the case of a machine), in practice the approach of the law is more abstract here, concentrating more on the illegitimacy of allowing a person to gain an advantage (in the shape of an enforceable contract) through their own wrongful act.[94] And such reasoning is equally applicable to the activities of AIEMs as it is to human and other contractors.

[92] *Chitty on Contracts*, 36th edn, para 11-003 ff.

[93] See eg *The Universe Sentinel* [1983] 1 AC 366 (wrong); *The Siboen & The Sibotre* [1976] 1 Lloyd's Rep 293 and *Atlas Express Ltd v Kafco (Importers and Distributors) Ltd* [1989] QB 833 (breach of contract).

[94] Compare Lord Scarman's dicta in *The Universe Sentinel* [1983] 1 AC 366, 401; also *Borrelli v Ting* [2010] UKPC 21, and Lord Hodge in *Times Travel (UK) Ltd v Pakistan International Airlines Corpn* [2021] UKSC 40, [2023] AC 101, [1]–[13]. These authorities throw into considerable doubt the reasoning in earlier cases like *Pao On v Lau Yiu Long* [1980] AC 614, which had regarded it as important to inquire whether the duress victim's will had been overborne.

What of lawful act duress, a category finally cemented in our law by the 2021 decision in *Times Travel (UK) Ltd v Pakistan International Airlines Corpn*?[95] In theory, the position could be a little different, the requirement here being a showing of either seriously reprehensible but not illegal behaviour, or (for example) threats to prosecute a person or their connections with a view to inducing them to contract.[96] Here there is an element of personal morality involved, which could in theory cause difficulties in cases where an amoral element of AI featured in the contracting process. Admittedly, as we observe in connection with unjust enrichment, any mismatch with the ordinary law is likely to be small.[97] Nevertheless on balance we would see much attraction in changing the law, in parallel to that applying to unconscionability, and providing that where an act of an AIEM is alleged to constitute duress it should be enough if the same act would have done so if performed by a human or corporation.

VII. Contractual Performance

No issues connected with contractual performance arise directly from the use of AIEMs. Depending on the terms of a contract, a party can clearly in principle use an AIEM as an aid to performance;[98] indeed, it seems likely that direct performance by AI will become a great deal commoner.[99] However, a number of matters may arise more indirectly, and they are worth noting briefly.

A. Vicarious Performance

Under the present law, the question whether a contractual obligation must be performed personally or can be delegated to a third party is a matter of contractual interpretation in the light of the parties' intention.[100] While no clear rule or presumption emerges from the authorities, it seems that performance of most straightforward commercial contracts can prima facie be delegated;[101] but the

[95] [2021] UKSC 40, [2023] AC 101. In that case its existence was accepted (though not on the facts before the court) by a majority of the court.

[96] Eg *Williams v Bayley* (1866) LR 1 HL 200; *Mutual Finance Ltd v Wetton & Sons Ltd* [1937] 2 KB 389.

[97] If only because the incidence of lawful act duress is itself likely in practice to be very limited.

[98] For example, in choosing goods of the correct quality to supply under a sale contract, monitoring service levels under a contract for logistical or other services, or helping a financial adviser decide between investments.

[99] For example, goods being delivered by an autonomous vehicle or AI-enabled drone, or securities advice being given by an AIEM acting as adviser.

[100] See eg *Davies v Collins* [1945] 1 All ER 247, 250 (Lord Greene MR); also, the earlier *British Waggon Co v Lea* (1880) 5 QBD 149, esp 153 (per Cockburn CJ).

[101] Compare Paull J in *Garnham Harris & Elton Ltd v Alfred W Ellis (Transport) Ltd* [1967] 1 WLR 940, 947.

nature of the contract, and degree of risk[102] or personal skill[103] involved, may give a contrary result.

How far can these principles be carried over to the delegation of performance to an AIEM? The answer is not entirely clear, particularly since the element of personal skill might well become rather less important as machines became more intelligent and able to replicate or even exceed human abilities, and professional advice is one of the areas where the use of AI is increasing fast. It would be possible to leave the matter to be worked out as a matter of case law over time; but in our view this would lead to undesirable uncertainty in the interim. We suggest that it would be better to clarify the matter in any reform of AI law.

It is respectfully suggested that since many people and businesses might have understandable concerns about receiving services via AIEM rather than human agency, the best solution would be a presumptive rule that recognised this. In our view the best solution would be a brief statutory provision confirming that in any contract for the provision of services, a contracting party has a presumptive right to personal performance rather than performance by an AIEM. This would, however, be a prima facie rule only, and would be stated to be subject to any express or implied agreement to the contrary between the contracting parties.

B. Duties of Care

The difference between contractual and tortious duties is often over-stated. In practice, very large numbers of contractual duties amount, as in tort, to some form of a duty of care: an express or implied obligations to take care, for example, or a duty to see that care is taken by oneself or those whose services one uses, or to show standards of reasonable skill and competence (the latter, for example, predominates in the field of construction or professional services contracts).

In all these cases, where AIEMs intervene complications arise under the present law in the same way as they do in connection with tortious negligence. They arise in particular from a point we make in greater detail in that connection: namely, that there is under the present law no such thing as a negligent machine. It follows from this proposition that in so far as a contractor who is obliged to take care utilises an AIEM, and personally[104] shows all due care in using and supervising it, then they will not be in breach of any contractual duty

[102] See *Garnham Harris & Elton Ltd v Alfred W Ellis (Transport) Ltd* [1967] 1 WLR 940, above, where Paull J held that the right to delegate was excluded in the case of a valuable and easily stealable load of peculiar attraction to thieves.

[103] Hence professional duties generally cannot be delegated: see eg *Moresk Cleaners Ltd v Hicks* [1966] 2 Lloyd's Rep 338, 343 and *Southway Group Ltd v Wolff & Wolff* (1991) 57 BLR 33.

[104] Or, corporately, where neither the company's directing mind and will nor any employee has been at fault.

even if the AIEM makes an error that would in the case of a person be clearly negligent. Any victim will thus be forced to prove personal fault in the controller of the AIEM (or alternatively in its manufacturer or someone involved in programming or operating it[105]) in order to receive compensation.

Furthermore, it makes no difference that the duty is a non-delegable one to ensure that care is taken: if a machine cannot fail to take reasonable care, there will be nothing for this duty to bite on either. It is arguable that the result might be different where the duty is to procure that work is done to a reasonably competent standard,[106] since it could in theory be said that an AIEM could at least fail to do this: but even this is uncertain.

As with tort, it is our view that this needs to be changed. In contract, as in tort, there is no justification for affording fundamentally differential treatment to those who are injured by the failings of machines or humans. For the purposes of any contractual duty to take care or procure that care be taken, or any like duty, it should be provided that where that duty is undertaken by an AIEM, then any mistake by the latter which would have amounted to negligence in a human shall be treated as if it were human fault for the purposes of any liability.

C. Good Faith

English law, as is well-known, recognises no doctrine of good faith in contract performance in general.[107] But it does recognise it, or something like it, in three situations. First, there is nothing to prevent parties introducing an *express* duty of good faith. This is increasingly common, and in principle such duties are enforceable.[108] Secondly, there may – especially in long-term contracts – be a specific if implicit obligation not deliberately to mislead the other party or defeat the object of the contract.[109] And thirdly, where one party has a unilateral power fairly drastically to change the terms of the contract or to make a decision that will drastically change the other party's position, the court may well imply an obligation not to use the power in bad faith; that is, not to use it other than for a legitimate purpose.[110]

[105] For example, a programmer who failed adequately to install, or even perhaps code, a vital update.

[106] A standard that appears in a typical duty of care deed in the construction context.

[107] *Chitty on Contracts*, 35th edn, para 2-038 ff; and eg *Interfoto Picture Library Ltd v Stilletto Visual Programmes Ltd* [1989] QB 433, 439 (per Bingham LJ); *Monde Petroleum SA v WesternZagros Ltd* [2016] EWHC 1472 (Comm), [2016] 2 Lloyd's Rep 229, [249].

[108] For instance, in long-term energy production contracts, or joint venture or shareholding agreements, where it largely means a duty to be honest and not deliberately to subvert the contract or its workings. See eg *Scottish Power UK plc v BP Exploration Operating Co Ltd* [2015] EWHC 2658 (Comm), [2016] 1 All ER (Comm) 536 and *Connoisseur Developments Ltd v Koumis* [2023] EWHC 855 (Ch). But, as was made clear in cases such as *Faulkner v Vollin Holdings Ltd* [2022] EWCA Civ 1371, the meaning of such clauses is highly contextual.

[109] *Yam Seng Pte Ltd v International Trade Corp Ltd* [2013] EWHC 111 (QB), [2013] 1 CLC 662, [132]–[146]; also *D&G Cars Ltd v Essex Police Authority* [2015] EWHC 226 (QB), [173]–[177].

[110] eg *Abu Dhabi National Tanker Co v Product Star Shipping Ltd (No 2)* [1993] 1 Lloyd's Rep 397, 404 (per Leggatt LJ); *Paragon Finance plc v Nash* [2001] EWCA Civ 1466, [2002] 1 WLR 685, [32]–[36]

None of these doctrines currently fits very comfortably with the use of an AIEM. All of them tend to be concerned with acts done by a contracting party with a particular (normally inadmissible) intent, or alternatively with matters like deliberately deceitful or misleading conduct, or with moral or ethical issues of what counts as honesty and fair dealing. As we suggest in the tort chapter,[111] none of these is very appropriate when it comes to performance guided by machine learning. The idea of deliberate deceit or fraud on the part of a machine, however smart it may be, is distinctly problematical. So too with the effort involved in trying to divine the purpose of a non-human entity; and as regards talking about an action taken with an improper motive, this becomes almost impossible as soon as we move away from human to machine action.

In short, under the present law we take the view that good faith is likely to be something of an irrelevance when it comes to contracts concluded by or through AIEMs: faith, whether good or bad, is not something easily attributed to a machine. Furthermore, perhaps surprisingly, this is not something we see as particularly problematical. In so far as any nascent notion of good faith is aimed at the penalisation of behaviour that is fraudulent, opportunistic or ill-motivated, and in so far as this is behaviour largely beyond the capacity of any machine, we see no practical need to suggest any change in this respect. This is, in our view, an area where there is a strong case for letting sleeping dogs lie.

VIII. Conclusions

The analysis presented in this chapter demonstrates that many of the legal challenges in contract law could be addressed through statutory clarification. Below is a summary of our key recommendations.

A. Contract Formalities and Agreement

We see possible difficulties over what should count as a meeting of the minds between two AIEMs, given that it might be problematical to determine whether two machines, as opposed to humans, have shown the necessary intent to agree. Rather than leaving this to being worked out by practice and case law, we think it safer to legislate.

We suggest that the best way to do this is by imposing a limited formal requirement specific to contracts of this sort. It might provide, for example, that agreement

(per Dyson LJ); *Redwood Master Fund Ltd v TD Bank Europe Ltd* [2002] EWHC 2703 (Ch), [2006] 1 BCLC 149; *Braganza v BP Shipping Ltd* [2015] UKSC 17, [2015] 1 WLR 1661, [20], [102] (per Lady Hale and Lord Neuberger).

[111] See Chapter 4 below.

exists if, and only if, either: (a) the facts satisfy any definition previously agreed between the controllers of the AIEMs involved; or (b) the exchange between the two AIEMs contains particular specified code apt to indicate agreement which would be apparent to a reasonable expert in the relevant protocols.

B. Signature: What is to Count as a Signature?

Where an agreement requires to be signed, either because of a legislative requirement or because of some other business arrangement between the parties such as a 'no oral alterations' clause, issues may arise as to what counts as a signature by a machine. The criterion of what amounts to a signature by an individual depends on the latter's intent to authenticate the document, something which is hard to apply to a machine. We propose tentatively a provision stating that for a valid signature in such a case there must in the code produced under the agreement be either: (a) an explicit reference to 'signature' or 'authentication'; or (b) something which would be understood as such by a reasonable expert coder.

C. Deeds

Deeds executed by AIEMs are problematic. Because of the workings of section 44 of the Companies Act 2006, a company is effectively unable to issue a deed through an AIEM; and in the case of both companies and individuals the requirement that a deed be witnessed by one or more persons present at the time may present serious practical difficulties.

We suggest here two legislative reforms. First, a document appearing on its face to be a deed issued on behalf of a company should be capable of being valid as a deed provided it is produced by an AIEM of which that company is the controller. Secondly, provision needs to be made for remote witnessing of deeds produced by AIEMs, such that if the production of such a document is communicated in real time to the would-be (human) witness, it shall not be invalidated merely because the actual server on which the production occurred was in a different place.

D. What Counts as Substantive Agreement

Because of possible difficulties over whether an intent to agree can be attributed to a machine, including an AIEM, we think that the matter ought to be put beyond doubt. Apart from the proposal above – that there should be a limited formality requirement for an agreement entirely between AIEMs – we would propose legislation providing that where the circumstances would indicate a binding agreement entered into directly between natural or legal persons, the validity of that agreement should not be denied on the ground only that it was concluded on one or both sides by or through an AIEM.

E. The Objective Theory of Contract: Reasonable Belief by a Counterparty that an Offeror Intends to Contract on Given Terms

Issues of belief in a particular fact can often be awkward in the AI context. One such case is the rule that where a person makes an apparent offer, this can be accepted so as to give rise to a contract only if the counterparty reasonably believed that the offeror intended to make a binding offer in those terms. This raises a logical difficulty where the offeror is a human and the offeree an AIEM. If an AIEM cannot intend to be bound to particular terms, *a fortiori* it cannot believe that someone else is.

Nevertheless, there are, in our opinion, very good reasons to circumvent this dry logical problem if we can. We think the best solution here is a statutory extension of the 'objective meaning' test, with inquiry limited in cases like this to the question of whether a reasonable person with a basic knowledge of AI in the position of the offeree would have seen an agreement here. If the answer is yes, then the agreement should be capable of being enforced as a contract.

F. Undue Influence and Other Equitable Grounds for Attack

When an issue arises over whether a third party is affected by notice of the existence of some equitable vitiating factor, such as undue influence, unconscionability or the like, at present there are problems over what we do about facts made available to an AIEM under that party's control. Unlike facts made available to a human employee, which generally are attributed to the employer, it is unlikely that any attribution is possible here.

We see this as unsatisfactory. In our view, it should be provided by legislation that for the purposes of the law of undue influence and other equitable vitiating factors affecting contracts, information available to an AIEM should be treated for all purposes as information available to its controller.

G. Unconscionability

When it comes to the ambit of unconscionability as regards contract, there is in our view considerable doubt as to how far an AIEM controlled by a contracting party can be properly regarded as guilty of unconscientious conduct, and if so how far this will be attributed to the controller. We take the view that this problem should be nipped in the bud by suitable legislation to clarify matters. Such legislation, we suggest, ought to provide that for the purpose of any jurisdiction to impugn a transaction as unconscionable on account of the relative position or bargaining power of the parties, account should be taken of both the actions of any AIEM and the state of mind of its controller, and a decision made as to whether the conscience of a reasonable person in the position of the latter would be affected had they known of the actions of the former.

H. Duress

Although we see few problems with AI as regards most of the law of duress, we see a possible potential difficulty with lawful act duress, which can apply in the case of seriously reprehensible but not illegal behaviour by one party against the other. At least arguably, there is an element of personal morality involved in applying this criterion, which could in theory cause difficulties where AI is involved.

In this case we would advocate a statutory clarification, in parallel to that applying to unconscionability, to establish that where an act of an AIEM is alleged to constitute duress, it should be enough if the same act would have done so if performed by a human or corporation in the same situation and with access to the same degree of knowledge.

I. Duties of Care in Contract

As regards the law of tort, we advocate a legislative change to the effect that where a function is undertaken by an AIEM, then any mistake by the latter which would have amounted to negligence in a human shall be treated as if it were human fault for the purposes of any liability.

We see no reason in this connection to differentiate duties of care owed in tort, and duties to take care (or see that care is taken) in contract in this connection. Accordingly, we would call for a similar change to be made here, again subject to any contrary agreement between the parties.

4

Intelligent Machines, AI and the Law of Tort[1]

I. Introduction

Issues over AI in the law of contract, dealt with in Chapter 3, predominantly turn on such matters as agreement, contractual intent, interpretation and vitiating factors (though, as we point out, a number of other awkward questions do arise in addition). In tort, by contrast, the emphasis shifts subtly. As with contract, much of tort can take AI in its stride, but there are four specific areas where the influence of AI, and in particular the need to deal properly with acts involving the use of AIEMs, needs careful discussion. These are attribution, conduct, knowledge and intent, and reliance. In addition, there is a fifth, more specialised, topic: namely, strict product liability, and how this can be adapted to deal with claims arising from allegedly defective AIEMs. This chapter seeks in section II to deal with these issues in turn.

II. AI and Tort: Areas of Difficulty

A. Attribution

Most difficulties with the application of AI to tort arise when harm or loss has been caused as a result of the acts of, or input from, an AIEM. The AIEM may have acted on its own, or in combination with human activity. The emphasis in this chapter is on whether, and if so in what circumstances, such acts or omissions ought to give rise to liability, and whether any changes may be needed to the law in this respect. But this leaves unanswered a logically prior question. A machine itself cannot incur liability, own property or enter into liability insurance contracts – at least in the absence of legal personality, which we argue elsewhere should not be accorded to AI of any sort.[2] If so, then if we say the act of a machine should create

[1] On AI and tort generally, compare M Hervey and M Lavy, *The Law of Artificial Intelligence*, 2nd edn (London, Sweet & Maxwell, 2024) Chs 6–8.

[2] In Chapter 2 when deliberating the key concepts of private law that are in need of reconsideration to face the challenges posed by AI and AIEMs.

liability, whose (personal or corporate) liability are we talking about? We need, to put it shortly, rules of attribution for machines.[3]

The present law, unsurprisingly, says nothing about this specifically. When AIEMs' actions are involved, we are therefore left to apply the ordinary rules of tort as they apply to human or corporate actors. These are for the most part clear enough. There is, for example, no doubt that a tort can be committed through the intermediacy of a non-human object, something that clearly includes an AIEM. AI-related examples might include a person programming a drone to fly low over a neighbour's land while themselves remaining outside the boundary,[4] or programming ChatGPT to write material on the Internet that turns out to be defamatory of a third party.[5] Similarly there can obviously be liability for personal negligence in failure to control any potential inanimate source of harm, including an AIEM, so as to stop it injuring others. And by extension, there could theoretically be liability in nuisance or under the rule in *Rylands v Fletcher*[6] if an AIEM caused interference with someone else's use of land amounting to a nuisance,[7] or was incorporated in something classified as a dangerous thing likely to cause damage in the event of an escape. Where appropriate, rules of agency[8] and vicarious liability[9] will apply here so as to make principals and employers liable for their agents and employees who themselves use AIEMs. And, of course, while AI is not itself a product for the purposes of strict product liability under the EU Product Liability Directive,[10] there is nothing to stop a physical product becoming defective because of AI incorporated in it.

But the limitations of the existing law need to be noted. There are in particular no rules imposing automatic liability on anyone for the acts of AI. Furthermore, much of the current law on agency and vicarious liability has the difficulty that it is

[3] Compare similar observations in B Soyer and A Tettenborn, 'Artificial Intelligence and Civil Liability – Do We Need A New Regime?' (2023) 30 *International Journal of Law & Information Technology* 385.

[4] See the non-AI case of *Anglo International Upholland Ltd v Wainwright* [2023] 5 WLUK 613, [8], and *cf* too *MBR Acres Ltd v Curtin* [2025] EWHC 331 (KB). So too with causing an animal incursion: *League Against Cruel Sports Ltd v Scott* [1986] QB 240 (foxhounds).

[5] No such case is reported, though in Ireland a lawyer is reported to have contemplated suing Meta for what its chatbot has said: see *The Daily Telegraph*, 8 June 2025. In any case it seems accepted that a user of, say, ChatGPT is generally liable for what they cause it to produce: compare *R (Ayinde) v Haringey LBC* [2025] EWHC 1040 (Admin), [2025] PNLR 22 (lawyer liable for wasted costs arising out of misguided AI output in document filed in court).

[6] (1868) LR 3 HL 330.

[7] Repeated overflight by a malfunctioning AI-enabled drone might be a possible instance.

[8] On the liability of a principal for an agent's torts, see Reynolds, F and Watts, P (eds), *Bowstead & Reynolds on Agency*, 23rd edn (London, Sweet & Maxwell, 2023) para 8-177 ff.

[9] See A Tettenborn (ed), *Clerk & Lindsell on Torts*, 24th edn (London, Sweet & Maxwell, 2023) Ch 6 (hereinafter referred to as *Clerk & Lindsell on Torts*).

[10] A 'product' being defined as 'goods or electricity': Consumer Protection Act 1987, s 1(2), reflecting the terms of the underlying Directive 85/374/EEC. AI is clearly not goods; and it would be a very big stretch to call it electricity. New EU legislation from 2024 replacing Directive 85/374/EEC (Directive (EU) 2024/2853) does include AI in the concept of 'product' and create a limited liability for its malfunctions: but this will not affect English law (though it may in due course affect the law of Northern Ireland owing to the vagaries of the Brexit settlement).

predicated on the idea of a human actor and legal subject as agent or employee.[11] As we see below,[12] this does not easily translate to the case of acting through a smart but non-conscious machine.

It is highly arguable, notwithstanding all this, that those who use AI should – even in the absence of personal fault – shoulder at least some of the risks that something may go wrong. In view of this point, the present position is in our view unsatisfactory. We need, we suggest, a bespoke solution to deal with the problems of liability for AI. The answer we think lies in creating a form of statutory liability for a machine modelled on similar principles to the concept of representation, but doing it in a special way. This would be by carrying over to tort the solutions which we put forward in Chapter 5 to the problems of agency and vicarious liability, which currently cause severe problems in this context.

First, agency. In Chapter 7, we suggest that in the case of an act or intervention by an AIEM, an automatic statutory attribution should attach to its 'controller': that is, the person (or corporation) in whose name the machine operated or purported to act, and who had made, or caused to be made, the arrangements for it to operate in that way.[13] This, it is suggested, would produce a satisfactory result as regards tort. A human agent acting within the scope of their agency has always had their acts attributed to their principal, with the result that the latter is potentially liable in tort.[14] Indeed, it seems that in respect of some torts, notably negligent misrepresentation and deceit, the rules in tort and contract are much the same.[15] It is our view that in tort we should endeavour to introduce parity of treatment here between defendants who act through human agents and those who act through AIEMs, with as far as possible the same rules applying to both. This solution advanced above comes close to doing this.

In a similar way, it is our view that the statutory liability proposed in Chapter 5 to supplement vicarious liability would greatly benefit the adaptation of the law of tort to the widespread use of AIEMs. This liability, to anticipate, would attach to any controller (defined as above) making use of an AIEM. It would, during the period of that use, cause that person to be treated as if the acts of the AIEM in

[11] For example, an agent has to be able to agree to act and to be given authority; and vicarious liability depends on (a) the existence of a contract of employment or similar agreement between employer and tortfeasor, and (b) a wrong committed by the latter. Neither idea is easily applicable to an inanimate entity, however smart. On the other hand, there are cases where this seems to have been overlooked: see eg the Canadian decision in *Moffatt v Air Canada*, 2024 BCCRT 149 (information produced by airline chatbot).

[12] See Chapter 7.

[13] See pp 120–121.

[14] See the reference above to *Bowstead & Reynolds on Agency*, 23rd edn, para 8-177 ff.

[15] See eg *Kooragang Investments Pty Ltd v Richardson & Wrench* [1982] AC 462; also, *Armagas Ltd v Mundogas SA* [1986] AC 717, 781 ff (per Lord Keith). The reason is that here the normally more generous rules of vicarious liability, notably a wide scope for liability even in respect of unauthorised acts, are largely disapplied.

question were those of a human employee of theirs so long as the person made use of the AIEM (a) regularly, and (b) as part of the operations of its business or profession. There would be one exception. The statutory liability would not apply in so far as the AI controller could show that the act of the AIEM would not appear to a reasonable person to be an act closely related to the regular activities of the controller's business or profession.[16]

Admittedly, here the parallel would not quite be exact. It would not apply to non-business liability. Again, while applying the rules of vicarious liability work well enough for strict liability and negligence (especially since it is suggested below that there is a strong case for introducing the idea of a negligent AIEM), it is more difficult as regards deliberate torts, or wrongs requiring intent on the part of the actor. This is because the vicarious liability of an employer is premised on the idea of a tort committed by the employee, who thus has to be proved to have committed all the elements of it[17] – something which will be hard to apply if, as we suggest elsewhere,[18] a machine cannot form an intent in any meaningful sense.

On the other hand, this may not matter very much in practice. Vicarious liability is of little practical importance in the non-business context. And, while it is true that humans frequently commit deliberate torts in the course of employment (for example theft, assault or abuse), and there is some fairly complicated law on how far those employing them can be liable in such cases,[19] these situations nearly always involve wrongs which an AIEM is unlikely to be involved in. If so, continuing to require the necessary intent or knowledge to be brought home to the AI controller in such cases so as to make the latter personally liable is unlikely to cause much injustice.

B. The Problem of Conduct

Liability in tort often requires conduct characterised in a particular way. Particular torts very frequently require as a condition of liability that the defendant's conduct be characterised as (for example) negligent, or unreasonable, or intentional, or malicious.[20] In this section we discuss whether, and how, this can be carried across to torts committed through the medium of AI, or through the activities of an AIEM. Four particular issues arise here.

[16] See pp 125–127.

[17] See on this *Clerk & Lindsell on Torts*, 24th edn, para 6-63.

[18] See p 36.

[19] See *Clerk & Lindsell on Torts*, 24th edn, para 6-51 ff, and cases such as *Lister v Hesley Hall Ltd* [2002] 1 AC 215, *Dubai Aluminium Co Ltd v Salaam* [2002] UKHL 48, [2003] 2 AC 366, *Various Claimants v Catholic Child Welfare Society* [2012] UKSC 56, [2013] 2 AC 1, and *Trustees of the Barry Congregation of Jehovah's Witnesses v BXB* [2023] UKSC 15, [2024] AC 567.

[20] *Clerk & Lindsell on Torts*, 24th edn, para 1-069 ff, usefully discusses this matter.

i. AI and Fault: A Delinquent Person, or a Delinquent Machine?

Fault, central to negligence and also highly relevant to a number of other heads of liability such as nuisance[21] or even in some cases trespass,[22] immediately creates difficulties with activities directed or modulated by AI. At present, English law is uncompromising in this respect. The idea of fault presupposes a human act or omission, coupled with a human mental state (or its negative, blameworthy inadvertence). Thus, although an otherwise blameless employer will be liable for the fault of an employee or someone else in an analogous position,[23] failure in the same situation on the part of a mere machine, such as a computer or AIEM, used by the employer will not suffice.[24] In this latter case the employer escapes because not at fault; and the machine cannot be liable at all. So too if a negligent householder burns down their neighbour's house by carelessly mishandling a gas-fired boiler they will be liable, but if exactly the same mistake is made by an apparently sound AI-enabled heating control unit installed by the householder there will, it seems, be no responsibility.[25] In cases of this kind, the only way liability can be established is by proof of personal fault in someone, for example an employee controlling or programming the AI in question, or failing to use or supervise it properly.

Is this position satisfactory? To us it seems concerning. First, we see it as counter-intuitive that the increasing use of AI to do things previously done by humans should actually *reduce* the legal protections available to claimants, whether clients or third parties, when things go wrong. Furthermore, at least two arguments from horizontal equity – treating like cases alike – tend the same way. For one thing, the need to compensate deserving victims consistently suggests that, assuming a decision or act is visibly wrong, it cannot be right to dismiss one claimant's complaint if the action was taken by an algorithm but allow suit by a claimant in an otherwise identical position where it was made by a human. And conversely, similar considerations apply to defendants. It seems odd that an employer who would have been liable for the error of an employee should escape responsibility for exactly the same mistake should the action be taken through the medium of AI simply because no human can be shown to have been at fault.

[21] See *Overseas Tankship (UK) Ltd v Miller Steamship Co Pty Ltd* [1967] 1 AC 617, 639 (in nuisance, 'fault of some kind is almost always necessary').

[22] See *League against Cruel Sports Ltd v Scott* [1986] QB 240 (trespass can be committed by negligently allowing a pack of hounds onto land).

[23] Under the principle of vicarious liability: *Clerk & Lindsell on Torts*, 24th edn, Ch 6. For who is equivalent to an employee despite not technically being one, see generally *Cox v Ministry of Justice* [2016] UKSC 10, [2016] AC 660.

[24] There is very little authority here, possibly because the point is regarded as obvious. But see *Target Holdings Ltd v Redfern* [1996] 1 AC 421, 432 (Lord Browne-Wilkinson), where payment due to a computer failure is treated as a matter of course as being non-negligent. In the context of healthcare, the point is made in D Schönberger, 'Artificial Intelligence in Healthcare: A Critical Analysis of the Legal and Ethical Implications' (2019) 27 *International Journal of Law & Information Technology* 171, 197.

[25] This is implicit in decisions such as *Filliter v Phippard* (1847) 11 QB 347.

If the argument above is correct, then clearly some change is necessary. It also seems clear that, at least for the sake of certainty, such clarification should be legislative rather than worked out by case law. One solution would be to eliminate the troublesome problem of fault entirely by introducing a rule of strict liability where harm was done as a result of the workings of AI.[26] But this is, in our view, unacceptable. A general rule that any harm whatever done by AI was automatically compensable would clearly be unworkable; there would have to be at least some notion of malfunction or defectiveness, which would itself be problematical. And even if this difficulty disappeared, such a solution would suffer from the same horizontal equity objections as the status quo, only the other way round. With strict liability for AI, those complaining of a given action would now be *better* protected if that action happened to have been taken by an AIEM than if it was that of a human. This is equally unattractive.

Following on from this reasoning, the conclusion seems unavoidable:[27] even though under the present law there is no such thing as a negligent AIEM, this needs to be altered. However incongruously, we need to find some means of imputing fault to a machine. Some years ago, the European Parliament toyed with an idea which might have had this effect: namely, ascribing some kind of legal personality to AIEMs.[28] But this outré and over-complex solution makes little sense, quite apart from the oddity of regarding a machine as a moral agent;[29] and this quite apart from the fact that in order to make sense of the law of tort the duty to compensate has to be vested in some natural or a legal person who can own the money to do it with.[30]

We prefer a simpler and neater legislative solution, making use of the concept of the controller referred to above. In any case where an action is taken, or a

[26] As suggested in part by the European Parliament in 2020, in a resolution proposing strict liability for 'any harm or damage that was caused by a physical or virtual activity, device or process' driven by a 'high-risk' AI system (see 2020/2014(INL), Art 4.1). The Commission has, however, stopped working on AI liability regimes, at least for the moment, since February 2025.

[27] In the EU context, there was a further suggestion from the European Commission that would retain the requirement for personal fault, but would: (a) put further duties on the defendant to reveal the workings of any AI used, and (b) introduce a reversed burden of proof as regards causation (for an account see eg O Dheu and J De Bruyne, 'Artificial Intelligence and Tort Law: A "Multi-faceted" Reality' (2023) 31 *European Review of Private Law* 261). But this seems over-complex, and the proposal was sidelined in February 2025.

[28] European Parliament Resolution with Recommendations to the Commission on Civil Law Rules on Robotics (2015/2103(INL)) (European Parliament, 16 February 2017) para 59(f).

[29] Which, even if true, is largely irrelevant, since there is precious little of personal morality in much of negligence law anyway.

[30] True, one could say a corporation was just as artificial a seat of personality as an intelligent machine. But the property-holding powers of a corporation make limited sense except in the context of detailed rules on capitalisation, agency and powers of disbursement, none of which is easy to apply to an algorithm. A similar point has been made by Simon Chesterman: see S Chesterman, 'Artificial Intelligence and the Limits of Legal Personality' (2020) 69(4) *International & Comparative Law Quarterly* 819, 822–27. See too the interesting and perceptive article by B Brozek and M Jakubiec, 'On the Legal Responsibility of Autonomous Machines' (2017) 25 *Artificial Intelligence and Law* 293; also, R Brown, 'Property Ownership and the Legal Personhood of Artificial Intelligence' (2021) 30 *Information & Communications Technology Law* 208.

determination made, by an AIEM acting on behalf of a controller, the court would be required to ask whether that action would, if taken by a person in the same position and circumstances, have been negligent. If it would, then there should be automatic personal liability in the controller as if the act of the AIEM had been an act of an employee of the controller in the course of that person's employment. Just as an employer is liable for the negligence of an employee despite not being personally negligent in employing or supervising the latter, liability could not be negatived by a plea either of lack of personal fault, or of reasonable reliance on the workings of an apparently impeccable machine. It would also be made clear that this statutory liability was in addition to, and not in replacement of, any personal liability in the controller or anyone else.[31]

For example, applying this solution, if (say) an AIEM used by a financial adviser recommends a particular investment strategy that turns out to be disastrous, the focus of the enquiry should be: if the recommendation had come from a human employee in an appropriate position within the firm controlling the AIEM, would it have been regarded as negligent so as to make the firm liable? Again, if an industrialist uses an AIEM for quality control and a dangerous product nevertheless gets on to the market and causes severe property damage, then if a reasonable human inspector would have picked up the defect the industrialist should be automatically liable in negligence.[32]

ii. AI and Fault: The Problem of Superhuman AI

The above situation deals with the case where AI falls below reasonable human standards. In practice, however, as AIEMs become smarter a serious converse problem may arise. Far from their falling short of the standards of a person of reasonable competence, we may increasingly find ourselves dealing with situations where the capabilities of AIEMs substantially exceed human abilities. Take, for example, medical diagnosis and operating procedures,[33] financial or investment advice,[34] or the process of monitoring industrial or commercial premises to guard against emergencies like fire and flood. All of these processes are ideally suited to the capabilities of AI to digest and analyse vast amounts of information in order to draw conclusions from it – jobs likely to involve far more informational inputs than any human could be expected to handle. In all these cases it seems a racing

[31] As is the case with vicarious liability: it is always open to the victim to sue the employer for breach of their own personal duty of care.

[32] There might also be the prospect of strict product liability: on which, see p 74 ff below.

[33] On which see generally M Hervey and M Lavy, *The Law of Artificial Intelligence*, 2nd edn (London, Sweet & Maxwell, 2024) para 8-044 ff; J Devenney, 'Developing Product Liability Networks for AI Systems in the Medical Context' (2025) 76(1) *Northern Ireland Legal Quarterly* 118.

[34] D Quest, 'Robo-advice and Artificial Intelligence: Legal Risks and Issues' (2019) 34 *British Journal of International Banking & Finance Law* 6; S Afghan, 'What Should Be Our Ethical, Legal and Regulatory Standards for AI in Financial Services? Part 1' (2022) 37 *Journal of International Banking Law & Regulation* 472, 480 ff.

certainty that before long AI will be performing functions like this better than humans.

This will raise issues concerning the controller's personal liability. It seems inevitable that in future, when deciding whether humans have been negligent, courts may also have to decide whether a reasonable person in the defendant's position ought to have declined to act in person and instead entrusted the decision to some AIEM (assuming such a thing to have been available).[35] De facto, indeed, there may well come to be areas where it is almost de rigueur to use AI or risk a negligence suit.

Such a rule, for that matter, almost certainly represents the existing law. There seems little doubt that if it is apparent that a machine can do a job more safely or effectively than a human, then it is potentially negligent for a human to insist on acting personally. We therefore need no change. However, one provision might be helpful by way of clarification. In any statutory reform, it should, in our view, be provided that nothing should prevent any court from deciding that in all the circumstances a defendant has been negligent in failing to utilise AI where its use would have been reasonable.

iii. Reasonableness in Tort: An Obstacle, or a Machine-Friendly Standard?

The idea of unreasonableness in tort law shades into that of fault. Indeed, very often they are two sides of the same coin: thus negligence, for example, is often said to consist in failure to show the degree of care or vigilance expected of a reasonable person. Nevertheless, they are not quite the same thing. In contrast to decisions about simple inadvertent fault, the reasonableness inquiry leans more towards the objective assessment of an act or decision by reference to a balancing of its effects on the interests of the actor, society and others who may be involved and the balancing of the relevant interests. Furthermore, it should be remembered that in deciding whether a particular defendant is at fault, the reasonableness or otherwise of their conduct is also a vital, though sometimes overlooked, consideration. It can, for example, qualify the principle that it is negligent to cause foreseeable harm to third parties. Negligence as a tort consists not simply in the causing of foreseeable damage to another, but in doing so *unreasonably.* To the extent that the defendant's action involves something of social or other utility, or reflects considerations such as necessity, it may be acceptable to take the risk of a certain amount of damage; even though that damage is entirely foreseeable, it will nevertheless not engender liability.[36]

[35] See *Clerk & Lindsell on Torts*, 24th edn, para 9-86.

[36] This is the well-known rule in *Bolton v Stone*: see *Bolton v Stone* [1951] AC 850, esp 858, 860, 863–64 and 869, and *Clerk & Lindsell on Torts*, 24th edn, para 7-176 ff. Ideas of this kind are also reflected in two pieces of legislation: the Compensation Act 2006 and the Social Action, Responsibility and Heroism Act 2015.

Reasonableness is also relevant in other tortious situations. For instance, although there is no general rule that unreasonableness renders wrongful an act otherwise unexceptionable,[37] in a few cases this is not so, and the unreasonableness of the defendant's action can make all the difference. One example is torts such as malicious prosecution and malicious abuse of process, where invoking the legal process becomes tortious when the defendant acts unreasonably.[38] So too in nuisance, where in some cases proof of the unreasonable nature of the defendant's activity can tip the balance in favour of liability even though such liability would not normally exist;[39] and elements of trespass where the defendant's conduct consists, say, in the unreasonable use of a right of way or overflight.[40]

Conversely, the reasonableness the defendant's conduct is on occasion an integral part of a defence to liability. Clear examples include the right of defence of person or property, limited to actions reasonable in the circumstances;[41] the tortious defence of necessity;[42] and the defence of reasonableness in the statutory tort of harassment.[43] In cases of this kind, all the facts are in account in determining what is reasonable, not excluding at times the particular circumstances or difficulties of the defendant.

It is fairly certain that in future reasonableness in this sense will arise in connection with decisions taken by AI. For example, AI is increasingly likely to be used remotely to control emergency intervention equipment such as sprinklers, hoses and fire-extinguishers whose operation may in the nature of things affect not only the premises concerned but also neighbouring properties or even passers-by. This is something that will necessarily involve balancing the interests of the owners of the property protected and those of third parties who may suffer collateral injury. More controversially, but with the same result, it could be used by venue owners in controlling crowds, sometimes with the result that those crowds then spill out and interfere with neighbouring property. Users of AI-controlled drones may well find that their drones occasionally fly over others' land. Yet again, AI is already impinging noticeably on lawyers' activities, especially when it comes to digesting large quantities of information, and will likely soon take at least some part in decisions on whether to sue or prosecute.[44]

[37] See the well-known decision in *Bradford Corpn v Pickles* [1895] AC 587, essentially rejecting the doctrine of abuse of rights as a matter of English law.

[38] See *Clerk & Lindsell on Torts*, 24th edn, para 15-35 ff, on the lack of 'reasonable and probable cause'.

[39] See for example *Hollywood Silver Fox Farm Ltd v Emmett* [1936] 2 KB 468 (noise disturbance to neighbouring landowner normally acceptable, but not when engaged in deliberately to harm claimant).

[40] See eg *Harrison v Duke of Rutland* [1893] 1 QB 142 (misuse of highway); compare *Bernstein v Skyviews & General Ltd* [1978] QB 479, esp 488 (flying over land trespassory if, and only if, it amounts to unreasonable interference with the use to which owner might wish to put it).

[41] See the discussion in eg *Cope v Sharpe (No 2)* [1912] 1 KB 496.

[42] *Clerk & Lindsell on Torts*, 24th edn, para 3-87.

[43] Protection from Harassment Act 1997, s 1(3)(c) ('in the particular circumstances the pursuit of the course of conduct was reasonable').

[44] True, in the case of prosecution administrative rules may well intervene but that does not alter the point in the text.

All this raises the issue: how will reasonableness play out in the AI context? Under the present law, the position is not completely clear. However, it is suggested that since AIEMs are likely to be seen by courts merely as inanimate tools, it will probably be held that reasonableness can only be judged by reference to the (human or corporate) persons making use of them. In other words, if, say, the operation of an automatic fire-suppressant system controlled by an AIEM causes damage to third parties through widespread wetting or spreading of foam, the question will be whether the company which made use of it was acting reasonably in installing and relying on it (or whether the supplier or installer themselves took reasonable care). And if a landowner uses an AIEM to monitor a structure on their land in case it creates a nuisance by damaging or engulfing a neighbour's territory,[45] the issue will be whether the landowner themselves acted reasonably in entrusting this function to the machine rather than to human employees or agents. If they did, then there will be no liability.

If a claimant suffering damage as a result of the AIEM's operations wishes to succeed, they will thus have to argue that in all the circumstances it was unreasonable for the controller to rely on the equipment in the first place without some further human back-up. Furthermore, in deciding this the court tends in nuisance and similar cases to look at the issue from the point of view of this particular defendant's own position, circumstances and weaknesses.[46]

Is this the rule we want? The point is actually quite nuanced. One might argue that, given the close connection between negligence and reasonableness, the approach to both should be the same. If we accept this argument, it follows that we should embrace the concept not only of the negligent machine but equally of the unreasonable machine, and make the controller of it statutorily liable for the errors of both.

On balance, however, it is suggested that here there is a strong argument in favour of retaining the status quo. In contrast to ordinary issues of fault, questions of reasonableness in tort look to the human, and indeed moral, side of the equation: a point emphasised by the fact that at least in some cases the question of liability is looked at with one eye on this particular defendant's own position and resources.[47] If so, it is probably better to make it clear that whenever a question of reasonableness arises in connection with a decision taken by an AIEM, this is to be taken by reference to the position of the controller of the AIEM concerned or the person being sued.

[45] Compare the facts of cases such as *Goldman v Hargrave* [1967] 1 AC 645 or *Leakey v National Trust* [1980] QB 485.

[46] See eg *Goldman v Hargrave* [1967] 1 AC 645, 663; also, *Lambert v Barratt Homes Ltd* [2010] EWCA Civ 681, (2011) 131 Con LR 29.

[47] See *Goldman v Hargrave* [1967] AC 645 and *Leakey v National Trust* [1980] QB 485, referred to above.

iv. Foreseeability of Loss or Damage

Tort liability for negligence is predicated on the damage to the claimant being foreseeable.[48] More accurately, it depends on a showing that damage of the type caused,[49] to a person in the claimant's position,[50] could have been foreseen (though there is no need for foreseeability of the precise means by which the damage occurred[51]). In addition, for most torts that do not involve fraud or intent to cause loss, such as nuisance or conversion, the defendant's liability for individual heads of consequential loss also depends on such loss being foreseeable.[52]

Presumably under the present law the issue is one of foreseeability to the reasonable human or corporate defendant, even if AI in some form has intervened in the transaction. To say damage was foreseeable to X means that X would have been at fault in not foreseeing that damage: if a machine cannot itself be at fault (as we argue elsewhere), then clearly it is difficult to apply foreseeability to it. Admittedly it may be that the presence of an AIEM might have an indirect effect on liability; for example, it has been suggested that the ability of AI to strike out on its own might have the effect of making foreseeable that which would not otherwise have been within a reasonable person's contemplation.[53] But this does not alter the point we are making.

Is the present solution the right one, or should we contemplate introducing the idea of 'damage foreseeable to a reasonable AIEM', in the same way as we have suggested that we should accept the idea of a negligent machine? The matter here is fairly evenly balanced. On the whole, however, in our view it is better to let sleeping dogs lie. AI, and AIEMs, vary enormously. It would, we think, be very hard for courts to come up with a convincing criterion of what should have been foreseeable to an AIEM in the position of the one involved in a particular case; and such difficulties ought, if possible, to be avoided. Furthermore, the whole criterion of remoteness of loss has a moral responsibility element to it,[54] which makes it more appropriate in our opinion to continue to anchor it to the question of human rather than algorithmic abilities.

[48] *The Wagon Mound* [1961] AC 388; *Clerk & Lindsell on Torts*, 24th edn, para 2-149 ff.

[49] *Overseas Tankship (UK) Ltd v Miller Steamship Co Pty Ltd* [1967] 1 AC 617; *Topp v London Country Bus (South West) Ltd* [1993] 3 All ER 448.

[50] *Bourhill v Young* [1943] AC 92.

[51] *Hughes v Lord Advocate* [1963] AC 837.

[52] *Overseas Tankship (UK) Ltd v Miller Steamship Co Pty Ltd* [1967] 1 AC 617, 640 (per Lord Reid) (nuisance); *Kuwait Airways v Iraq Airways Co* [2002] UKHL 19, [99], [2002] 2 AC 883 (conversion). See too *Cambridge Water Co Ltd v Eastern Counties Leather Co Ltd* [1994] 2 AC 264 (*Rylands v Fletcher* liability).

[53] A point made by the Law Commission: see *AI and the Law: A Discussion Paper* (2025) 11.

[54] 'For it does not seem consonant with current ideas of justice *or morality* that for an act of negligence, however slight or venial, which results in some trivial foreseeable damage the actor should be liable for all consequences however unforeseeable and however grave …' (per Lord Simonds in *The Wagon Mound* [1961] AC 388, 422) (emphasis added).

C. The Issue of Knowledge

A fair number of tort law rules and principles are predicated on a showing that a defendant (or indeed in some cases a claimant[55]) was actually aware of particular facts at the time they acted. Liability in deceit, for example, requires the making of a statement knowing it to be false (or at least being knowingly reckless as to whether it might be);[56] the economic tort of inducing a breach of contract requires actual knowledge by the defendant of the existence of the contract affected.[57] Again, a person's liability for damage done by an animal of a non-dangerous species in their keeping depends on their having had actual knowledge of the beast's dangerous features.[58] And matters can go further. For example, even conversion, normally a strict liability tort, can at times depend on knowledge: thus a bailee who returns goods to their bailor is normally protected from liability even if the bailor does not own the goods, but this does not apply if the bailee has actual knowledge that there is a rival claimant who in the event turns out to have been the true owner.[59]

Note that all these are requirements of actual knowledge. Nothing short of this will do. A defendant who *ought* to have known they were telling an untruth is not liable for deceit, however foolish they may have been;[60] nor is a person liable for inducing a breach of contract that they ought to have known about but in fact did not.[61] To create strict liability under the Animals Act 1971 it is not enough that the animal's keeper was in a position to know an animal's dangerous characteristics;[62] and so on. Moreover, the knowledge must have been not only available but present to the defendant's mind at the relevant time: a person who has been told something in the past but forgotten it,[63] or has written information present in their possession but not in their consciousness, does not have knowledge in this sense so as to make them liable.

True, in some of these cases there may also be liability on the basis of constructive, as against actual, knowledge. There can be liability in negligence for the acts of dangerous animals; a person who tells an untruth having forgotten what they were told a day earlier may find themselves liable for negligent misrepresentation;

[55] This will happen if, for example, a defence of *volenti non fit injuria* is raised, or if a person who is sued in respect of a misstatement puts causation in issue by arguing that the claimant knew the truth all along.

[56] *Derry v Peek* (1889) 14 App Cas 337.

[57] *Emerald Construction Co Ltd v Lowthian* [1966] 1 WLR 691; see too *Unique Pub Properties Ltd v Beer Barrels & Minerals (Wales) Ltd* [2004] EWCA Civ 586, [2005] 1 All ER (Comm) 181.

[58] See the Animals Act 1971, s 2(2). The point could matter in so far as agriculturalists choose to utilise AI to supervise their stock.

[59] See *Hollins v Fowler* (1874–75) LR 7 HL 757; *Clerk & Lindsell on Torts*, 24th edn, para 16-78 ff.

[60] *Derry v Peek* (1889) 14 App Cas 337, 376: also *AIC Ltd v ITS Testing Services (UK) Ltd* [2006] EWCA Civ 1601, [2007] 1 All ER (Comm) 667, [256]–[259] (Rix LJ).

[61] Made clear in *Unique Pub Properties Ltd v Beer Barrels & Minerals (Wales) Ltd* [2004] EWCA Civ 586, [2005] 1 All ER (Comm) 181, above.

[62] See *Clerk & Lindsell on Torts*, 24th edn, para 20-14 (knowledge must be 'actual and present as a matter of fact').

[63] Compare *Derry v Peek* (1889) 14 App Cas 337, 343 (Lord Halsbury).

and so on. But these are different forms of liability, on a different basis, and subject to different rules.[64]

What about AIEMs in this connection? The difficulty here is that knowledge in this sense is very difficult to ascribe to a computer or AIEM in a meaningful way. To begin with, as we point out elsewhere,[65] there are enormous difficulties with the assertion that an AIEM 'knows' something. What we tend to mean when we say this is that data representing a given fact, or from which this fact can logically be inferred, is present somewhere in, or accessible to, some storage medium accessible to it. But is this the same thing as 'knowing' as regards the matter being present to the consciousness of a human? Arguably not: even if it is readily retrievable at a few microseconds' notice at the time the relevant action is taken, there is a respectable argument that of itself the mere presence of electronic data on a storage medium is really equivalent at most to inadvertence. It is, in our view, more like the situation where a short time ago I received a piece of paper stating some fact, filed it away and then forgot about it when I turned to dealing with other matters. No doubt we would say that I ought to know that fact: it strains language to say I know it.

If this is right, then a further point follows. In the case of a human, distinguishing actual from constructive knowledge, or knowing from merely negligent wrongdoing, is fairly unproblematical. It is a matter of asking whether at a particular time the information was, or was not, present to their mind – something which lawyers do the whole time. In the context of AIEMs, however, things are different. We can call expert evidence that information was present in an AIEM's memory at a given time, but we cannot meaningfully characterise it as being present to the computer's consciousness at that or any other time. In short, there is a powerful argument that, while an AIEM can have constructive knowledge or something like it, drawing a line between 'knows' and 'ought to know' becomes difficult, if not impossible.[66]

How does the law deal with this issue at present? There is little authority but, in line with its treatment of AIEMs as inanimate tools, it is possible to surmise the position. Where information is present in AIEM memory, we suggest that this will not, without more, be ascribed to the person standing behind the machine. The controller will, however, prima facie be treated as someone who ought to know it, provided that they have the ability to seek and retrieve it fairly readily.[67] Nevertheless, the effect of the presence of the information stops there. Unless the

[64] The measure of damages in deceit, for example, is very different from that for negligent misrepresentation, with foreseeability being out of account: so too other matters, such as the availability of a defence of contributory negligence.

[65] See in particular, the discussion on the subject in Chapter 2.

[66] Similar difficulties might arise in insurance law, especially when it comes to constructive knowledge of the insurer. These will be deliberated in Chapter 8.

[67] Or possibly if they have invited another party to place information on the AIEM, for example through a website, as an alternative to passing it directly to them. In such a case they might well be estopped from denying that they have notice of it.

person in control actually has the fact present to their mind at the same time as they have the ability to control the AIEM,[68] they will not be regarded as actually knowing it.

So, for example, if A, the controller of an AIEM, makes a statement that information on the AIEM demonstrates to be untrue, they may be liable for negligent misrepresentation, but there is no scope for liability for deceit. Again, if a farmer has on an AIEM details of the dangerous characteristics of one of their bulls but is not actually aware of those characteristics, they may be liable in negligence for injury suffered by anyone gored by it, but will not on that account only be strictly liable under the Animals Act 1971.

Is this the right position? Or does it need altering by legislation? In one case it is our view that change is clearly necessary. Suppose an AIEM, acting autonomously, gives advice or otherwise does something when information is available to it which would have made a human negligent if the action had been done by the latter. In such a case there should be parallel liability. We suggest elsewhere[69] that in such a case the controller of the AIEM should be liable without being able to plead that they had relied on an apparently competent machine. This should apply here too.

Might reform need to go further, however? Even if under the existing law an AIEM cannot know something, it would be possible for legislation to treat it as if it did. For example, whatever the position at common law statute could provide that in the case of information actually present on the storage of an AIEM, for the purposes of tortious liability that information should count as actually known to the controller.

Such a solution has a superficial attraction. Someone relying on a statement from an AIEM in possession of knowledge showing that information to be false might feel short-changed if unable to recover if they would have had a claim against a human representor in the same situation: so too with the victim gored by the bull in the above example. Nevertheless, despite this reasoning it is suggested that there are strong arguments against adopting it.[70] This is for two reasons. First, the practical difficulties remain of distinguishing, in the AI context, between actual and constructive knowledge. What knowledge would have to be present in the AIEM storage to trigger any such rule? The answer to the question would remain intractably unclear and that is always a strong argument against asking a court to find it.

But there is also a second, more significant, consideration. Practicalities aside, the normative case for extending the idea of knowledge to cover information

[68] This being analogous to the case of the employer who, knowing the true state of affairs, allows an innocent agent to present a false picture: compare *London County Freehold Properties Ltd v Berkeley Property Co Ltd* [1936] 2 All ER 1039, as interpreted in *Armstrong v Strain* [1952] 1 KB 232; and also *Standard Chartered Bank Ltd v Pakistan National Shipping Corp (No 2)* [2000] 1 Lloyd's Rep 218, esp 225.

[69] See p 77.

[70] In Chapter 8, we adopt a similarly cautious approach when examining the extent to which information may be attributed to the insurer in cases where underwriting decisions are made by AI.

on an AIEM is also remarkably shaky. Where actual knowledge is relevant to tortious liability, the reason is essentially moral: deliberate wrongdoers deserve to be treated more harshly than inadvertent ones. Liars rightly receive more severe treatment from civil courts than those guilty of mere negligent misrepresentation; it should be easier to sue those who knowingly hold on to dangerous animals than those who have no knowledge of their dangerous features; deliberately causing A to break a contract with B is more serious than doing this through mere negligence; and so on. But these moral reasons only make sense where the knowledge is that of the human or corporate defendant themselves. Even under the present law, someone else's knowledge does not suffice to create liability for knowing wrongdoing unless actually shared by, and present in the mind of, the defendant.[71] There is no reason not to apply exactly the same principle to information in the metaphorical hands of a machine, since the moral case for liability is no stronger here either.

D. Intent

Just as knowledge is often a crucial element in legal liability, a good deal of the law of tort also turns on issues of intent. An obvious instance is torts that require a specific intent in the defendant to establish liability in the first place. Examples include assault, false imprisonment, deceit, conspiracy and causing loss by unlawful means: none of these torts can be committed by a mere inadvertent act. But the matter goes a good deal further. Even such torts as conversion or trespass to land, often thought of as strict liability torts in the sense that the defendant is potentially liable despite having believed, reasonably, that they were acting within their rights, nevertheless require at least an intentional action of going onto land or handling the property concerned. The same may very well be true of libel, at least as regards the publication of the statement complained of.[72] Hence someone who merely negligently destroys property,[73] imprisons another

[71] Thus, apart from vicarious liability, a person is not liable for deceit merely because an agent of theirs acting within their employment knows the truth: eg *Kwei Tek Chao v British Traders & Shippers Ltd* [1954] 2 QB 459 (forwarding agents acting for sellers of goods produce falsified bills of lading; sellers innocently present bills to buyers; sellers not liable), and *cf Bradford Third Benefit Building Society v Borders* [1941] 2 All ER 205, 223, 226 (per Lords Wright and Porter). So too under the Animals Act a keeper of an animal of a non-dangerous species is only liable on account of the knowledge of another if that other is in charge of the animal: see s 2(2)(c). This comes to much the same thing.

[72] This seems implicit in cases such as *Huth v Huth* [1915] 3 KB 32 and *Byrne v Deane* [1937] 1 KB 818, both of which talk of ways of inferring that a defendant has intentionally associated itself with content and thereby published it. Would there be publication of a libel for legal purposes if a person wrote a note to themselves which they then negligently allowed to blow into the street? It seems unlikely.

[73] *The Arpad* [1934] P 189, 232 (Maugham LJ); *BMW Financial Services Ltd v Bhagwanani* [2007] EWCA Civ 1230, [2007] CTLC 280 (not conversion negligently to crash car, causing it to be unavailable to owner).

without intending to do so,[74] or interferes with another's land[75] is not, it seems, liable for any of these torts.

This is significant as regards AI. As with the related problem of knowledge, the difficulty lies in the nature of AIEMs. Just as it is hard to regard an AIEM as 'knowing' something in the sense of having it to mind, we also argue elsewhere[76] that in the nature of things a machine, being without the capacity for desire, equally cannot 'intend' to act in a particular way, or to bring about a particular consequence. If this is right, then it seems that, at least under the present law, where a person acts through the medium of an AIEM the interposition of the latter must be disregarded for the purposes of any of the deliberate torts; the relevant intent is, and is only, that of the controller or the person making use of the machine. So if a person unintentionally causes a drone under their control to take off and fly over neighbouring land, or software governing crowd control facilities goes wrong and pens up visitors with no reason, it would seem that there would be no liability: there could be no relevant intent in the machine, and there would be none in the person controlling it.

Is this position acceptable? In defence of it, it could be argued that in the deliberate or semi-deliberate torts mentioned above the law has made a social policy choice – a person only deserves to be made liable as a result of a deliberate human act – and that we should continue to respect that choice where AI is involved. We take the view, however, that on balance the law ought to be changed here so as to give rise at least in some cases to liability for the acts of an AIEM. This is for two reasons. First, the requirement for a deliberate act in the case of the deliberate torts we see as a matter not so much of moral deservingness as of taxonomy: wholly inadvertent damage, raising different issues from liabilities arising out of conscious acts, naturally falls to be treated differently. And if so, extending liability where AIEMs are involved is unlikely to do much harm to the scheme of the law. And secondly, in line with our argument elsewhere on vicarious liability,[77] we see the need for equity between employers who act through humans and those who act through AI: those injured through what is essentially the same act should not see their right to a remedy differing sharply according to whether an AIEM was involved.[78]

We therefore suggest that where a controller of an AIEM deliberately entrusts some function to an AIEM, such as dealing with property, crowd control, or

[74] See *Clerk & Lindsell on Torts*, 24th edn, para 14-28 ('To be liable in false imprisonment, it must be demonstrated that the defendant had the necessary intention, as well as the ability, to detain the claimant').

[75] True, in *League against Cruel Sports Ltd v Scott* [1986] QB 240 a master of hounds was held liable for negligently allowing them to invade neighbouring land. But even here it was emphasised that the hounds had been deliberately taken out in the vicinity of the land concerned: there would, it is suggested, be no liability in trespass were dogs to invade another's land owing to simple negligence by a kennelman in failing to shut the door of their enclosure.

[76] See p 71.

[77] See Chapter 7, p 123 ff.

[78] See p 123 ff.

whatever, their liability for any of the deliberate torts should go largely in parallel to vicarious liability. If they would have been liable had they employed a human in the same capacity and the latter had, within the scope of their employment, acted with the necessary intent to create tortious liability, then they should be similarly liable if the same function had been entrusted to an AIEM.

E. The Problem of Reliance

A claimant seeking to sue for misrepresentation, whether deliberate or negligent, has as a general rule[79] to show reliance on what the defendant said. This means, it is suggested, that they must show that the statement was present to their mind at the relevant time,[80] and also that that awareness played a causal part in any decision they took.[81]

Does this kind of reasoning work where the representee utilises an AIEM and the representation is made to it? Our view is that it works partly, but only partly. In principle, causation is susceptible of being established: with enough evidence (if necessary from an expert in computing and AI) it must be possible to show either that but for the information received by the AIEM it would have acted differently, or at least that the information fed to it had some influence in leading it to act as it did. Indeed, there are already cases saying that a machine can be duped for the purposes of the law of deceit, such that if it is then the person in control of it can sue whoever fed it the false information that caused it to take particular action.[82]

The difficulty lies in the further requirement that the representation be present to the mind of the representee: as we said elsewhere, it is difficult to say that a machine can 'know' or be 'aware' of a fact in the same way as a human can. This means that this requirement may well be impossible technically to satisfy, especially if we are dealing with implicit representations, as where a defendant sells or pledges goods that they know are not their own, but says nothing about title.

It is possible that this problem could be surmounted by judicial decision. But our view is that this is a matter better suited to legislation dealing specifically

[79] Subject to a possible exception where the claimant does not rely on a particular positive statement but instead founds on an implied representation that a transaction is unexceptionable when it is not. An example is where a person sells or pledges goods that they know are not their own but says nothing about title. The claimant can sue even if they never even thought about the question of ownership: see *Advanced Industrial Technology Corp Ltd v Bond Street Jewellers Ltd* [2006] EWCA Civ 923, and *ED&F Man Capital Markets v Come Harvest Holdings Ltd* [2022] EWHC 229 (Comm), [440]–[447].

[80] *Marme Inversiones 2007 SL v Natwest Markets plc* [2019] EWHC 366 (Comm), [286] (per Picken J). See too generally *Leeds City Council v Barclays Bank plc* [2021] EWHC 363 (Comm), [2021] QB 1027. It remains to be seen whether this proposition is affected by the decision of the Privy Council in *Credit Suisse Life (Bermuda) Ltd v Ivanishvili* [2025] UKPC, [2025] 3 WLR 789.

[81] *Hayward v Zurich Insurance Co plc* [2016] UKSC 48, [2017] AC 142.

[82] eg *Renault UK Ltd v Fleetpro Technical Services* [2007] EWHC 2541 (QB), [2008] Bus LR D 17; *cf* too *IG Index plc v Colley* [2013] EWHC 478 (QB).

with the use of AI in this context. In our opinion, legislation should provide two things. First, when any issue arises as to whether there has been adequate reliance on a representation by an AIEM, then it should be enough to prove that the representation was a cause of the AIEM acting as it did. And secondly, for the avoidance of doubt it should be provided that if a statement would have been taken to be an implied representation if made to a human, and the latter would have been able to sue on the basis of it, the statement should be deemed to have affected an AIEM.

F. A Specific Problem in AI and Tort: 'Defective' AI and Strict Product Liability

The sixth area where AI is likely to cause difficulties within the law of tort is more specialised, but nevertheless important enough to deal with here. At present AI is not as such covered by the strict liability regime in Part I of the Consumer Protection Act 1987,[83] since a 'product' within that Act is defined as any 'goods or electricity',[84] and AI falls under neither rubric.[85] It follows that the effect of the Act as regards AI is simply that in so far as the incorporation of defective AI in a physical product, including an AIEM, makes it defective,[86] then we are talking of a defective product overall, to which the 1987 regime applies. But if the only complaint is that an AI algorithm caused loss and damage, there can be no statutory strict liability.[87]

This position has the advantage of reflecting a well-established pattern of liability: producers of physical products insure against strict responsibility, whereas producers of the incorporeal assets that go into those products, such as AI software, carry errors and omissions insurance based on a theory of negligence liability. Any extension of strict productsliability so as to engulf software writers would undoubtedly upset this balance considerably, a fact which suggests that there is something to be said for leaving matters unchanged.

On balance, however, we are of the view that the present position remains unsatisfactory and ought to be changed. Despite the incorporeal nature of AI, its present importance in social and commercial life means that it is vital to bring it within the pre-existing strict liability scheme by amending the definition of 'product' to

[83] Legislation in turn based on the 1985 EU Product Liability Directive (Council Directive 85/374/EEC) but remaining in force without substantial change post-Brexit.

[84] Consumer Protection Act 1987, s 1(2)(c).

[85] It is clearly not goods. And despite its basis in electronics it would, it is suggested, be stretching matters beyond breaking point to say it counted as 'electricity'.

[86] For example, machinery controlled by AI which is rendered dangerous to human life because of a glitch in the AI concerned.

[87] Compare the uncompromising decision by the Court of Justice of the European Union, that disembodied information is outside the current Product Liability Directive: Case C-65/20, *VI v Krone-Verlag GmbH KG* [2022] CEC 740.

include it.[88] But while we see this as relatively uncontroversial, this in turn raises further issues about what is to count as 'defective' AI. Any product liability scheme necessitates a definition of a defective product;[89] any parallel liability for harm done by AI equally demands at least some definition of defective AI.[90]

The position under the Consumer Protection Act 1987 as respects physical products is this. A product is defective, and thus potentially liable to make its producer liable for any damage it does, 'if the safety of the product is not such as persons generally are entitled to expect'.[91] Such a definition has two good points as regards AI. For one, it rightly stresses the objective nature of safety and its complete independence from any idea of fault or foreseeability of harm. In addition, it also correctly emphasises the strong social interest in favour of promoting people's reasonable expectations of security.

AI differs from a paradigmatic product by being a purely intellectual creation without the familiarity or physical footprint of a car or a microwave, it also raises two particular difficulties. First, AI is both very new and for the moment fairly unfamiliar. For the foreseeable future it may therefore be difficult for a court to reckon what degree of 'safety' the public expects, or has a right to expect, from it.[92] This being so, it might be better to define defectiveness by reference to function – does the algorithm do what it was being used to do? – rather than expectations of safety. Even if we do not as yet know what degree of safety we can legitimately expect from an AI application, we can at least have a good idea of what it is meant to do and whether it is doing it.

Secondly, there could be a problem over the application of the 'development risks' defence in the Directive, namely that 'the state of scientific and technical knowledge at the relevant time was not such that a producer of products of the same description as the product in question might be expected to have discovered

[88] As has already been done in the EU. In December 2024, the 1985 Directive was replaced and updated by a revised provision (Directive 2024/2853) which does encompass AI (see Art 4(3): 'product' now includes 'electricity, digital manufacturing files, raw materials and software'). But as post-Brexit EU legislation this will not affect Great Britain, though it may be brought into effect in Northern Ireland under the Windsor Framework. See generally N Nikolinakos, 'Aligning Liability Rules with the Digital Age and Circular Economy: The Revised EU Product Liability Directive' (2025) 31 *Computer & Telecommunications Law Review* 126.

[89] See s 2(1) of the Consumer Protection Act 1987 ('… where any damage is caused wholly or partly by a *defect* in a product …') (emphasis added). This can on occasion be far from straightforward: see eg the coverage in *Clerk & Lindsell on Torts*, 24th edn, paras 10-55–10-66.

[90] For the obvious reason that a generalised liability for any harm caused by any AI decision whatever is entirely unworkable.

[91] See s 3(1) of the Consumer Protection Act 1987, anglicising the original EU Product Liability Directive, Art 6.

[92] It has been said that the issue is one of entitled, not actual, expectation: see eg *A v National Blood Authority* [2001] 3 All ER 289, [31] (per Burton J) and *Gee v DePuy International Ltd* [2018] EWHC 1208 (QB), [2018] Med LR 347, [94] (per Andrews J). Nevertheless, this itself remains difficult without an industry standard in the light of which defectiveness can be reckoned. These issues are doubtless at present occupying the minds of both theorists and regulators at national and EU level; but for the moment we are far away from imposing national, let alone international, standards. The point is discussed in Devenney (n 33).

the defect'.[93] The fact that AI may develop a mind of its own arguably might trigger this defence, though the matter is uncertain.[94]

Third, there is a difficulty of timing. With defective products the invariable cut-off is the time of production: problems appearing later, unless mere manifestations of some pre-existing defect, are out of account.[95] But the utility of AI lies precisely in its adaptivity; that is, in the ability of the algorithms embodied in it to change and improve in the light of experience, without the original producer necessarily having the final word. It may, therefore, be appropriate to impose liability for miscalculations by AI even in respect of subsequent malfunctions in taking account of experience.[96] The point might well be significant. Take, for example, a case of AI used to preserve safety in a dangerous environment such as a mine or quarry. If after a number of unexpected incidents it failed properly to take these new dangers into account and as a result an accident occurred which would not otherwise have done so, there would be a strong case for liability.

It is tentatively suggested that as regards defective AI, we need a definition on the following lines, which would capture both AI with an unexpected glitch and AI which was simply inadequate as designed. AI in a device should be regarded as defective if: (a) it does not perform, or fails to perform properly, the function reasonably to be expected of it; and (b) as a result of this failure, it is likely, or more likely, to cause damage to a claimant.

III. Conclusions

As demonstrated by the analysis presented in this chapter, the deployment of intelligent machines is anticipated to generate more challenges in the domain of tort law than in any other area of law. This outcome primarily stems from the fact that traditional tort doctrines are grounded in inherently subjective premises, although we expect that the arising issues will remain amenable to resolution. A summary of our recommendations is provided below.

A. The Problem of Attribution

We see a major difficulty in the application of tort to the actions of AI, in that there are no rules about when the acts of an AIEM are to be attributed to its controller,

[93] See the Consumer Protection Act 1987, s 4(1)(e).

[94] Devenney (n 33) argues that because this very possibility of future waywardness is known, the defence is automatically excluded. With respect, this seems tendentious.

[95] See the Product Liability Directive, Art 7(b).

[96] A point neatly made in T Cabral, 'Liability and Artificial Intelligence in the EU: Assessing the Adequacy of the Current Product Liability Directive' (2020) 27 *Maastricht Journal of European & Comparative Law* 615, 624.

and that the existing laws of agency and vicarious liability cannot readily be applied to those acts. In this chapter, we suggest legislation to deal with this. The legislation proposed there would provide that, subject to exceptions, acts and omissions of an AIEM would be treated for the purposes of agency law as having been performed by an authorised agent of its controller, and in addition as the acts of an employee of the controller committed within the latter's course of employment.

B. The Negligent AIEM

The lack of rules about the attributability of the actings of AI is paralleled by another difficulty we see as a serious problem: the lack, under the present law, of any concept of a negligent machine, or any possibility of regarding a machine, intelligent or otherwise, as being at fault. Since much of the law of tort, including most of vicarious liability, depends on showing that some actor somewhere was at fault, this needs to be legislatively dealt with.

Our solution is legislation to the effect that in any case where an action is taken, or a determination made, by an AIEM acting on behalf of a controller, a court would be required to ask whether that action would, if taken by a person in the same position and circumstances, have been negligent. If it would, then there should be automatic personal liability in the controller as if the act of the AIEM had been an act of an employee of the controller in the course of that person's employment. Furthermore, this should extend not only to physical acts and omissions, but also to negligent advice.

C. Representations and Reliance

Before a claimant can sue for negligent – or fraudulent – misrepresentation, they must prove reliance on the latter. This requirement has been interpreted as meaning that the representation must, at least in a minimal sense, have been actually in their mind at the time they acted. Unfortunately, this creates a problem with AI. This is because, while we can always tell (at least in principle) whether data is present in, or retrievable from, AIEM storage, it makes little if any sense to ask whether that information is at any particular time present to its mind.

In our view it is necessary here to enact legislation to deal robustly with the matter. This, we suggest, should provide two things. First, when any issue arises as to whether there has been adequate reliance on a representation by an AIEM, then it should be enough for the person alleging it to prove that the representation was a (physical) cause of the AIEM acting as it did. And secondly, for the avoidance of doubt it should also be provided that if a statement would have been taken to be an implied representation if made to a human, and the latter would have been able to sue on the basis of it, the statement should be deemed to have affected the AIEM.

D. AI and Strict Product Liability

At present AI causes difficulties with strict product liability under the Consumer Protection Act 1987. First, being intangible it cannot as such amount to a 'product', even though its incorporation in a physical product may make the latter itself defective. And secondly, the self-renewing nature of AI, and its essential difference from any existing physical product, make the concept of 'defective AI' a difficult one.

We take the view that both these issues need to be dealt with legislatively. First, in our view the definition of a 'product' under section 1(2)(c) of the Consumer Protection Act 1987 should be extended to cover AI. Secondly, there should be a statutory definition of 'defective' AI. AI in a device, or used in connection with it, should be regarded as defective if: (a) it does not perform, or fails to perform properly, the function reasonably to be expected of it; and (b) as a result of this failure, it is likely, or more likely, to cause damage to a claimant.

5

Intelligent Machines, AI and Equity

I. Introduction

Equitable institutions run through private law, including not only trusts and real property law but also, importantly, commercial law. This chapter is not a summary of equitable rules or doctrines as such, which would be well beyond the scope of this book.[1] Rather, it aims to state our views on how a number of particular equitable institutions may be potentially affected by the growth of AI, and whether changes may need to be made to accommodate this fact.

This subject is likely to be of considerable practical importance in the next few years. Take a few examples. Trustees managing substantial funds will in many cases already find themselves increasingly using or relying on AI input, whether directly or indirectly, for the purposes of investment, portfolio management and buying and selling investments.[2] In future, moreover, others subject to equitable duties may also find themselves more and more in contact with AI. Examples could include its use in such processes as collating information relevant to how trusts are to be administered and their funds or pension monies distributed; in financial tools aimed at helping mortgagees to decide whether, how and when to realise their security; helping receivers manage property or assets which they have taken under their control; and so on.

We can begin with what we see as an obvious point. Under the present law it is pretty certain that machines, being unendowed with legal personality and thus unable to have rights in or against property, or to be subject to legal duties, cannot be actual characters in the drama of equity. They cannot therefore be actual beneficiaries[3] or trustees;[4] nor, it is submitted, can they in the nature of things be receivers or mortgagees. Nor, for the same reason, can they owe fiduciary obligations; and again, for the same reason, the rules relating to delegation in trusts

[1] For a seminal text on the subject, see J McGhee KC (ed), *Snell's Equity*, 35th edn (London, Sweet & Maxwell, 2024) (hereinafter referred to as *Snell's Equity*).

[2] See generally L Brown, 'Artificial Intelligence & Trusts and Trustees: A New Dawn of Investment Opportunities and Risks?' (2025) 31 *Trusts & Trustees* 210.

[3] 'But the court will not enforce a non-charitable trust which is for an abstract object and not for the benefit of any *person*.' See L Tucker et al (ed), *Lewin on Trusts*, 20th edn (London, Sweet & Maxwell, 2023) para 5-053 (hereinafter referred to as *Lewin on Trusts*).

[4] 'In general terms, therefore, a trustee must be a *person* capable of taking or holding the legal estate …': *Lewin on Trusts*, para 2-014.

cannot apply to actions delegated to AIEMs. (We deal with the subject of legal personality in more detail in Chapter 2, and for reasons that appear there express the view that no change in the law here is either necessary or desirable.)

It follows from this that in so far as AI becomes involved in the administration of trusts, or in other cases where equitable obligations are in issue, the question must largely be – as it is in the case of contract and tort – how far the acts of machines can, or ought to be, attributed to their controllers or the other human or corporate persons standing behind them, and how far the use of AIEMs may impact on existing rules.

As regards attribution, we refer to our suggestion in Chapter 4 that a new category of person be introduced in connection with liability in contract and tort, the 'controller' of an AIEM. This would be the person who makes use of an AIEM, or of space on it, for the purposes of their business or other activities. Where appropriate, certain activities of the AIEM would be attributed to that person. For the sake of consistency and simplicity,[5] we advocate, with the odd exception,[6] that the same idea be carried over into equity.

II. Equity and AI

With many aspects of the law of trusts, it seems fairly clear that the law can take the interposition of AI in its stride without serious problems. It is worth remembering that unlike contracts, trusts are unlikely often to be created automatically by machine interaction.[7] If so, then issues such as interpretation, certainty and intention to create a trust relationship are unlikely to be seriously affected. These will continue, at heart, to depend on the law's rules for the evaluation of the intentions of human actors, and we see no reason to deal with them here.

Nevertheless, there are a number of situations in equity where the intervention of AIEMs is likely to become more relevant, and more apt to cause problems. One such concerns two general doctrines of equity: first, the rules of actual or constructive notice, which run through a great deal of commercial and property law, and secondly, the rules of rectification of contracts and other instruments. These are dealt with in the first part of this chapter.

The other part of this chapter concerns specific equitable rules and obligations. We are thinking here of the established obligations imposed by equity on trustees, mortgagees and other fiduciaries to act in good faith, or take reasonable

[5] Especially since equitable duties may well overlap to a large extent with other duties elsewhere in the law of obligations, and there is every reason to avoid unnecessary differentiation between them; *cf* the very perceptive A Burrows, 'We Do This at Common Law but That in Equity' (2002) *22 Oxford Journal of Legal Studies* 1.

[6] Notably in connection with the duty of care owed by trustees. See p 91 ff, below.

[7] It is perfectly possible that trust-like duties to account, such as *Quistclose* trusts (named after *Barclays Bank Ltd v Quistclose Investments Ltd* [1970] AC 567) may arise, but that is a different matter.

care, and the rules about delegation of trustees' functions. Other examples of the rules that may be affected include liabilities for knowing receipt of trust property, and dishonest assistance in a breach of trust, not to mention general doctrines of equity such as actual and constructive notice. These are already fairly complex subjects but as soon as an element of AI is introduced, the complexities are likely to increase.

III. Doctrines of Equity

A. Actual and Constructive Notice

Rules based on actual or constructive notice run through equity. For example, property rights obtained for value override previous equitable interests or rights to follow property only if the acquirer is free of actual or constructive notice of the latter;[8] and a similar rule applies to the right of a payee to keep payments made to them in breach of trust or fiduciary duty.[9] In commercial law, whether a later chargee can hold the priority of a security entered into in the teeth of a negative pledge clause may depend on whether they have actual notice of the clause's terms;[10] and so on.

Outside machine learning situations, the position is relatively clear.[11] Actual notice consists of positive knowledge, of matters specifically brought to a someone's attention in such a way that a reasonable person would take notice and investigate,[12] or alternatively of a person's wilful blindness to the existence of facts whose existence they suspect but which they choose not to investigate.[13] Constructive notice, by contrast, is constituted by knowledge that a reasonably prudent person in the position of the person in question,[14] if necessary with the aid of skilled advice, would have discovered had they made appropriate enquiries in the course of a transaction.[15] Put another way, it signifies knowledge which is available to a person, in circumstances such that if they do not take account of it they are to be regarded as in some way at fault.

[8] *Snell's Equity*, 35th edn, para 4-043 ff.

[9] ibid para 4-017 ff.

[10] *Wilson v Kelland* [1910] 2 Ch 306, 313; also *Snell's Equity*, 35th edn, Ch 40, section 7.

[11] *Snell's Equity*, 35th edn, para 4-027 ff; see too, in connection with property transactions, s 199 of the Law of Property Act 1925.

[12] Hence implying some degree of specificity and excluding vague third-party rumours: *cf Barnhart v Greenshields* (1853) 9 Moo PC 18, as explained in *Reeves v Pope* [1914] 2 KB 284.

[13] See particularly *Baden v Société Générale pour Favoriser le Développement du Commerce et de l'Industrie en France SA* [1993] 1 WLR 509, 575–576 (per Peter Gibson J).

[14] This is an important qualification, since what amounts to constructive notice can depend on the status of the defendant, more being expected of, say, a large bank than of a small trader: see eg *Sinclair Investments (UK) Ltd v Versailles Trade Finance Ltd* [2011] EWCA Civ 347, [2012] Ch 453, [109] (per Lord Neuberger).

[15] Eg *Berwick & Co v Price* [1905] 1 Ch 632, 638–39 (per Joyce J).

How does AI fit in here? As more and more business and other activities, such as carrying out due diligence or deciding whether to enter into a given transaction, are undertaken through AI, the issue will increasingly be raised: how far should information imparted, or available, to an AIEM be relevant to the actual or constructive knowledge calculus when it comes to those acting through such devices?

Under the present law, the answer is, perhaps surprisingly, hardly at all.[16] This is because the ideas behind notice cannot be readily carried across to information contained on, or available to, an AIEM. In law, we suggest elsewhere that an AIEM cannot have knowledge in the same sense that a human can.[17] Nor can it be at fault, since there is no such thing as a negligent machine;[18] and equally it cannot plausibly be regarded as an agent of anyone, including for the purpose of receiving or holding information.[19] It seems to follow from these two propositions that even if data is made available to an AIEM, or even present on its storage, there is little room for a holding that, for that reason alone, it is to be regarded as available to its controller.[20]

But this position is not immutable. Whatever the present law says, it would always be possible for legislation artificially to attribute a machine's possession of information to its controller or someone else. The issue that needs to be dealt with here is whether, and if so, how far, such legislation would be appropriate. In our view, there are some cases where it would be.

Take first the category of actual notice. Despite its name, and unlike knowledge in other parts of the law,[21] this does not depend on actual knowledge currently present to the mind of the person concerned, but merely on a showing that the relevant information has been explicitly communicated to them in the past.[22] Because of this, there is, we suggest, little difficulty, and a good deal of practical good, in making it clear that it can apply to knowledge or data present in an AIEM. In principle, it is suggested that no distinction should be drawn here between knowledge communicated to a person and knowledge communicated to, or contained on, an AIEM. In either case, it is suggested that it makes good sense to provide that the controller of the AIEM who has its acts attributed

[16] Hardly ever, but one cannot say never. If A specifically requests or permits B to give information to a machine controlled by A, for example by asking for it to be uploaded to A's website, then it is true that A will be regarded as in possession of it. But it is suggested that this is essentially on the basis of estoppel, or some similar doctrine.

[17] See p 27 ff.

[18] See p 21.

[19] See Chapter 5.

[20] Of course it remains open to a party to show that the controller itself could reasonably have been expected to gain access to that information or even was aware of it. But this is a different matter and would have to be specifically demonstrated.

[21] See p 27.

[22] In other words, a person may have actual notice of a fact previously made clear to them, or the contents of a document sent to them, even if at the relevant time they have forgotten about it or are otherwise not conscious of it. See *Re Montagu's Settlement Trusts* [1987] Ch 264; also *Eagle Trust plc v SBC Securities Ltd* [1993] 1 WLR 484, 494 (per Vinelott J) and *Lewin on Trusts*, para 44-126.

to them should equally be regarded as affected by actual notice of any such information.

However, the limits to this principle need to be noted. The suggestion above deals with data or knowledge actually communicated, and says nothing about any other kind of actual notice. Intelligent machines being incapable of holding suspicions, or of forming intentions in any meaningful sense, it is suggested that there is no convincing way of attributing to their controllers the alternative form of actual notice, namely notice inferred from wilful blindness to inconvenient matters which a person suspects might be present but deliberately turns away from. Here, we suggest, only the position of the controller themselves should be in account.

What of constructive notice? Despite the fact that constructive notice is related to fault, which is not easily attributable to a machine,[23] there is something to be said for a limited artificial statutory extension of the doctrine to AIEMs. In our view, it should in certain particular situations be possible to fix their controllers with constructive notice of facts that would have been accessible to them.

This should be the case, we think, where such machines possess (or have ready access to) data from which a reasonable human in the position of the controller,[24] had they had it to mind, would have inferred a relevant fact. The reason for this is connected with horizontal equity. Imagine two purchasers of assets encumbered with some equity. One, A, entrusts the decision whether to go ahead with the transaction to a person; the other, B, to an AIEM. Imagine too that both the person employed by A and the machine used by B have access to identical information. We suggest that for the purposes of notice both A and B should be treated in the same way.

B. Rectification and Mistake

Rectification is an equitable doctrine under which an instrument – traditionally a contract or deed, but it can apply to any written instrument[25] – can be corrected judicially to make it reflect the parties' intentions.[26] The remedy is subject to the usual discretionary principles applying to equitable relief, and will not be granted if oppressive or likely adversely to affect third-party rights.[27]

[23] See p 21.

[24] The individuation is important. Just as the status and sophistication of a human or corporation is relevant to whether they are fixed with constructive notice as a result of information being made available directly to them (see *Sinclair Investments (UK) Ltd v Versailles Trade Finance Ltd* [2011] EWCA Civ 347, [2012] Ch 453), so too where AI is involved the sophistication of the controller should be in account, in order to preserve maximum parity.

[25] Including, for example, a conveyance (eg *Re Colebrook's Conveyance* [1972] 1 WLR 1397; *Ralph v Ralph* [2021] EWCA Civ 1106, [2021] 4 WLR 128, [26] ff), a share transfer (eg *Re Int'l Contract Co* (1872) 7 Ch App 485), and a voluntary disposition of property (see eg *Re Butlin's ST* [1976] Ch 251, and also *AMP (UK) plc v Barker* [2001] Pens LR 77).

[26] *Snell's Equity*, 35th edn, para 16-007 ff.

[27] ibid para 16-025 ff.

The availability of rectification depends fundamentally on an instrument having been drawn up as a result of the parties' mistaken belief that its wording reflected their true intention. Where the instrument concerned is unilateral, what matters is the error of the person executing it; if that intention was not reflected in the eventual document, the latter is rectifiable.[28] If the instrument is multilateral, the error must be that of all parties,[29] and the real agreement between them must in addition be outwardly manifested in some express or implied way.[30] There is also a further situation where rectification is available. Where one party to a bilateral instrument, A, is mistaken as to whether it expresses their true intention and the other party, B, is aware of A's mistake, then the instrument can be rectified to correspond with A's actual intention.[31]

Issues of rectification could very well arise where AI is deployed by one or other party or otherwise appears in the picture. Examples might be where a contract is made on one or both sides by an AIEM; where an AIEM utilised by a pension provider decides who is entitled to rights under a pension scheme; or where a share transfer is made by an AIEM in a broking or investment house in favour of someone not entitled to benefit.

One point can be dealt with quickly. Hitherto the doctrine has been applied to written documents,[32] whereas AIEMs' output will typically be in purely electronic form. But this is unlikely to cause much difficulty. Provided that there is some output that is relatively permanent and intended to be in some way authoritative, it seems inconceivable that courts will not hold the remedy applicable to it.

More awkward, however, at least at first sight, is the issue of the application of the requirement of error. Here we need, it is suggested, to treat unilateral and other transactions separately. In the case of unilateral transactions, where it needs to be shown that the instrument failed to reflect the intent of the person executing it, the question immediately arises of whose error is to count here. Does the law limit itself to taking account of mistake by one or more persons (natural or artificial) behind the AIEM, or can it also in a suitable case regard the AI itself as mistaken and if so give a remedy accordingly?[33] The better position seems to be at present that although a machine can be regarded as having been duped for the purposes

[28] ibid para 16-021.

[29] See Peter Gibson LJ in *Swainland Builders Ltd v Freehold Properties Ltd* [2002] EWCA Civ 560, [2002] 2 EGLR 71, [33]; also *Persimmon Homes Ltd v Hillier* [2019] EWCA Civ 800, [2020] 1 All ER (Comm) 475.

[30] *FSHC Group Holdings Ltd v Glas Trust Corpn Ltd* [2019] EWCA Civ 1361, [2020] Ch 365, [75]–[77], also [80]–[87].

[31] *Roberts v Leics CC* [1961] Ch 555 is the classic example. See too *Holaw (470) Ltd v Stockton Estates Ltd* (2000) 81 P & CR 29, [41].

[32] 'Courts of Equity do not rectify contracts; they may and do rectify instruments purporting to have been made in pursuance of the terms of contracts': James VC in *Mackenzie v Coulson* (1869) LR 8 Eq 368, 375.

[33] An example might be where AI caused a pension fund to assign pension rights to the wrong person, or on the basis of a miscalculation.

of the law of deceit,[34] for the purpose of pure error it is only human mistake that counts.[35] A machine, after all, cannot easily be said to have an intention which is able to be subverted by error, or be said to have acted contrary to an intention it holds. If so, it would seem to follow that where there is no human error, rectification is unavailable in the case of transactions initiated by an AIEM.

With bilateral transactions, such as contracts, in our view the matter falls to be treated similarly, though the reasoning is slightly different. In *FSHC Group Holdings Ltd v Glas Trust Corpn Ltd*[36] the Court of Appeal laid down the formal requirements for rectification in such cases. Where it was alleged that a bilateral document had failed to record the true agreement of the parties, it had to be shown first that there had been some outward manifestation of the misrecorded prior agreement, and secondly a subjective intention in both parties to agree in those terms. The first of these raises no difficulties as regards an AIEM; whether there is such a manifestation is simply a matter of evidence. But not so the second. As we point out elsewhere, it is all but impossible to ascribe a subjective intention to agree to a machine. From this it follows that where rectification of an AIEM-mediated agreement is sought, this will only be available where there is evidence of a contrary common intention on the part of the humans behind the machines.

Equally, we take the view that similar reasoning must apply in the *Roberts v Leicestershire CC*[37] situation: that is, where there has been a failure by a written document to record one party's true intent which was known to the other, and rectification is sought by the former so as to enforce the contract on their terms. If a machine cannot itself form an intention, it is suggested that it equally it cannot have a belief in the intention of another party. From this it follows that once again the only relevant knowledge is that of the person behind it.

We think that this situation is unsatisfactory. Imagine, for example, a case where an AIEM without human intervention causes a documentary transfer of assets to be made to the wrong person because of a misstated name or address; or a situation where there is clear evidence of an AI malfunction that causes an agreement concluded between AIEMs to be entered into in terms X but formally recorded in terms Y. We see no reason why rectification, or some remedy equivalent to it, should not be available here.

It is suggested that the neatest way to do this would be legislation as follows. It should be provided that, whenever rectification is sought of a document or other permanent record, any requirement that the expression differ from a person's

[34] The classic instance being the facts of *Renault UK Ltd v Fleetpro Technical Services* [2007] EWHC 2541 (QB), [2008] Bus LR D 17 (automated purchasing: machine manipulated to give unauthorised discount). See too *IG Index Plc v Colley* [2013] EWHC 478 (QB).

[35] As held in Singapore: see *B2C2 Ltd v Quoine Pte Ltd* [2020] SGCA(I) 02, [2020] 2 SLR 20 (malfunction of computer in computerised Bitcoin trading: plea of error: error to be that of person in charge of machine, not machine itself).

[36] [2019] EWCA Civ 1361, [2020] Ch 365. Compare D Whayman, 'The Rectification (and Construction) of Computer-Generated Documents' (2019) 30 *King's Law Journal* 489.

[37] [1961] Ch 555.

intention should be deemed satisfied in the case of an AIEM if it is shown either: (i) that the difference arose from a malfunction in the machine;or (ii) that the difference was caused by given false data in the memory of the machine. This would essentially bring the position with documents executed through the intermediacy of AIEMs as nearly as possible into line with those executed by purely human means.

IV. Equitable Duties and Liabilities

A. Duties of Good Faith

In contrast to the common law of contract and tort, where they play a very minor role at best, good faith duties are a pervasive theme in equity. Trustees have always been under a duty to act in good faith;[38] so too, whether or not they also owe a duty of care (see above), fiduciaries in the course of their operations,[39] partners,[40] donees of fiduciary powers,[41] mortgagees exercising powers of intervention or sale,[42] receivers, and others.

The content of the good faith duty in equity clearly varies according to the context. But in essence it includes four features. One is an obligation to exercise powers or discretions as a result of conscious thought, rather than automatically or at someone else's dictation.[43] Another is a prohibition on a person in a fiduciary position vis-à-vis another, such as a mortgagee, exercising a power without good reason in prejudice of that other's rights or interests.[44] In addition, fiduciary

[38] See eg *Armitage v Nurse* [1998] Ch 241, 253–54 (per Millett LJ) ('The duty of the trustees to perform the trusts honestly and in good faith for the benefit of the beneficiaries is the minimum necessary to give substance to the trusts'), and D Hayton, 'The Irreducible Core Content of Trusteeship' in A Oakley (ed), *Trends in Contemporary Trust Law* (Oxford, Oxford University Press, 1997) 57.

[39] eg *Bristol & West Building Society v Mothew* [1998] Ch 1, 18 (per Millett LJ). Company directors have analogous duties to act in a way that they in good faith think is for the benefit of the company and its members: Companies Act 2006, s 172(1). This largely reflects the duty of good faith they owed at common law (eg *Re Smith & Fawcett Ltd* [1942] Ch 304, 306): see the 2006 Act, s 170(4). This will be particularly relevant in the AI context in the case of the use of AI by corporate directors, whose appointment is permitted under the present companies legislation (Companies Act 2006, s 155). It will become less so when s 156A of the Act, introducing a prima facie requirement subject to exceptions that all company directors must be human, comes into force.

[40] See R I'Anson Banks (ed), *Lindley & Banks on Partnership*, 21st edn (London, Sweet & Maxwell, 2024) Ch 16.

[41] *Lewin on Trusts*, para 29-001 onwards; also eg *Imperial Group Pension Trust Ltd v Imperial Tobacco Ltd* [1991] 1 WLR 589 and *FS Capital Ltd v Adams* [2025] EWCA Civ 53, [93].

[42] *Cuckmere Brick Co Ltd v Mutual Finance Ltd* [1971] Ch 949; *Downsview Nominees Ltd v First City Corpn Ltd* [1993] AC 295; *Mortgage Express Ltd v Mardner* [2004] EWCA Civ 1859, [9].

[43] eg *Wilson v Turner* (1883) 22 Ch D 521 and the more recent *Turner v Turner* [1984] Ch 100.

[44] As in *Downsview Nominees Ltd v First City Corpn Ltd* [1993] AC 295 (first mortgagees of business refused to realise security by sale and assignment of rights to junior mortgagee, choosing instead to trade disastrously).

powers must not be exercised for improper motives such as spite or dislike,[45] or for a collateral purpose.[46] And it also seems that there may sometimes in addition be a more nebulous duty to take reasonable steps to promote the beneficiary's interests.[47] All this immediately raises the question: where the operations of AIEMs intervene in the decision whether to undertake a particular course of action, how might these duties be affected?

As regards the first and second of these features, it is suggested that the intervention of AI will make little if any change. When it comes to the duty to exercise independent judgement, if a trustee is required to reach a conclusion for themselves and not act at the dictation of another person, *a fortiori* they cannot do so at the whim of an algorithm: in both cases there will be an abuse of power. And so too with the fiduciary obligation not unnecessarily to prejudice another's interests without some objective justification. This is essentially an objective obligation: there either is such unacceptable unfair prejudice or there is not, and the fact that the decision may have been reached through the intervention of an AIEM is beside the point.

Unfortunately, however, the same cannot be said of the other aspects of the duty, namely the obligation not to misuse one's position for ulterior or improper motives. This is because here the subjective motivation with which a power was exercised are central to the determination of whether there has been a breach. A machine, we submit, can neither form an intention nor act from a particular motive, at least in the sense that humans can; and equally it cannot in any normal sense be said to act from spite or dislike. It follows that in such cases the only issue will be the state of mind of the controller of the AIEM concerned: the operations of any intervening AI will be disregarded.

Is this situation satisfactory? Perhaps surprisingly, it is our tentative view that it probably is. In so far as the rule against improper motive is based on human wrongdoing, there seems nothing wrong in excluding references to the thought processes of an AIEM that is incapable of such things. Furthermore, such a solution is unlikely to do much injustice. In many cases where a trustee is found to have acted from an improper or collateral motive the decision itself often remains one that could have been reached had it not been tainted by its motivation. If so, then if the decision is based on input from an AIEM there is no reason why it should not stand in the absence of proof of wrongdoing by the controller, or (though proving this this might be a tall order) the making available by the controller of biased or partial data to the machine with a view to influencing its advice.

[45] eg *Klug v Klug* [1918] 2 Ch 67; *cf Re Pauling's Settlement Trust* [1964] Ch 303, 333.

[46] *cf Quennell v Maltby* [1979] 1 WLR 318 (mortgagee of dwelling-house colluding with freeholder to eject protected tenant).

[47] See eg *Item Software (UK) Ltd v Fassihi* [2004] EWCA Civ 1244, [2005] 2 BCLC 91, especially at [41]–[44] (company director).

B. Fiduciary Duties

Fiduciary duties are a massive subject in themselves and are still expanding fast.[48] We can do little more here than scratch their surface. In essence, however, while there is no fixed concept of a fiduciary,[49] such duties amount to four (apart from the duty of good faith, dealt with above). First, a fiduciary, at least within the confines of their function, must act entirely in the interests of the beneficiary without regard to their own benefit.[50] Secondly, a fiduciary must not without the informed consent of the beneficiary engage in self-dealing: that is, must refrain from taking part as a direct or indirect counterparty in any dealings on behalf of the beneficiary.[51] Thirdly, more generally a fiduciary must avoid putting themselves in a position where their duty and interest conflict;[52] and fourthly, they must not without properly informed consent make a profit out of their position.[53]

One might have thought fiduciary obligations as described above would sit slightly ill with AIEMs. The duties they create are, after all, on one level intensely moral. They are duties related to selflessness and suppression of one's own interests,[54] and arise, it has been said, at least partly out of an instinct that fiduciaries, being human, need to be kept out of temptation's way by strict rules denying them the right to benefit from questionable transactions.[55] Hence the inflexibility of the duties involved, and (for instance) the rules that a transaction arising out of self-dealing can be set aside even if ostensibly quite fair at the time,[56] and that

[48] For example they now form a large part of professional obligations: see RM Jackson and JL Powell, *Jackson & Powell on Professional Liability*, 9th edn (London, Sweet & Maxwell, 2021) para 2-198 ff.

[49] As Millett LJ has said, a fiduciary 'is not subject to fiduciary obligations because he is a fiduciary; it is because he is subject to them that he is a fiduciary'. See *Bristol & West Building Society v Mothew* [1988] Ch 1, 18 (derived from PD Finn, *Fiduciary Obligations* (Sydney, Law Book Co, 1977) p 2).

[50] See *Bristol & West Building Society v Mothew* [1998] Ch 1, 18 (per Millett LJ); also *Arklow Investments Ltd v Maclean* [2000] 1 WLR 594, 598; *Children's Investment Fund Foundation (UK) v Attorney General* [2020] UKSC 33, [2022] AC 155, [47]–[49] and [91].

[51] See *Ex p James* (1803) 8 Ves Jr 337; *Holder v Holder* [1968] Ch 353.

[52] eg *Longstaff v Birtles* [2001] EWCA Civ 1219, [2002] 1 WLR 470; *Ratiu v Conway* [2005] EWCA Civ 1302, [2006] 1 All ER 571.

[53] Something that often, but no means invariably, comes up in the context of either secret commissions (eg *Imperial Mercantile Credit Association v Coleman* (1873) LR 6 HL 189 (stockbroker); *McWilliam v Norton Finance (UK) Ltd* [2015] EWCA Civ 186, [2015] PNLR 22 (credit broker)) or business opportunities arising from inside knowledge (see in particular *Boardman v Phipps* [1967] 2 AC 46 and *Rukhadze v Recovery Partners GP Ltd* [2025] UKSC 10, [2025] 2 WLR 529).

[54] A fiduciary 'owes a duty of single-minded loyalty to his principal, meaning that he cannot exercise any power in relation to matters covered by his fiduciary duty so as to benefit himself': *Hopcraft v Close Bros Ltd* [2025] UKSC 33, [2025] 3 WLR 423, [90] (per Lord Reed).

[55] eg *Murad v Al-Saraj* [2005] EWCA Civ 959, [2005] WTLR 1573, [74] (per Arden LJ); *Rukhadze v Recovery Partners GP Ltd* [2025] UKSC 10, [2025] 3 WLR 423, [46] (per Lord Briggs), [198] (per Lord Leggatt).

[56] '[I]f a trustee sells the trust property to himself, the sale is voidable by any beneficiary ex debito justitiae, however fair the transaction': *Tito v Waddell (No 2)* [1977] Ch 106, 241 (per Megarry V-C); see too eg *Ex p James* (1803) 8 Ves 337, 345, 348–49.

a profit made out of a fiduciary position must be repaid even if made entirely innocently and even if the beneficiary themselves could never have made it.[57] Surprisingly, however, it is suggested that the use by fiduciaries of machine learning or AIEMs is likely to cause few difficulties. This is, ironically, because of the very strictness of the duties imposed, and their resulting independence of any wrongful or improper intent on the defendant's part.

Thus, as regards the duty to act entirely in the beneficiary's interest, the criterion is essentially whether a given decision or activity is reconcilable with the need to have regard only to the benefit of the counterparty. This is a question which normally can be answered yes or no without reference to any state of mind or intention on the defendant's part. It follows, we suggest, that even if a decision is taken, or at least informed, by an AIEM, the law can take this in its stride and there is no need for any different approach. Even more so is this true in the case of self-dealing: either a transaction amounts to self-dealing, such that it is voidable at the suit of the beneficiary,[58] or it does not, and the intervention of a computer makes no difference. So too, it is suggested, with the third duty. A computer having no duties or interests of its own, the only issue is whether the person whose interests it represents is in a position of conflict. Since this again is a question that can be answered without reference to any knowledge or intention,[59] the fact that an AIEM with no facility for forming an intention may have played some part in the decision or course of action involved is beside the point.

The only slight difficulty arises where it is sought to recoup profits or gains made by a fiduciary. In many cases, it is true, here too the issue will still be a simple objective one where the interposition of AI will not matter: did these profits arise out of the defendant's fiduciary position, and if so did the beneficiary give informed consent to their being made?[60] But not always: imagine a case where information imparted in confidence in the course of a fiduciary relation such as a joint venture existed on an AIEM controlled by the defendant, but there is no evidence that the defendant actually knew about it or of any connection between it and the defendant's gain. A claim to claw back the profit might face some difficulty here:[61] and there is something to be said for a presumption of a connection between the two, it being left up to the defendant to disprove it if they can.

[57] *Boardman v Phipps* [1967] 2 AC 46, 105 (per Lord Hodson); *Rukhadze v Recovery Partners GP Ltd* [2025] UKSC 10, [2025] 2 WLR 529.

[58] See *Re Cape Breton Co* (1885) 29 Ch D 795, 803 (per Cotton LJ); also, *Armstrong v Jackson* [1917] 2 KB 822, 823–24 (per McCardie J).

[59] eg *Bristol & West Building Society v Mothew* [1998] Ch 1, 18–19 (Millett J).

[60] See eg *Boardman v Phipps* [1967] 2 AC 46, 102–103 (per Lord Cohen); 105 (per Lord Hodson); more recently, see generally *Hopcraft v Close Bros Ltd* [2025] UKSC 33, [2025] 3 WLR 423.

[61] Compare the comments of Lord Cohen in *Boardman*, above, at 102: it would be possible for information to reach a trustee which would not have done so had they not been acting as such, but for this nevertheless not to give rise to a duty to pay over any profits arising from its use.

There is, however, one further difficulty that may arise with fiduciary duties on the other side of the equation. This concerns informed consent. At present, a fiduciary wishing to avoid a finding of breach of fiduciary duty can do so on the basis of consent by the beneficiary, but only where that consent is informed[62] – that is, where the fiduciary shows that the beneficiary not only acquiesced in what happened, but had in addition been provided with full information about any matters that might affect their decision,[63] taking into account their sophistication or lack of it.[64] This may cause difficulty where the beneficiary conducts their affairs through an AIEM: should the fact that full information was present in the machine's memory suffice to show informed consent by its controller?

It is suggested that the answer is no, since this would deprive the informed consent rule of much of its efficacy. The only exception would be where the beneficiary had expressly or impliedly told the fiduciary that all information, instead of being transmitted expressly to them, could instead be communicated to the AIEM. This seems to us to be unsatisfactory, and to call for reform. The best solution, we suggest, would be legislation stating two things. First, it should make clear that the availability of information or data on an AIEM would not of itself show knowledge in the controller for the purpose of any rule requiring consent. Secondly, however, this should be without prejudice to any rule of law under which the beneficiary was precluded from denying that they had received the necessary information.

C. Delegation of Functions in Equity

This is an issue that particularly affects trustees. The prima facie position is that the nature of a trustee's position is such that a trustee must act, and take decisions, personally.[65] However, this is now considerably modified. The position is today regulated largely by the Trustee Act 2000, under section 11 of which there is now a general power to delegate any function other than a trustee's core obligations, the latter being enumerated as essentially the determination of who to distribute trust property to, the apportionment of expenses to income or capital, and appointment of other trustees.[66] Where functions are properly delegated, trustees are under a

[62] *Boardman v Phipps* [1967] 2 AC 46, 109 (per Lord Hodson); *New Zealand Netherlands Society 'Oranje' Inc v Kuys* [1973] 1 WLR 1126, 1132 ('full and frank disclosure').

[63] *Johnson v EBS Pensioner Trustees Ltd* [2002] EWCA Civ 164, [2002] Lloyd's Rep PN 309, [72], [83]; *Hopcraft v Close Bros Ltd* [2025] UKSC 33, [211] onwards.

[64] *McWilliam v Norton Finance (UK) Ltd* [2015] EWCA Civ 186, [2015] PNLR 22, [51]–[54] (Tomlinson LJ).

[65] *Re Lucking's Will Trusts* [1968] 1 WLR 866; *Bartlett v Barclays Bank Trust Co Ltd* [1980] Ch 515.

[66] See s 11(2). Trustees of land are, in addition, unable to delegate their function under s 11 of the Trusts of Land and Appointment of Trustees Act 1996: see the Trustee Act 2000, ss 13(4), 13(5). Charity trustees have a rather narrower power of delegation, specifically limited to certain functions (Trustee Act 2000, s 11(3)).

personal duty of care in choosing and supervising their delegates,[67] but are otherwise not liable for their delegates' defaults.[68]

In addition, to take account of the fact that trustees may be temporarily unable to act for personal or other reasons, a trustee may by statute[69] delegate any function of theirs by power of attorney to another for up to a year. But here the rule is stricter: in this case the trustee is strictly liable for any default on the part of the delegate.[70]

The latter of these powers we see as unlikely to raise any serious difficulties as regards AIEMs. The right of temporary delegation clearly envisages delegation only to someone having legal personality.[71] Any delegation to a machine, however smart, would fairly obviously be a breach of trust in and of itself, not to mention an unlawful abdication of the trustee's powers, and the issue of liability for any malfunction is therefore unlikely to arise as such.

The former power is potentially more problematic. One point is that some typical trustee functions – the curation of relatively small investments, or the care of particular kinds of trust assets, for example – may in coming years be functions that can perfectly well be performed by AIEMs. At present, however, it would seem that the delegation power under section 11 of the Trustee Act 2000 is limited to human or corporate delegates.[72] There is much to be said, in our view, for an amendment of the section stating that where appropriate and compatible with a trustee's duty of care under section 1 of the same Act, the delegation of at least functions to an AIEM shall be permissible. To that limited extent, a trustee's duty to take decisions personally needs to be qualified.

The other point is that the issue of fault, which does cause problems in the context of AIEMs, will arise in fairly acute form here. However, this is probably better covered below, under the trustee's duty of care.

D. The Duty of Care

Duties to take care arise as much in equity as at law. Admittedly, fiduciaries do not owe duties of care merely because they are fiduciaries[73] (though they often owe concurrent duties to exercise reasonable care in carrying on their business in some other capacity, as for example with lawyers or accountants). However, categories of fiduciary do owe self-standing duties of care or due diligence. Two such duties in particular need some attention.

[67] Trustee Act 2000, s 1.

[68] Trustee Act 2000, s 23.

[69] See s 25 of the Trustee Act 1925 (as amended by the Trustee Delegation Act 1999).

[70] Trustee Act 1925, s 25(7).

[71] Thus s 25(3) of the 1925 Act, allowing delegation to be to a trust corporation, refers to the 'persons' to whom delegation is allowed.

[72] 'Subject to the provisions of this Part, the trustees of a trust may authorise *any person* to exercise any or all of their delegable functions as their agent' (emphasis added). A machine is not a person.

[73] *Bristol & West Building Society v Mothew* [1998] Ch 1, 16 (Millett LJ).

i. Trustees

A trustee owes a duty to take care in respect of the custody and investment of trust assets, and to preserve the trust property, both under the general law[74] and also in respect of certain specific functions under section 1 of the Trustee Act 2000.[75] Under section 5 of the same Act this duty is fleshed out in the specific case of investment: the trustee must, in investing trust property, where necessary take advice from a person they reasonably believe to be financially experienced,[76] though there is an exception where the trustee reasonably considers this unnecessary.[77] In addition, where a trustee lawfully employs an agent,[78] or custodian of trust assets,[79] to look after those assets, they are liable to take care in the appointment and supervision of such people, and are protected if they do take such care.[80]

AI is clearly going to be relevant here, in particular as regards investment decisions which are likely to be increasingly entrusted to it. At present, however, this is unlikely to have much effect on the liability of trustees.[81] In so far as a trustee reasonably entrusts investment decisions to AI, they will not be liable for the errors of that AI, even if these are errors that would not have been made by a reasonable person. True, a trustee is bound where necessary to take advice on investment policy, and this duty will not be satisfied by following the advice of an AIEM.[82] However, under section 5(3) of the Trustee Act 2000 there is no duty to take advice where the trustee 'reasonably concludes that in all the circumstances it is unnecessary or inappropriate to do so'.[83] It is submitted that a reasonable decision to rely on computerised, rather than personalised, advice will potentially be protected by that section.

Although elsewhere we suggest that there needs to be introduced into the law the concept of a negligent machine, and that in certain cases controllers of such a

[74] eg *Speight v Gaunt* (1883) 9 App Cas 1; *Re Lucking's Will Trusts* [1968] 1 WLR 866, 874 (per Cross J).

[75] These include, most importantly, exercising powers of investment, appointing and supervising agents, insuring trust property and compromising claims. See the Trustee Act 2000, Schedule 1.

[76] See ss 5(1) and 5(2).

[77] See s 5(3).

[78] Which, subject to any contrary terms in the trust instrument, they are allowed to do except as regards decisions over distribution, income/capital balance, appointment of trustees, or further delegation: see above, and s 11(2).

[79] See s 17.

[80] See s 23(1).

[81] Though there may be an indirect effect. If and when AI investment advice becomes substantially better or more cost-effective than human advice, it may become the duty of the trustee under s 1 of the Trustee Act 2000 to employ it.

[82] Since advice must come from 'a *person* who is reasonably believed by the trustee to be qualified to give it by his ability in and practical experience of financial and other matters relating to the proposed investment' (s 5(4) (emphasis added)), and an AIEM, however smart and otherwise qualified, is not a 'person'. This point is made in L Brown, 'Artificial Intelligence & Trusts and Trustees: A New Dawn of Investment Opportunities and Risks?' (2025) 31 *Trusts & Trustees* 210.

[83] See s 5(3).

machine should be liable for such fault,[84] it is our tentative view that this should not apply to the duties of care owed by trustees under the Trustee Act 2000. The scheme of that Act, as we see it, is largely to protect trustees from liability except in the case of personal fault (or the fault of their human employees, where appropriate): this is evidenced by a number of exculpatory provisions in the Act.[85] Any ascription to trustees of the fault of AI used by them would, in our opinion, cut across these protections, and for that reason defeat the purpose of the statutory arrangement.[86]

ii. Other Fiduciaries

Trustees aside, other fiduciaries may owe duties of care over and above the more general one of good faith (dealt with below). Mortgagees in selling, for example, owe a well-established duty to take care to obtain the best price available in the circumstances of the sale.[87] So too receivers appointed by a lender or other creditor, if they choose to run a business they have taken over, owe an obligation to the business owner to show due diligence,[88] and furthermore, if they sell an asset under their receivership owe a duty to the owner, and possibly to any surety of theirs,[89] to get a proper price. (Indeed, depending on the degree of control exercised over the receiver, the appointing creditor may also be liable if this duty is broken.[90]) And it is worth adding that company directors by statute owe a duty of proper care to the companies they direct.[91]

With these duties of care, many of the same issues arise as with duties to take care arising from contract and tort.[92] Moreover, given that many of these equitable duties concern complex financial and business decisions of a type potentially rather suited to AI approaches, the point is likely to matter. The point is the same

[84] See Chapter 4 in particular.

[85] Notably, ss 21–23 of the Trustee Act 2000. There are exceptions to this (see eg s 25(7) of the Trustee Act 1925, dealing with substitutes appointed by power of attorney), but they are narrowly drawn.

[86] It should be noted that this argument is limited to the liability of trustees themselves.

[87] *Cuckmere Brick Co Ltd v Mutual Finance Ltd* [1971] Ch 949. 'In the circumstances of the sale' emphasises that the mortgagee can choose the time of sale without being accountable, but that having chosen it, it must obtain the best price possible: see eg *Tse Kwong Lam v Wong Chit Sen* [1983] 1 WLR 1349.

[88] *Medforth v Blake* [2000] Ch 86. It is suggested that in respect of any asset taken into the receiver's control a similar duty of care in its custody and control will be imposed.

[89] See *Standard Chartered Bank Ltd v Walker* [1982] 1 WLR 1410 and *American Express International Banking Corpn v Hurley* [1985] 3 All ER 564. Note, however, the doubts expressed by Lightman J in *Burgess v Auger* [1998] BCLC 478.

[90] Compare *Standard Chartered Bank Ltd v Walker* [1982] 1 WLR 1410 (control and liability) with *American Express International Banking Corpn v Hurley* [1985] 3 All ER 564 (no control, no liability).

[91] Companies Act 2006, s 174; Dame M Arden et al, *Buckley on the Companies Acts*, 15th edn (London, LexisNexis, 2000) para 1000 ff. This will become less important in the AI context as and when s 156A of the Companies Act 2006, prohibiting with a few exceptions the appointment of non-human directors, comes into force.

[92] See Chapters 3 and 4 in particular.

as bedevils contractual and tortious duties: the lack of any legal concept of a negligent machine. Where a person subject to such a duty makes use of an AIEM and the AIEM makes an error that would be negligent if made by a person, it will be difficult under the present law to argue that there has been a breach of the duty of care. In the absence of proof of personal fault in selection or supervision of the AIEM the person making use of it will be innocent of any negligence; and – the machine being incapable of negligence – the concepts of vicarious liability, or even non-delegable duty, cannot help.

Our suggested solution to this problem is the same as with other duties of care, as we suggest elsewhere.[93] In contrast to our recommendations as regards trustees, we would call for a statutory liability in the controller of the AIEM where the machine makes an error that if committed by a human would amount to negligence.[94]

E. Knowing Receipt and Dishonest Assistance

Apart from duties of care, referred to above, most breaches of equitable obligations are not as such fault dependent. In other words, it is enough for a person seeking a remedy for their breach, such as equitable compensation, to prove the failure to observe or respect the obligation, without going on to show that the person subject to it was either negligent or a knowing wrongdoer. This is true of breach of trust, and of most other breaches of fiduciary duty. However, the position is different where it is sought to make third parties other than the trustee or fiduciary liable to compensate the victim. Here two further liabilities come into play: the equitable wrongs of unconscionable receipt of assets transferred in breach of duty; and dishonest assistance in a breach of trust. Both of these are fundamentally fault-based.[95]

Knowing receipt deals with the case of the defendant through whose hands trust assets or other property wrongfully transferred in equity has passed, but who no longer controls them. In practice, cases of knowing receipt normally involve trust money, but they can equally involve chattels[96] or securities,[97] provided that at the time of receipt an equitable interest subsisted in someone else.[98] Liability depends not on deliberate wrongdoing, but on a fairly flexible fault-based standard somewhere between that and simple negligence.[99] The essential issue is whether, at the time of receipt or at a later time while the asset was still in their hands, the

[93] See p 61 ff.

[94] For details the reader is referred to p 61 ff.

[95] *Snell's Equity*, para 30-067 onwards.

[96] As in eg *Re Montagu's ST* [1987] Ch 264.

[97] eg *Byers v Saudi National Bank* [2023] UKSC 51, [2024] 2 WLR 237.

[98] ibid.

[99] See the summary of this complex subject by Hoffmann LJ in *El Ajou v Dollar Land Holdings plc* [1994] 2 All ER 685, 700.

defendant had gained such a degree of actual knowledge[100] of the surrounding facts as to make it unconscionable for them to dispose of it or deal with it as if it were their own.[101] In most cases at least, the answer to this question would seem to depend on whether the defendant had actual notice of facts that would put a reasonable person in their position[102] on inquiry.[103]

Dishonest assistance differs from knowing receipt. The essence of this wrong is that even if trust assets have not passed through the defendant's hands, they may still be liable if in some way they have actively assisted in the commission of a breach of trust or a similar fiduciary obligation.[104] Typical examples include a bank handling money transfers or a lawyer dealing with client funds in respect of a dubious transaction, or a third party assisting a trustee or fiduciary in the wrongful dissipation of assets. Like knowing receipt, this head of liability is emphatically fault-based.[105] For the last 30 years it has been clear that the standard here is one of dishonesty;[106] that is, where a defendant is more than merely negligent[107] and engages in conduct which, in the light of what that defendant actually knows,[108] would be regarded by right-thinking people as lacking probity.[109]

How might this liability be affected by the conduct of business through AIEMs by, say, a trader, a bank or a broker? Take first knowing receipt. Here, unconscionability is relatively unproblematical. Being essentially an objective (although moral) standard, it carries over fairly easily to transactions carried out electronically: the question is simply, it is suggested, whether what happened would be seen as unconscionable if done by a human. In our view, however, there is much more difficulty in the requirement that any assessment of unconscionability must take account of what the defendant actually knows. Suppose that a potential acquirer of assets uses AI, say, to seek out possible bargains or perform due diligence on assets offered to them. Should information picked up by that AI but not actually known to the controller be attributed to the latter for the

[100] The knowledge must, it seems, be actual. Mere negligent failure to gain it will not suffice: *cf Armstrong DLW GmbH v Winnington Networks Ltd* [2012] EWHC 10 (Ch), [2013] Ch 156, [131]–[132].

[101] See *Bank of Credit & Commerce International (Overseas) Ltd v Akindele* [2001] Ch 437, 455 (Nourse LJ) (where the voluminous earlier authority is distilled).

[102] The relevance of the defendant's position is suggested in *Snell's Equity*, para 30-072 by analogy with the rules on constructive notice, above. In our view this is right.

[103] *MacMillan Inc v Bishopgate Investment Trust plc* [1995] 1 WLR 978, 1000.

[104] See generally *Snell's Equity*, para 30-077 onwards.

[105] *Royal Brunei Airlines Sdn Bhd v Tan* [1995] 2 AC 378, 387 (per Lord Nicholls).

[106] ibid 392: see too *Group Seven Ltd v Nasir* [2019] EWCA Civ 614, [2020] Ch 129.

[107] See *Royal Brunei Airlines Sdn Bhd v Tan* [1995] 2 AC 378, 391–92.

[108] That is, it requires actual knowledge or at least a deliberate blindness: the means of knowledge is not enough. See *Royal Brunei Airlines Sdn Bhd v Tan* [1995] 2 AC 378, 389; *Group Seven Ltd v Nasir* [2019] EWCA Civ 614, [2020] Ch 129, [58].

[109] *Royal Brunei Airlines Sdn Bhd v Tan* [1995] 2 AC 378, 389; *Barlow Clowes International Ltd v Eurotrust International Ltd* [2005] UKPC 37, [2006] 1 WLR 1476, [11]–[16]. The criterion of what counts as dishonest is, it is now clear, objective: see eg *Group Seven Ltd v Nasir* [2019] EWCA Civ 614, [2020] Ch 129, referring to *Ivey v Genting Casinos (UK) Ltd* [2017] UKSC 67, [2018] AC 391.

purpose of deciding whether they are acting unconscionably? Under the present law it is suggested that the answer is no. Although an agent's knowledge readily binds a principal where the agent is a legal or a natural person, there is no authority that any similar rule applies to data on a machine.[110]

Somewhat similar reasoning, moreover, applies to dishonest assistance. Since it is now clear that dishonesty in law does not involve personal bad intent but simply behaviour that a decent person would see as dishonest,[111] the same argument applies to it as to unconscionability in knowing receipt: it is fundamentally an objective standard, and the interposition of AI should make no difference. On the other hand, it is also clear that the question of (objective) dishonesty has to be judged in the light of the information actually known to the defendant,[112] and to the latter's subjective motives.[113]

If so, here again the problem arises of what to do about data in the 'hands' of AI but not those of the human controlling it. Currently, in the light of the lack of any general principle of attribution in such cases, it would seem that such data is out of account: but should it be? It is our view that in this respect different criteria may have to be applied in the case of knowing receipt, and that of dishonest assistance. This is because the rationale of the claims is subtly different.

As regards a claim in knowing receipt, the essence of such a claim is that a person should not deal with or dispose of assets in circumstances where information that is, or has been made, directly available to them indicates that the assets are not theirs to deal with. This in turn implies at least a duty in a potential recipient positively to consider what information is available to them before engaging in any such dealing. If this is right, it is suggested that there is no good reason to distinguish here between information collated in paper files, resting in the hands of agents, or contained on the storage medium of an AIEM under the defendant's direct control. If the information concerned is reasonably accessible, whether by the AIEM or otherwise, the defendant should deal with the relevant assets at their peril. It should, therefore, be provided that for the purpose of liability for knowing receipt any knowledge gained by an AIEM should be deemed to be the knowledge of its controller.

Turning now to dishonest assistance, in our view the thinking is – at first sight surprisingly – not quite the same. True, as with knowing receipt, liability is fault-based: but here the required fault is not so much failure to take account of facts made known to one, as actual moral obliquity: this is implicit in the requirement that the defendant must have done something that any decent person would recognise as dishonest. We do not think that it would be right to

[110] See p 120 ff.

[111] See *Group Seven Ltd v Nasir* [2019] EWCA Civ 614, [2020] Ch 129, above.

[112] *Royal Brunei Airlines Sdn Bhd v Tan* [1995] 2 AC 378, 391; *Clydesdale Bank plc v Workman* [2016] EWCA Civ 73, [2016] PNLR 18, [50].

[113] *Clydesdale Bank plc v Workman* [2016] EWCA Civ 73, [2016] PNLR 18, [52].

place this liability on someone merely on account of knowledge that they could have, but did not, retrieve from a machine under their control, since this would essentially replace a criterion of dishonesty with one of liability for negligence. If this is right, then it would seem appropriate to provide expressly that for the purposes of determining liability for dishonest assistance data on an AIEM under a person's control should not, without more, count as facts known to its controller. The words 'without more' are important, however. If the information is in fact known to the controller, clearly the result should be different: and so also if a person, knowing that they have utilised an AIEM in a transaction, deliberately fails to check the information on it in case there is something contrary to their interests.

V. Conclusions

Equity has evolved incrementally through judicial decisions, guided by principles of fairness, conscience, and moral justice. While inherently flexible, our analysis has illustrated that the use of intelligent machines poses significant challenges to this area of law, necessitating a measure of statutory intervention. A summary of our conclusions is provided below.

A. Attribution

For the purposes of deciding whether, in relation to the rules of equity, a given act or omission by an AIEM is to be attributed to a given person, we envisage that the general statutory test propounded in Chapter 5 for determining who is the 'controller' of the AIEM will apply.

B. The Doctrine of Notice

When an issue arises as to what counts as notice of equitable interests, there is under the present law no clear rule about how we treat knowledge available to an AIEM but not to its controller. It is possible that such knowledge falls to be disregarded except in so far as the controller themselves are at fault in not appreciating it, but we cannot be certain.

We see this situation as unsatisfactory. In our view, for the purposes of the doctrine of notice it makes good sense to provide that the controller of the AIEM who has its acts attributed to them should equally be regarded as affected by actual notice of any such information. This should be the case where such machines possess (or have ready access to) data from which a reasonable human in the position of the controller, had they had it to mind, would have inferred a relevant fact.

C. Rectification and AIEMs

In a number of cases, the availability of the remedy of rectification depends on findings that the terms of the document departed from the subjective intention of one or other of the parties executing it. This raises difficulties in the case of documents executed by AIEMs, which have no capacity to subjectively intend anything.

Yet it is our view that this is unsatisfactory, and that at least in some cases rectification should be an available remedy even here. We suggest legislation to the effect that, whenever rectification is sought of a document or other permanent record, any requirement that the expression differ from a person's intention should be deemed satisfied in the case of an AIEM, if it is shown either: (i) that the difference arose from a malfunction in the machine; or (ii) that the difference was caused by given false data in the memory of the machine.

D. Informed Consent as a Defence to an Equitable Claim

When informed consent is raised as a defence to a claim based, for instance, on breach of fiduciary duty, the issue may arise as to the status of information communicated to an AIEM of which the complainant is the controller but not present to the mind of the latter. Will such information render the consent informed by being attributed to the controller? The probable position is that it will not, but pending litigation the matter must be seen as uncertain.

We think this matter should be clarified. There should be a statutory provision that, for the purpose of deciding whether a defence of informed consent applies, knowledge contained on, or available to, an AIEM would not without more show knowledge in the controller. Secondly, however, this should be without prejudice to any rule of law under which the beneficiary was otherwise precluded from denying that they had received the necessary information.

E. Delegation by Trustees

Trustees have power under section 11 of the Trustee Act 2000 to delegate certain management powers, such as the curation of investments, to professionals or experts for whose faults they will not be liable. But this is currently limited to human or corporate delegates. In our view this is unsatisfactory in an age where the use of AI in investment management is burgeoning. We would urge an amendment of the section stating that where appropriate and compatibly with a trustee's duty of care under section 1 of the Trustee Act 2000, the delegation of such functions to an AIEM shall be permissible. It should also be added that this power prevails over the general rule that a trustee must take decisions personally.

F. Equitable Duties of Care

In equity as in law, liability for negligence is currently bedevilled in the case of AI by the lack of any concept of a negligent machine. We regard this as unsatisfactory. In our view, the suggested statutory liability of a controller of an AIEM, coupled with the provision for liability in the controller where the machine makes an error that, if committed by a human, would amount to negligence, should be stated to apply whatever the source of the duty of care.

G. Knowing Receipt

The essence of a claim for knowing receipt of property transferred in breach of trust or fiduciary duty is a complaint that the defendant has dealt with or disposed of assets in circumstances where information made available to them indicates that those assets are not theirs to deal with. The issue then arises: is information available to an AIEM of which the defendant is controller, but not in the mind of the defendant themselves, relevant here?

We take the view that this is a matter that should be cleared up legislatively, and that in this case such information ought to be attributed to the controller. Accordingly, we would advocate a statutory provision saying that, for the purpose of liability for knowing receipt, any knowledge gained by, or in the control of, an AIEM should be deemed to be the knowledge of its controller.

6

Intelligent Machines, AI and Unjust Enrichment

Unjust enrichment[1] is a wide and slightly amorphous area of law, dealing with a range of topics running from the rendering of benefits by mistake, duress or undue influence,[2] through recoveries for benefits supplied in the expectation of something that fails to materialise,[3] or under a contract or other arrangement which for some reason then goes off,[4] to the recovery of misclaimed tax[5] or ultra vires payments by public bodies.[6]

A great deal of the subject turns either on fairly recondite points of law,[7] or on what are essentially issues of accounting between the parties.[8] These raise few if any difficulties as regards the use of AI or the adjustment of liabilities between parties who use AIEMs to conduct their business, and we will largely pass them by. Furthermore the same thing can be said of some of the classic grounds for allowing restitutionary recovery, such as where A pays B for goods or services that are not forthcoming,[9] or where owing to fraud or a software glitch A's assets go to benefit B without any consent on the part of A.[10] Once again, these are issues decided at a fairly high level of abstraction. No particular issues are likely to arise in such cases from the intervention of an AIEM, and we see no reason to discuss them in detail.

However, there are a number of areas, especially those dealing with general principles running through the law of unjust enrichment, or with defences to

[1] On which, see generally C Mitchell et al, *Goff & Jones's Law of Unjust Enrichment*, 10th edn (London, Sweet & Maxwell, 2022), hereinafter referred to as *Goff & Jones*.

[2] ibid Chs 9–11.

[3] ibid Ch 13.

[4] ibid Chs 13–15.

[5] See eg *Woolwich Equitable Building Society v IRC* [1993] AC 70. Most such cases are now subsumed by statute but, as this case shows, this is not an absolute rule.

[6] *Goff & Jones*, Ch 22.

[7] For example, how far a person is barred from claiming restitution because they cannot offer counter-restitution, or because any prejudice they have suffered has been passed on to someone else; or whether a proprietary remedy is available: see ibid Chs 31, 32, 37–40.

[8] For instance, the issue of the amount of enrichment, embodying questions such as how far a benefit is conferred on someone by payment of a debt to a debtor who might not have insisted on payment, or how much a service rendered to a defendant goes to enrich them if they might not otherwise have been willing to pay the market price for it: see ibid Ch 4.

[9] ibid Ch 12.

[10] ibid Ch 8.

claims, where the use of AI may cause difficulties. These do on occasion suggest a need for either elucidation or change. In this short chapter we will deal with a number of these.

I. Grounds for Recovery

A. Mistake

Mistake of one kind or another often provides the basis of a right to recover in unjust enrichment. It features not only in obvious areas like money paid in error,[11] but also (for example) provision of other benefits by mistake,[12] a good deal of the law of subrogation[13] and for that matter things like the right to undo the effects of a declaration of trust or trust deed which is set aside because it has been found to have been made under a misapprehension.[14] Indeed, it is true to say that the subject of error plays a vastly larger part here than it does in the law of contract, where (except in the case of misrepresentation) the intervention of the rule *pacta sunt servanda* means that as a matter of English law the scope allowed to error as a vitiating factor is notoriously narrow.[15]

As regards human or corporate subjects, mistake traditionally is defined as an erroneous belief as to present or past fact or as to law, present to the mind of a party,[16] that causes that party to act in a particular way, such as transferring money or conferring some other benefit.[17] The reference to a belief present to a party's mind is important: although the law accepts that a belief may in certain cases be more or less implicit,[18] a mere failure to advert to an external fact that might otherwise change one's behaviour will not of itself do.[19]

This immediately raises two issues with persons operating through an AIEM, issues bearing some similarity to those arising in connection with contracts.[20] First, we need to ask whether the concept of mistake is inherently limited to a

[11] See notably *Kelly v Solari* (1841) 9 M & W 54 and *Barclays Bank Ltd v WJ Simms, Son & Cooke (Southern) Ltd* [1980] QB 677.

[12] See *Goff & Jones*, para 9-01 ff.

[13] See eg cases such as *Banque Financière de la Cité v Parc (Battersea) Ltd* [1999] 1 AC 221 and *Menelaou v Bank of Cyprus* [2015] UKSC 66, [2016] AC 176.

[14] See eg *Re Hastings-Bass* [1975] Ch 25 and *Pitt v Holt* [2013] UKSC 26, [2013] 2 AC 108.

[15] See generally *Chitty on Contracts*, 36th edn, Ch 9.

[16] Or, in the case of a corporation, to the mind of the person acting for it.

[17] *Chitty on Contracts*, 36th edn, para 9-01 ff.

[18] For example, a person who inadvertently pays a creditor twice is unlikely on the second occasion to have actively considered whether they had already paid, but this does not prevent recovery. See too *Re Griffiths* [2008] EWHC 118 (Ch), [2009] Ch 162 (transfer executed by person not knowing he was suffering from terminal illness).

[19] See Lord Walker in *Pitt v Holt* [2013] UKSC 26, [2013] 2 AC 108, [108]. Compare too Lord Mance in *Swynson Ltd v Lowick Rose LLP* [2017] UKSC 32, [2018] AC 313, [79]–[80].

[20] See ch 3 above.

human mistake on the part of the claimant or their agent, or whether there can be such a thing as a mistaken machine. One Singapore case, concerned with error in contract, suggests that the former is true, and that any misapprehension on the part of a machine is in law out of account.[21] On the other hand, there is also authority in England that deceit can be practised on a machine even if no human is duped, which logically entails that a machine can at least in some cases be seen to be subject to error in such a way as to affect the rights of its controller.[22]

This issue of principle remains highly uncertain. It is our view that it needs to be clarified by legislation rather than being left to be cleared up through an agglutination of perhaps inconsistent case law. The better position, we suggest, is that there is no reason in principle why, at least in some cases, a machine should not be regarded as having been mistaken and a remedy granted accordingly. We would, therefore, propose a provision that a claim that a party acted under a mistake, or for relief arising from a mistake, shall not be defeated merely because no human being was in fact in error.[23]

However, this in turn raises a second issue. Assuming that there is no bar as such to giving a remedy in respect of a non-human mistake, what counts as such a mistake? As we saw above, a human mistake generally requires a belief either present to a person's mind, or at the very least taking the form of a tacit assumption at the back of it. The mere fact that a human would not have rendered a benefit had a fact X, which they never contemplated at all in any way, been brought to their attention will not do. But how, if at all, does this apply to an AIEM? An AIEM, after all, cannot (as we point out elsewhere[24]) have a belief present to its mind in the same way that a human can; still less does it make much sense to talk of a machine making a tacit assumption. If this is right, then there must be a need to clarify what is meant by a mistake on the part of a machine.

Our view is that any legislation should provide for this. We suggest a provision that, for the purposes of the law relating to relief for mistake, mistake on the part of an AIEM should be deemed to be established when either of two criteria is satisfied. One is that the machine had present in memory, or had access to, data that were false to a material extent, and that had those false data not been present the machine would not have acted as it did. However, we also need to deal with situations typified by the case of tacit assumptions. What if, for example, the same debt is paid twice by an AIEM, say through a software malfunction? There should, in our view, be an alternative rule limited to restitution: namely, that where a restitutionary claim would normally be available in respect of a benefit rendered by inadvertence, the fact that there was no human intervention will not of itself defeat the claim.

[21] See *Quoine Pte Ltd v B2C2 Ltd* [2020] SGCA(I) 2, [2020] 2 SLR 20.

[22] *Renault UK Ltd v Fleetpro Technical Services Ltd* [2007] EWHC 2541 (QB), [2008] Bus LR D 17 (liability for the tort of deceit); and *cf* also *IG Index plc v Colley* [2013] EWHC 478 (QB).

[23] Compare our conclusions at p 43 ff.

[24] See p 44.

B. Undue Influence

For the purpose of the law of unjust enrichment, it is suggested that mistake is best viewed as merely one particular instance of a wider genus of justifications for recovery, namely lack of consent (or impaired consent) to a benefit being obtained by a defendant at the claimant's expense. Undue influence is another instance of the same idea, as is duress (dealt with in the next section).

In summary, the central instance of undue influence as a ground for restitution is influence or pressure exerted by one person, A, over another person, B, who is particularly susceptible to influence by A. Such influence normally, but not invariably, arises either because B is in a position of familial or social subordination to A, or because it is clear that B relies on A to look after their interests.[25] Importantly, the question whether such a situation of ascendancy exists in respect of A is answered largely objectively: there is no need for any proof of actual wrongdoing,[26] still less of knowing misfeasance.

Undue influence must normally be proved positively in order to obtain redress, but it may be regarded as proved in the case of certain relationships, such as trustee and beneficiary, or lawyer and client, in the absence of some independent explanation for the conferring of the benefit.[27] When such influence is so established, any benefit received by A from B is prima facie recoverable by B unless it is shown that B gave clear and informed consent to A obtaining it, and hence that it did not in fact stem from the influence concerned.[28]

As with duress (dealt with below), in most cases it seems to us that relief for undue influence is unlikely in practice to give rise to problems with AIEMs. The relationships that give rise to undue influence are overwhelmingly personal rather than commercial or corporate,[29] and the fact that machines may be involved peripherally, for example in advising on decisions, is unlikely to make much difference. Furthermore, since the emphasis in undue influence cases is on preserving the freedom of action of the victim rather than on

[25] See *Snell's Equity*, para 8-009 ff; *Goff & Jones*, Ch 11.

[26] See eg *Hammond v Osborn* [2002] EWCA Civ 885, [2002] WTLR 1125 (no defence that conduct unimpeachable); also, the older *Allcard v Skinner* (1887) 36 Ch D 145, 171.

[27] *Royal Bank of Scotland plc v Etridge (No 2)* [2001] UKHL 44, [2002] 2 AC 773, [8] (per Lord Nicholls); *Snell's Equity*, paras 8-014, 8-018 ff.

[28] See *Snell's Equity*, para 8-031; and eg *Nature Resorts Ltd v First Citizens Bank Ltd* [2022] UKPC 10, [2022] 1 WLR 2788, [13]. Independent advice is one way to show this, but the issue is fundamentally one of consent, not information as such: see *Goldsworthy v Brickell* [1987] Ch 378, 401 (per Nourse LJ) and *Royal Bank of Scotland plc v Etridge (No 2)* [2001] UKHL 44, [2002] 2 AC 773, [111] (per Lord Hobhouse).

[29] Can a company be unduly influenced? It seems unlikely in most cases, but cannot be ruled out: for example, where the person in control of a family company is unduly pressured to use the latter's assets in some way. Compare the duress case of *Mutual Finance Ltd v John Wetton & Sons Ltd* [1937] 2 KB 389, discussed below.

establishing wrongdoing by the influencer, the fact that the latter may have made use of an AIEM and not be guilty of personal fault is in most cases likely to be beside the point.[30]

There is one clarification, however, that may be required. If an issue arises over whether a person in the position of B above has given informed consent, what happens where that person utilises an AIEM in connection with the transaction? What is the status of information provided or made available to that AIEM? Our view is that under the present law information provided in such circumstances falls to be disregarded, and that the information necessary to show informed consent must reach (or at least be available to) B themselves. This seems to us implicit in the idea that what matters in undue influence cases is genuine consent, rather than the mere provision of information.[31] Nevertheless, the matter is not absolutely clear. In the interests of certainty it is our view that it ought to be confirmed by statute, with a provision that, for the purposes of the law of undue influence, any knowledge made available to an AIEM controlled by B is not, without more,[32] to be attributed to B.

There is one other area where the effect of AIEMs may need to be discussed in respect of undue influence, and that is where the case involves the interests of third parties obtained for value[33] and without notice.[34] However, this is largely concerned with the nature of notice in equity generally, and more specifically in practice with the validity of mortgages and securities granted to third parties.[35] For this reason, we take the view that this subject is best dealt with elsewhere.[36]

C. Duress

Duress consists, in essence, of a menace of violence,[37] or of a tort or breach of contract, that would affect the mind of a reasonable person, or alternatively the threat of a technically lawful act which nevertheless amounts to an unconscionable

[30] Imagine, for example, a bank or financial institution in a position unduly to influence a property owner, as in cases such as *Lloyd's Bank Ltd v Bundy* [1975] QB 326. The fact that any advice or pressure may have been computer-generated rather than human will be beside the point.

[31] See *Goldsworthy v Brickell* [1987] Ch 378, 401 and *Royal Bank of Scotland plc v Etridge (No 2)* [2001] UKHL 44, [2002] 2 AC 773, [111], referred to above.

[32] There could be more. For example, if B were offered advice and asked for it to be transmitted to an AIEM under their control, then it seems clear B would be estopped from denying that they had received it.

[33] A third party who has not given value being in no better position than the exerciser of the influence: *Huguenin v Baseley* (1807) 14 Ves 273, 289 (Lord Eldon).

[34] Imagine, for example, that A obtains a gift of assets by the exercise of undue influence over B, and then sells those assets to C, it being alleged that C had notice of the circumstances.

[35] As in cases such as *Royal Bank of Scotland plc v Etridge (No 2)* [2001] UKHL 44, [2002] 2 AC 773 and *Waller-Edwards v One Savings Bank plc* [2025] UKSC 22, [2025] 2 WLR 1263.

[36] See Chapter 6, p 81 ff.

[37] See eg *Barton v Armstrong* [1976] AC 104.

means of achieving a transaction that is to one's benefit.[38] Although it also arises in connection with the law of contract,[39] it is an established 'unjust factor' in the law of restitution, in that any transfer shown to result from it, even a non-contractual one, is prima facie reversible.[40]

In the case of unlawful act duress involving threats of violence or other wrongful acts, it is suggested that the intervention of an AIEM on either side is unlikely to make a large difference. Threats of violence can in any case be discounted: an AIEM is in the nature of things unlikely to make them or succumb to them. As regards other wrongful acts, the definition of duress is here essentially objective, and not dependent on a showing of either fault or a particular state of mind in the person alleged to have exercised it. Furthermore, while previously the main stress seems to have been laid on the question whether the will of the duress victim had been overborne,[41] which might have been problematic in the case of a machine without a will to be subverted, the emphasis today tends to be on the simpler issue of whether the duress was a form of unacceptable pressure[42] – which a threat of violence or a legal wrong nearly always is – and whether its exertion caused the transaction in question.[43] Such acts – for example, a demand made by an AIEM for payment for release of property to which the other party is in fact entitled free of charge[44] – remain equally wrongful whether human or machine-mediated, and the same thing goes for the illegitimacy of using such means as a way of extorting advantage. The result of a duress claim in situations like this is therefore likely to be the same in both cases. We regard this position as entirely satisfactory, and suggest there is no reason to recommend any change.

Lawful act duress is a little more difficult. It is implicit in the leading decision in *Times Travel (UK) Ltd v Pakistan International Airlines Corpn*[45] that for lawful act duress to form a basis for recovery the theory is that there is a need for proof of some conduct in the defendant that can be classed as in some way

[38] *Times Travel (UK) Ltd v Pakistan International Airlines Corpn* [2021] UKSC 40, [2023] AC 101, [78]–[80] (Lord Burrows, with whom the other members of the Court agreed on this issue). See too *Borrelli v Ting* [2010] UKPC 21, [2010] Bus LR 1718, [34], referring to 'illegitimate means' of pressure.

[39] See p 49.

[40] Generally, *Goff & Jones*, Ch 10; A Burrows, *Law of Restitution*, 3rd edn (Oxford, Oxford University Press, 2011) Ch 5.

[41] See eg Kerr J in *The Siboen and The Sibotre* [1976] 1 Lloyd's Rep 293, 336 ('coercion of will so as to vitiate consent'); also *Pao On v Lau Yiu Long* [1980] AC 614, 635–36 (per Lord Scarman).

[42] 'The rationale [of duress] is that his apparent consent was induced by pressure exercised upon him by that other party which the law does not regard as legitimate': Lord Diplock in *The Universe Sentinel* [1983] 1 AC 366, 384: see too Lord Goff in *Dimskal Shipping Co SA v International Transport Workers Federation* [1992] 2 AC 152, 165–66.

[43] And rightly so. The moral issue here is essentially the illegitimacy of manipulating a person into consenting by threatening a wrong, and the idea that manipulation of that kind should yield no advantage. This point is nicely made in *Goff & Jones*, para 10-03.

[44] As in cases such as *The Alev* [1989] 1 Lloyd's Rep 138.

[45] [2021] UKSC 40, [2023] AC 101.

reprehensible or unconscionable.[46] This may consist, for example, in the exercise of a right for a clearly illegitimate purpose,[47] or in deliberately leading another party into a position of weakness so as to make them vulnerable to a later demand.[48] While it may on occasion be possible for an act to be unconscionable for these purposes independently of the defendant's motive in doing it,[49] in most cases of this kind there seems to be a need for at least a degree of intent to act unfairly in order to manipulate the other party before relief can be granted. If so, it follows that outside a few specialist areas, lawful act duress may be hard in practice under the present law to show in the case of the acts of an AIEM, since (as we have argued elsewhere) intent of any kind is likely to be difficult to prove in a machine. The result is, at least in theory, a possible mismatch between the position of those who carry out activities in person and those who do so through an AIEM.

Is this justifiable? In a very strict sense, no: as far as possible we accept that the law should be technology neutral. On the other hand, two pragmatic arguments stand out in favour of leaving the status quo untouched. One is that, given the exceptionality of lawful act duress and the extreme rarity of cases where it has been successfully argued, any anomaly is likely to be of little practical significance. The other is that there is more of an air of personal immorality about lawful act than unlawful act duress. If so, then there is much to be said for limiting the inquiry to the acts of persons and disregarding the fortuitous fact of the intervention in a few cases of an AIEM.

In our view, in short, the law is perfectly capable of handling issues of duress as it is, and no changes are required. It may, of course, be that something needs to be done in respect of peripheral questions, notably whether a transaction affected by duress has been affirmed with knowledge so as to bar any right to undo it, but that is a different matter.

D. Failure of Basis

Restitutionary relief based on failure of basis deals with cases where, even in the absence of an unjust factor relating to flawed intent such as mistake or duress, benefits are conferred on the basis that an event will happen which never does, or on the assumption of the existence of a state of affairs which does not materialise or

[46] See [2021] UKSC 40, [2023] AC 101, [3]–[30]; also *Law Debenture Trust Corpn plc v Ukraine* [2023] UKSC 11, [2024] AC 411, [141]–[142].

[47] As on the facts in *Borrelli v Ting* [2010] UKPC 21, [2010] Bus LR 1718.

[48] As in *Progress Bulk Carriers Ltd v Tube City IMS LLC* [2012] EWHC 273 (Comm), [2012] 1 Lloyd's Rep 501.

[49] A possible example being money obtained through a threat to prosecute, as in cases like *Mutual Finance Ltd v John Wetton & Sons Ltd* [1937] 2 KB 389, as interpreted in *Times Travel*, above. In these cases the unconscionability of the demand seems to consist in the idea that it is per se unacceptable to use such a threat as a means to obtain money. It would seem that no distinction falls to be drawn here between threats emanating from a human and a machine.

which later ceases to obtain.[50] Examples include performance rendered or payment made under a contract that is, or becomes, ineffective;[51] services rendered under an arrangement that transpires to be legally ineffective;[52] performance rendered in the expectation of a counter-performance, whether contractual[53] or otherwise,[54] that never materialises; and many others.

The essence of this head of recovery is thus express or implicit conditionality: in other words, an agreement or common intent[55] that the claimant is conferring a benefit conditionally, such that if the condition is not satisfied the benefit or its value should be returned. This in turn raises potential issues where either party (or both) were making use of AI in contracting or determining whether to contract. Can the established instances of recovery for failure of basis be smoothly carried over to such a situation?

In most cases, it is our view that the answer is yes. Express agreement that a benefit is conditional is straightforward. As we point out in Chapter 3 on contract, since agreement in English law is largely viewed as an objective phenomenon rather than a subjective meeting of minds there is thus not even a theoretical obstacle to the enforcement of express contracts entered into by machine. If so, exactly the same argument applies to other express agreements making a benefit conditional on some state of affairs existing or coming into effect. And so too in slightly more complicated cases turning on issues of interpretation. The general rule – under which such interpretation of an arrangement turns on how it would have been viewed by reasonable people in the position of the parties[56] – causes few problems in contract,[57] and we see no reason why it should cause any more in unjust enrichment.

What of implied agreement? We suggest that much the same applies, though for slightly different reasons: namely, that in practice the issue of such agreement

[50] See *Goff & Jones*, para 12-01, referring to a 'joint understanding' relating to the state of affairs concerned.

[51] A straightforward example being the numerous cases concerned with financial swaps entered into by banks with public authorities that turned out to be ultra vires the latter, typified by *Westdeutsche Landesbank Girozentrale v Islington London Borough Council* [1996] AC 669 and more recently *Banca Intesa Sanpaolo SpA v Comune di Venezia* [2023] EWCA Civ 1482, [2024] 2 All ER (Comm) 23.

[52] eg *Barnes v Eastenders Cash & Carry plc* [2014] UKSC 26, [2015] AC 1 (void appointment of receiver by Crown meant no claim against company's assets as originally contemplated: restitutionary claim for services allowed against Crown).

[53] As where payment is made in advance for goods in the event never delivered or services never performed.

[54] eg *Chillingworth v Esche* [1924] 1 Ch 97 (pre-contract deposit relating to real estate sale; no contract ever signed) and *P v P* [1916] 2 IR 400 (premature wedding present recoverable when wedding later called off).

[55] The agreement or intent must be mutual: see *Burgess v Rawnsley* [1975] Ch 429, esp 442, 445, and also *Dargamo Holdings Ltd v Avonwick Holdings Ltd* [2021] EWCA Civ 1149, [2022] 1 All ER (Comm) 1244, [79], referring to a 'joint understanding' (per Carr LJ).

[56] A neat recent example, where restitution was refused, being *Barton v Morris* [2023] UKSC 3, [2023] AC 684.

[57] See the discussions carried out in Chapter 3.

is normally a pretty objective inquiry. As *Goff & Jones* remarks,[58] in clear cases, such as where a person pays for goods and does not receive them (or a good title to them), or where benefits are rendered on the basis of a proposed agreement that never takes effect, it is taken as obvious that the payment is in its nature conditional unless there is some clear indication to the contrary; there is no serious look at the parties' actual intentions, whether implicit or otherwise. A similar analysis might well apply elsewhere, for instance to benefits rendered under contracts that later turn out to be *ultra vires*, as in the 'swaps' cases; once again, it makes good sense to provide for a prima facie right to unravel the transaction on both sides.

Where this approach is adopted, it should make no difference that AI in some form may have featured on one or both sides involved in the negotiation and performance of the transaction. Difficulties may, however, arise in one case: namely, where interpretation is in issue and, but for the presence of an AIEM in the equation, turn on specific knowledge available to the parties to the transaction as part of the factual matrix. Here, are we limited to the knowledge and understandings of the humans behind the machines, or can we take account of the workings of the latter? At present, it is our view that the former is true. As we pointed out in our analysis of the interpretation of contracts,[59] however smart AIEMs may be, they can hardly understand a transaction in a particular sense or intend to agree a particular interpretation: if so, any knowledge they may have is not of great relevance. Nor is there any principled argument for imputing knowledge to the controller of an AIEM on the basis merely of the presence of information in the latter's storage. If so, then we are, as in the case of contract interpretation, thrown back on construing the intent of the humans behind the machine in the light of the knowledge available to them specifically.

Is this acceptable? We take the view that, overall, it is. Seeking to attribute any kind of intention or belief to an AIEM, even if allowed, would we think raise insuperable difficulties in practice. Furthermore, we see no reason in this context automatically to attribute knowledge of data on AIEM to the person controlling it: if so, there seems nothing wrong in continuing to look to whether that knowledge was reasonably available to the controller.

II. Defences

Most of the available defences to a claim in unjust enrichment[60] are fairly doctrinal in nature: for example, ministerial receipt, the impossibility of the claimant making necessary counter-restitution, or the passing-on of some charge to a third

[58] *Goff & Jones*, para 13-07.
[59] See p 40.
[60] On which, see generally *Goff & Jones*, Chs 27–35.

party such that the claimant is no longer out of pocket. All raise complex issues. But none, in our view, is particularly relevant to the issues raised by AI, since none of them depends in particular on knowledge, good faith, intent or any of the other phenomena that are difficult to apply to inanimate machines. We say no more about them here. Two defences are, however, more problematical: bona fide purchase, and change of position. To these we now turn.

A. Bona Fide Purchase

In a number of restitutionary situations a defendant who has purchased assets or services in good faith has a defence to a claim in unjust enrichment that might otherwise arise in respect of them. An obvious example concerns proprietary restitution, as where executors pay assets to the wrong person or otherwise exceed their authority,[61] or where A's asset is misapplied by B and its proceeds transferred by B to C.[62] In such cases the good title traditionally obtained, at least as regards equitable claims, by a good faith purchaser must logically also bar other claims relating to their receipt of that property.[63] But the principle also applies to at least some personal claims for restitution,[64] such as where A is sued as a recipient of the proceeds of money abstracted by B from C,[65] and claims for mistaken payment where the monies paid have gone to discharge an obligation owed to the defendant.[66]

It is not entirely clear whether actual notice of the claimant's rights is needed to defeat a good faith purchase defence, or whether at least some forms of constructive notice will do.[67] But in at least one case it seems to have been assumed that the latter is true.[68] If this is right, then the defence will fail not only if the relevant facts are specifically brought to a defendant's attention in circumstances where a

[61] See the facts of eg *Baker Ltd v Medway Building & Supplies Ltd* [1958] 3 All ER 540, 543; *Re Leslie Engineers Co Ltd* [1976] 1 WLR 292, 299.

[62] *Foskett v McKeown* [2001] 1 AC 102, 130 (per Lord Millett); *Vale SA v Steinmetz* [2021] EWCA Civ 1087, [2021] 2 CLC 508, [2] (per Males LJ).

[63] *Goff & Jones*, para 29-01. This is a fairly general principle: *cf Byers v Saudi National Bank* [2023] UKSC 51, [2024] AC 1191.

[64] See *Goff & Jones*, para 29-12 ff.

[65] See generally *Lipkin Gorman v Karpnale Ltd* [1991] 2 AC 548 (though the defence failed there for other reasons); also *Barclays Bank Ltd v WJ Simms, Son & Cooke (Southern) Ltd* [1980] QB 677, 695 (per Robert Goff J).

[66] eg *Aiken v Short* (1856) 1 Hurl & N 210, 214–15; also *Barclays Bank Ltd v WJ Simms, Son & Cooke (Southern) Ltd* [1980] QB 677 and *Lloyds Bank plc v Independent Insurance Co Ltd* [2000] QB 110.

[67] In the analogous defence of good faith change of position, while it is clear that a mere negligent failure to inquire will not defeat this plea, it has been said that dishonesty is not required: see below, p 111.

[68] In *Lipkin Gorman v Karpnale Ltd* [1991] 2 AC 548, 564–65 Lord Templeman drew an analogy between a restitutionary personal claim and a claim against a third party for assets transferred as a result of undue influence. Since in the latter case it is clear that constructive notice will do, presumably his Lordship meant to apply a similar rule to the former.

reasonable person would take notice of them,[69] or if they are wilfully blind to the existence of facts which they choose not to investigate,[70] but also in other cases. It will also be barred if they know facts that a reasonably prudent person in their position,[71] if necessary with the aid of skilled advice, would have discovered had they made appropriate enquiries.[72]

This immediately raises an issue which also arises in the context of equitable rights in assets (and is dealt with in that connection in Chapter 5). How far should the fact that a purchase took place through the intermediacy of an AIEM, which may have had data available to it but not necessarily to its controller, affect the defence?

Under the present law, the answer is that it probably does not.[73] As we point out elsewhere,[74] the idea of actual or constructive notice assumes human consciousness and human standards of behaviour. In law, an AIEM cannot have knowledge in the same sense that a human can; nor can it be at fault, since there is no such thing as a negligent machine. Equally it cannot be regarded as an agent, such that information stored on it is attributed to its controller. It follows that even where an AIEM is involved, the inquiry will still be into the state of mind of the humans involved.

Is this satisfactory? Not entirely, in our view. We see a strong case for legislation to modify the present situation for AIEMs in two ways, with the aim of equalising the position of those who do and do not act through them. It will be noticed that these largely parallel our suggestions in the case of notice in equity. First it should be provided that if data is in the storage of the AIEM, then in so far as the controller has the AIEM's acts attributed to them, knowledge of that data is equally attributed to them. Secondly, where data is stored on such machines from which a reasonable person in the position of its controller,[75] had they had it to mind, would have inferred a relevant fact, then the controller should be treated as having constructive notice of it. If either of these applied, then the defendant should lose the benefit of the bona fide purchase defence.

[69] Hence excluding vague third-party rumours and the like: *cf Barnhart v Greenshields* (1853) 9 Moo PC 18, as explained in *Reeves v Pope* [1914] 2 KB 284.

[70] *Baden v Société Générale pour Favoriser le Développement du Commerce et de l'Industrie en France SA* [1993] 1 WLR 509, 575–76.

[71] This is an important qualification, since it means that what amounts to constructive notice can depend on the status of the defendant, more being expected of a large bank than a small trader: see eg *Sinclair Investments (UK) Ltd v Versailles Trade Finance Ltd* [2011] EWCA Civ 347, [2012] Ch 453, [109] (per Lord Neuberger).

[72] eg *Berwick & Co v Price* [1905] 1 Ch 632, 638–39 (per Joyce J).

[73] If A requests or permits B to give information to a machine controlled by A, for example by asking for it to be uploaded onto A's website, then it is true that A will be regarded as in possession of it: but this is essentially on the basis that A will be estopped from denying that they have the knowledge themselves.

[74] See p 81.

[75] This is important: the sophistication of the controller should be in account to preserve a degree of parallel between the liabilities of those who do, and do not, use an AIEM. See *Sinclair Investments (UK) Ltd v Versailles Trade Finance Ltd* [2011] EWCA Civ 347, [2012] Ch 453 above.

B. Change of Position

Change of position can look similar to good faith purchase as a defence, but is actually rather different in conception, being only a defence pro tanto and also rather more restricted in its availability. The rule is essentially this: a person otherwise subject to a restitutionary liability who has irretrievably changed their position in good faith before learning of the facts relevant to the claim against them[76] has a partial defence up to the amount of the detriment they would suffer if forced to make restitution in full.[77] The simplest example is that of a person who has been mistakenly paid £1,000 and then, because they do not know of their potential liability to repay, spends £750 treating friends to an expensive meal out.[78] In principle they have a defence up to £750. But the defence is much wider and applies to most restitutionary claims.

The change of position must be genuine and irrevocable.[79] If money in respect of which there is a restitutionary claim goes to buy an asset which the defendant still has, for example, there may be a defence as regards any depreciation, but the recipient must still refund the asset's residual value.[80] Equally, a readily reversible change of position will not do, since it lies within the control of the defendant to reduce or eliminate any potential prejudice.[81]

Importantly, moreover, the change of position has also to have been in good faith. Moreover, this seems this has a fairly specialised, and demanding, meaning in this connection. Obviously, a defendant who pays knowing they are disentitled is excluded from pleading it.[82] But there is authority that this limitation goes further. Even if simple negligence will not bar the defence,[83] in at least some cases

[76] Including a change of position in anticipation of the enrichment: *Banca Intesa Sanpaolo SpA v Comune di Venezia* [2022] EWHC 2586 (Comm), [2023] Bus LR 384 (reversed on other grounds, [2023] EWCA Civ 1482, [2024] 2 All ER (Comm) 23).

[77] A point finally established in *Lipkin Gorman (A Firm) v Karpnale Ltd* [1991] 2 AC 548, where for reasons not relevant here the defendant was not a good faith purchaser, but nevertheless was allowed to rely on change of position.

[78] It must be shown that the expenditure would not otherwise have been incurred and that it did not form part of the defendant's usual expenditure: eg *Lipkin Gorman (A Firm) v Karpnale Ltd* [1991] 2 AC 548, 580 (Lord Goff); *Dextra Bank & Trust Co Ltd v Bank of Jamaica* [2001] UKPC 50, [2002] 1 All ER (Comm) 193, [38].

[79] For example, paying an existing debt, which would have had to be paid anyway, is generally seen as pecuniarily-neutral: *Scottish Equitable plc v Derby* [2001] 3 All ER 818, [35], and also *Credit Suisse (Monaco) SA v Attar* [2004] EWHC 374 (Comm), [98]. So too, at least in general, with paying off a mortgage, for the same reason: *Scottish Equitable plc v Derby*, above, and *Boscawen v Bajwa* [1996] 1 WLR 328, esp 340–41.

[80] *cf Credit Suisse (Monaco) SA v Attar* [2004] EWHC 374 (Comm), [98] (no defence based on purchase of securirties which had actually increased in value).

[81] eg *Hillsdown v Pensions Ombudsman* [1997] 1 All ER 862, 904 (tax paid on money received could be clawed back from the Inland Revenue).

[82] *Niru Battery Manufacturing Co v Milestone Trading Ltd* [2002] EWHC 1425 (Comm), [2002] 2 All ER (Comm) 705, [135] (Moore-Bick J); see too *Cressman v Coys of Kensington (Sales) Ltd* [2004] EWCA Civ 47, [2004] 1 WLR 2774, esp [21] and [41].

[83] *Niru Battery Manufacturing Co v Milestone Trading Ltd* [2002] EWHC 1425 (Comm), [2002] 2 All ER (Comm) 705, [125] (per Moore-Bick J).

imputed knowledge may be sufficient to negative good faith,[84] as will failure to act in a 'commercially acceptable way'.[85]

How is all this affected if an AIEM is interposed? As regards the mechanics of the defence – whether the change of position is truly the result of the enrichment, and the extent of any such change of position – the actions of AI used by the parties may peripherally be relevant, but the principles remain the same. The one difficulty arises in connection with the requirement of good faith. As a result of cases such as *Niru Battery Manufacturing Co v Milestone Trading Ltd*[86] and *Lipkin Gorman (A Firm) v Karpnale Ltd*[87] this question reduces to one of whether, in the light of the defendant's behaviour, it is equitable to make them provide restitution. In other words, in essence it is a test dependent on a specialised form of personal merit or deservingness.[88]

If this is right, then presumably it follows that under the existing law the question whether the benefit of the defence is lost has to be answered by reference to the behaviour of the people behind the machines; the behaviour of, or knowledge available to, the AIEMs is out of account, except in so far as it is available to, and ought to have been sought out by, the actual parties concerned. In short, the interposition of an AIEM makes little, if any, difference. Furthermore, in our view this position is right. In so far as issues of personal merit or deservingness are involved, there is no reason to change matters so as to take account of the actions of machines through which one or other party may have acted.

III. Conclusions

The law of unjust enrichment is grounded in the principle that a person should not be allowed to profit at another's expense without a legal justification. Traditionally, this area of law has relied on human interactions, contracts, and clear notions of benefit and detriment. The increasing use of artificial intelligence, however, raises novel challenges that test the conventional boundaries of unjust enrichment. We are of the opinion that certain statutory clarifications would be required in this field as summarised below.

[84] *Jones v Churcher* [2009] EWHC 722 (QB), [89]; also *Papamichael v National Westminster Bank plc* [2003] 1 Lloyd's Rep 34, [209]. See generally *Goff & Jones*, para 27-47 ff.

[85] *Niru Battery Manufacturing Co v Milestone Trading Ltd* [2002] EWHC 1425 (Comm), [2002] 2 All ER (Comm) 705, [135] (per Moore-Bick J), approved on appeal at [2003] EWCA Civ 1446, [2004] QB 985, [164] (per Clarke LJ). See too *Jones v Churcher* [2009] EWHC 722 (QB), [46].

[86] [2003] EWCA Civ 1446, [2004] QB 985.

[87] [1991] 2 AC 548.

[88] So much so that where a corporate entity is concerned it is the behaviour and knowledge of its senior management, and not its employees, that is in issue as regards whether it can rely on a change of position: see eg *Madoff Securities International Ltd v Raven* [2013] EWHC 3147 (Comm), [2014] Lloyd's Rep FC 95, [283].

A. Mistake, Unjust Enrichment and AIEMs

An issue may arise where an AIEM renders some benefit to a defendant (normally, but by no means exclusively, a payment of money) as a result of incorrect information in memory or made available to it. If the error did not affect the controller of the AIEM, can the 'mistake' on the part of an inanimate machine be in account?

In the context of unjust enrichment, we see no reason why not. To make the matter clear, we would urge a statutory provision stating that a claim that a party acted under a mistake, or for relief arising from a mistake, shall not be defeated merely because no human being was in fact in error.

We would also advocate that, for the purposes of the law relating to relief for mistake, mistake on the part of an AIEM should be deemed to be established when either of two criteria is satisfied. One is that: (a) the machine had present in memory, or had access to, data that were false to a material extent; and (b) had those false data not been so present or available, the machine would not have acted as it did. The other is that where a restitutionary claim would normally be available in respect of a benefit rendered by a human as a result of inadvertence, the fact that there was no human intervention will not of itself defeat the claim.

B. Undue Influence

We urge that, for the purposes of establishing a defence of informed consent under the law of undue influence, it should be provided that the knowledge of an AIEM controlled by B is not, without more, to be attributed to B.

C. The Defence of Bona Fide Purchase

Where a defence of bona fide purchase is raised to an unjust enrichment claim, it is presently not clear how far, if at all, account can be taken of information contained on, or available to, an AIEM under the control of the defendant for the purpose of defeating that defence.

We take the view that the better position here is that such information should, whether or not brought to the actual attention of the controller, be attributed to them. Statute should therefore provide two things. First, for the purposes of any defence of bona fide purchase, if data is in the storage of an AIEM, then in so far as the controller has the AIEM's acts attributed to them, knowledge of that data is equally attributed to them. Secondly, for the same purposes, where data is stored on such machines from which a reasonable person in the position of its controller, had they had it to mind, would have inferred a relevant fact, then the controller should be treated as having constructive notice of it.

7

Intelligent Machines and AI – Acting Through Others

I. Introduction

A large part of the commercial and professional law of obligations is concerned with the rights and liabilities of parties acting through others. In particular this involves the law of agency, the rules of vicarious liability and the ascription of actions to companies. The idea of liability through others is clearly vital when it comes to the use of AI. How far, if at all, can the ideas of agency or vicarious liability be extended so as to operate where one or other party is, or acts through, AI? When will the person who chooses to act through an AIEM or other machine be liable for the acts of the latter, and is the law satisfactory in this respect? These important inquiries form the subject of this chapter.

II. Agency Law

A. AI as Principal and/or Agent

i. Machines and AI as Principals

There is no doubt that a natural or juridical person can do a legal act through the intermediacy of a machine, whether intelligent or otherwise. A sale through a vending machine is a sale by the person that set it up. Again, a company X Ltd may automate its payment systems by setting up a computerised system which then from time to time instructs its bank to make payments to third parties. If so, the payments will be regarded as having been initiated by X personally, before being made by the bank acting as X's agent.[1]

But although a principal may act *through* a machine, it is equally obvious that it cannot actually *be* one. Under the present law there can be no question of a

[1] Whether a payment is not only made, but made by a particular person, may be important. Under the rule in *Owen v Tate* [1976] QB 402, for example, a debt is discharged if paid by or with the authority of the debtor, but not if paid without the debtor's agreement by a third party.

machine entering as principal in a legal relationship such as to create rights and duties in itself,[2] whether directly or indirectly. Since agency law is essentially a means of allowing a third party's act to ascribe legal rights and liabilities to, or alter the legal position of, another person, it follows that the latter must have the capacity to have rights and duties. But as long as AI and AI-equipped machines have no legal personality in their own right and hence no legal rights and duties to change or affect,[3] it follows that they cannot be principals.

ii. Machines and AI as Agents

Just as a principal may act through a machine, so may an agent. In the example in the previous paragraph, if (as is overwhelmingly likely) payment by the bank is made electronically through a computer system, then to that extent the bank will have acted as X's agent through the intermediacy of its own systems. So much is straightforward. But this leaves a much bigger issue: can a machine itself actually *be* an agent?

This is a trickier question. At first sight, it might seem that the answer was obviously 'Yes'. After all, even if as a matter of the civil law a machine cannot act legally through a person, there is no doubt that a person can act through a machine. And is there really that much difference between a person making a sale through a human employee, who clearly does act as an agent, and someone making exactly the same sale through (say) a chatbot, or an AI-enabled website?

If we look at the creation of liabilities in contract and tort, this parallel seems to be confirmed. A vending machine creates a contractual nexus between its owner and a user when the latter inserts coins or swipes a credit card to buy something,[4] in much the same way as a human employee in a shop creates a liability in the shop owner by taking payment. Exactly the same reasoning applies to a customer-facing interface or AI-equipped computer owned by a business, for example an airport terminal made available for the purchase of parametric insurance by would-be travellers.[5] The owner or controller of the machine here is essentially using it as a tool to do something they could have done themselves; its acts will be theirs, and a contract of insurance will be concluded. So too, for that matter, where both parties contract through machines and there is no immediate human input at all, for example where two parties set up their own

[2] It may of course act as the automatic mouthpiece of a corporation, though then it would not be acting as principal, but rather as a tool of communication.

[3] The Law Commission's recent discussion paper, published on 31 July 2025, *Artificial Intelligence and the Law*, considers the prospect of ascribing legal personality for AI but concedes that this might seem disconcertingly futuristic: see pp 21-23.

[4] This is clear from cases like *Thornton v Shoe Lane Parking Ltd* [1971] 2 QB 163.

[5] Typically something like flight delay insurance purchased from an airport terminal, the point of such insurance being that it is cheap to operate precisely because the processes of underwriting and payment can be almost entirely automated.

AIEMs to engage in an automated purchase of goods or exchange of currency (or cryptocurrency).[6]

Nor is this limited to contract. A computer programmed by A to make an automated phone call to B, C, D, etc to advertise a product sold by A will potentially engage A's liability in tort in respect of the contents of the call, in the same way as a human agent of A would. And a smart drone programmed by A to swoop low over B's land will render A liable in tort for trespass in the same way as if A had directed a model aircraft, or an employee in a microlight machine, over the same terrain.

Conversely, a machine can just as easily create rights in the party in control of it. An AI-equipped vending machine creates not only duties but rights in its owner, if only to claim the price of the goods;[7] and it has already been decided that where a company which uses dynamic pricing requires customers to fill in an electronic questionnaire to determine their circumstances, it can sue for deceit if a customer fills in false information with a view to duping the price-setting algorithm.[8]

So also, with matters of performance. Unless a term expressly or impliedly requires personal performance, A can perform a contractual obligation to B, for example to deliver goods or clean a house, by robot as much as in person.[9] And conversely with the receipt of benefits. If A on B's orders pays coins or notes into a machine, transfers bitcoin into B's wallet, or returns a library book to B by putting it on a conveyor belt in an outside wall and typing in a code, A is regarded as having paid B or returned the book. The fact that B never benefits because the money or the book is immediately stolen, or the Bitcoin wallet hacked by a fraudster, is beside the point.

This certainly looks very like agency.[10] An agent, after all, need not have the legal capacity to act or contract. A minor can be an agent;[11] and if a little child with limited understanding, why not an AIEM with similar surrogate

[6] So held in Singapore: *B2C2 Ltd v Quoine Pte Ltd* [2019] 4 SLR 17 esp [126]–[132] (automated trading on both sides in cryptocurrencies). It follows that we cannot accept the suggestion in L Scholz, 'Algorithmic Contracts' (2017) 20 *Stanford Technology Law Review* 128, 151–57 that contracts concluded through a 'black box' algorithm are probably not enforceable under ordinary contract doctrine.

[7] Which could be important, for instance, if relatively high-value items were bought with a stolen credit card or forged bills. The buyer, if caught, would remain liable in contract for the price.

[8] *Renault UK Ltd v Fleetpro Technical Services* [2007] EWHC 2541 (QB), [2008] Bus LR D17, esp [122]. A fairly similar case is *IG Index plc v Colley* [2013] EWHC 478 (QB) (entry of false information into systems of spread betting company).

[9] For instance, from early 2019 Amazon began using a smart pavement-trundling robot called the Scout to deliver goods to customers in Washington State. Clearly the goods would be regarded as being delivered by Amazon in such a case.

[10] eg S Chopra and L White, 'Artificial Agents and the Contracting Problem: A Solution via an Agency Analysis' (2009) *University of Illinois Journal of Law Technology & Policy* 363. See too S Chesterman, 'Artificial Intelligence and the Limits of Legal Personality' (2020) 69 *International & Comparative Law Quarterly* 819, 826, seemingly accepting at least to some extent an agency analysis.

[11] See the decisions in *Smally v Smally* (1700) 1 Eq Ca Abr 6; *Watkins v Vince* (1818) 2 Starke 368; *Re D'Angibau* (1880) 15 Ch D 228, 246; also, the Canadian *Travelers Guarantee Co of Canada v Farajollahi* [2012] BCSC 1283. This also demolishes a possible argument that the lack of liability of the agent for breach of fiduciary duty or breach of warranty of authority (both of which are problematic in the case of a small child) is fatal to an agency analysis.

sensibility? Furthermore, machine-based acting also to some extent recalls the idea of authority. My liability for obligations incurred in my name by a computer (or any other machine) is based not only on its acting in my name, but on the fact that I intentionally set it up and made the arrangements for it to operate in the first place. If I did not do this (for example because a fraudster X set up the machine to act ostensibly in my name),[12] then however much a third party may believe in good faith that they are contracting with me, I come under no obligation to them. This can be taken further, too. Although I am not automatically liable for what X's machine does in my name, if I discover the facts about X's activities but take no steps to prevent them or at least warn third parties about the fraud, I may find myself estopped from denying liability. The parallel between this situation and that of unauthorised agents acting with ostensible authority – a doctrine also based on estoppel[13] – is extremely plausible.

The agency analysis, in other words, looks convincing. We suggest, nevertheless, that ultimately it will not work. This is for a number of reasons. The first point is that, albeit plausible, it is actually unnecessary. All the above examples can be explained as instances of ordinary direct liability. For instance, my acting with you through the medium of an AI-equipped computer which I have set up is, it is suggested, in terms of legal analysis exactly the same as my interacting with you through any other instrument, such as a typewriter or teleprinter. My liability under agreements concluded through the machine arises under the ordinary objective theory of contract,[14] under which I am bound provided only that I behave as if I am agreeing. Conversely, if I have not so acted (for instance, if some rogue computer somewhere, equipped with malignant malware, acts in my name without my having had anything to do with it), I will not be responsible, not from any doctrine related to agency but simply because I never had anything to do with the transaction in the first place.

Furthermore, it is suggested that this reasoning applies equally where there are two parties to an agreement, A and B, both of whom contract through AIEMs. Unless one party deliberately set up its software to take advantage of an error by the other, there will, we suggest, be a contract between A and B on the terms apparently agreed between the machines;[15] conversely, if one of the supposedly contracting AIEMs was in fact a rogue machine with no connection to either party there will be no contract at all.

[12] A straightforward, and regrettably common, example being bogus bank ATMs.

[13] See eg *Freeman & Lockyer v Buckhurst Park Properties (Mangal) Ltd* [1964] 2 QB 480, 503 (per Diplock LJ). Despite some scepticism expressed in *Bowstead & Reynolds on Agency*, 23rd edn, para 8-014, it is our view that the doctrine remains pretty firmly anchored in the principle of estoppel.

[14] This theory has been neatly explained by OW Holmes in his classic book, *The Common Law* (Boston, Little, Brown and Company, 1881) 309, in the following fashion: 'The making of a contract depends not on the agreement of two minds in one intention, but on the agreement of two sets of external signs.'

[15] This seems implicit on the result of the Singapore decision in *B2C2 Ltd v Quoine Pte Ltd* [2020] SGCA(I) 02, [2020] 2 SLR 20 (upholding the validity of an entirely machine-concluded contract for the sale of cryptocurrency at a small fraction of its value).

The second problem concerns authority, an idea absolutely central to the law of agency. It is our view that, if properly understood, the present legal concept of authority cannot work between human and machine. Authority is a matter of permission. Implicit in the whole concept is the idea of abstract agreement between a principal on one hand, and on the other an agent assumed to have the physical ability to act in the principal's name, the terms of the agreement dealing with how the agent is authorised to exercise that ability. But it is submitted that this is a concept which cannot coherently be applied to any inanimate machine. I, or a writer of code if I am not sufficiently skilled, can certainly give an AIEM the *ability* to act in my name. But ability and permission are not the same thing. If the AIEM does not have legal (or any) personality, the idea of its having *permission* from me to do so makes no sense.[16]

Furthermore, if this is right then any analogy with ostensible authority also collapses. Ostensible authority requires, among other things, a very precise belief by the third party seeking to take advantage of it: namely, a belief induced by the principal that the agent with whom the third party deals has authority in the sense of the principal's permission to bind it.[17] But if, as we suggest, a machine cannot in a meaningful sense have permission to do anything, then a belief that it has such permission is equally impossible. In so far as a person who sets up a machine to act apparently in their name may be bound by what it does, the explanation therefore must lie elsewhere – for example, in estoppel more generally,[18] or in the objective theory of contractual intention.

Thirdly, there is a difficulty with liability for wrongs. True, you can become liable for a tort committed by someone else if you act according to a common design;[19] if you suggest to them an act in fact tortious and they do it;[20] or if you give them general authority to act for you in some respect and they commit a tort in the course of so acting.[21] But here too the concept of authority – of what you licensed or encouraged them to do – is paramount. In so far as you cannot

[16] A point nicely made in V Ooi, 'Contracts Formed by Software: An Approach from the Law of Mistake' (2022) *Journal of Business Law* 97, 105. See too the suggestive comment in the US *Restatement 3d of Agency*, § 1.04: 'To be capable of acting as a principal or an agent, it is necessary to be a person, which in this respect requires capacity to be the holder of legal rights and the object of legal duties. Accordingly, it is not possible for an inanimate object or a nonhuman animal to be a principal or an agent …. However, an animal or an inanimate object may serve as a person's instrumentality in a manner that may be legally consequential for the person.'

[17] '… [T]he third party cannot hold the principal liable if that party … did not believe that or care whether the agent had authority …': *Bowstead on Agency*, 23rd edn, para 8-023; *cf Tinkler v Revenue & Customs* [2019] EWCA Civ 1392, [2019] 4 WLR 138, [46] (per Hamblen LJ). In practice, such authorisation is generally unattainable, as these systems frequently include disclaimers indicating that they are 'AI systems, not human agents'.

[18] The estoppel could arise from a statement, for example, that the AIEM was an instrument set up by the person sought to be made liable.

[19] See generally *Fish & Fish Ltd v Sea Shepherd UK* [2015] UKSC 10, [2015] AC 1229, [19] (per Lord Toulson).

[20] See eg *Parkes v Prescott* (1869) LR 4 Ex 169, also *CBS Songs Ltd v Amstrad Consumer Electronics plc* [1988] AC 1013, 1058.

[21] As in *Brooke v Bool* [1928] 2 KB 578.

authorise a machine to do anything, and also in so far as a machine cannot itself commit a tort, the analogy immediately breaks down. Action through an AIEM or other machine is certainly possible: but it can only be explicable as directly instrumental liability and not one based on agency.

Fourthly, the idea that a machine is subject to the law of agency is contrary to at least two further established principles, as described below.

(a) Communication: the *Entores* problem. The rules relating to whether a person is bound by the acts of an inanimate entity are not the same as those in agency. Recall the judgment of Denning LJ in *Entores v Miles Far East Corpn*,[22] dealing with the case where A makes an offer to B by machine[23] which B accepts by responding to the machine, but B's acceptance never reaches A. The position, he says, is that A will be bound by B's acceptance, but only if A is some way at fault in not receiving the message. If the non-receipt is due to pure misfortune, A escapes. Yet if A had made the same offer through an agent X and the agent had received the acceptance, A would have been automatically bound.

(b) The ratification problem. If a machine is a genuine agent, presumably you should be able to 'ratify' an act it does supposedly in your name, but without your actual input. For example, if an AIEM goes rogue and enters into a contract in your name that is entirely outside what it was programmed to do, it should be possible for you to ratify what it has done and enforce (or be sued on) that contract. But can you? It is suggested that the answer is no. The essence of ratification involves the acceptance by A of a legal act supposedly done by B on A's authority. The duality is, it seems, essential: hence (for example) A cannot ratify B's act in forging A's own signature, since B did not affect to act *on behalf of* A but to *be* A.[24] But if this is right, then once again the fact that a machine cannot be authorised to do anything causes difficulties. If your AIEM affects to act in your name, it is not saying that it is acting for you, but rather that you are contracting through it. If so, it is suggested that in such circumstances ratification is a legal impossibility.

B. Agency and AI: Is Change Necessary?

i. AI as Principal

Under the present law AI, having no legal personality of any sort, cannot fill the role of principal. The question, however, is whether this is satisfactory, or whether

[22] [1955] 2 QB 327.

[23] There a telex machine, but the reasoning is equally applicable to messages transmitted by email, fax, AI trading software, or any other electronic means.

[24] See eg *Brook v Hook* (1870–71) LR 6 Ex 89, 100 (Kelly CB).

the law ought to be changed in some way. The answer to this query, it is suggested, is closely tied to the issue of whether AI ought to be accorded legal personality or in some way treated as a quasi-corporation. If the answer to that was 'Yes', then the case for allowing AI to act as principal would become unanswerable: after all, AI, being in itself an electronic rather than a physical entity, would in many cases be forced to act through human agency. However, when dealing with that question elsewhere,[25] we concluded that the giving of legal personality to AI would cause more problems than it would solve. If so, then the issue of allowing AI to act as principal falls away. No change is needed or called for.

ii. AI as Agent

Under the current law we have suggested that, while the use of AIEMs in the process of contracting and other activities may look a bit like agency, the appearance is deceptive. On a proper analysis, there are any number of reasons why an AIEM cannot actually be an agent in law. The question is whether this needs to be changed. For example, even if (owing to lack of personality) AI cannot engage its own liability, should it nevertheless be given powers to affect relations between its 'principal' and a third party in the same way as a human or corporate agent can?

Our view is that it would probably be going too far, and might be a source of confusion, to enact that a computer could be an agent *tout court*. However, it is suggested that there is a case, if only for the sake of legal certainty, for a limited approximation of the position of an AIEM with that of an agent.[26] We suggest three provisions: (1) a new head of statutory liability for the act of an AIEM; (2) new rules of ascription; and (3) provisions for ratification.

a. A New Statutory Liability for Acts Done in a Person's Name

While maintaining the existing rules allowing a person to act using a machine as a mere tool, there is a case for providing an alternative form of liability: namely, by creating an alternative class of statutory principal, and clear rules on when that person would be liable (or entitled) on the basis of anything done by an AIEM.

One possibility would be to create a widely-drawn legislative category of 'owner', 'operator' or some such, who would then automatically have the acts of the AIEM attributed to them for the purposes of creating rights and liabilities (perhaps subject to some defence in the former case where the machine had been deliberately manipulated by a third party, etc). But this could be problematic without a

[25] See our discussion in Chapter 2 on the key concepts of private law that require reconsideration in light of the emergence of AI.

[26] As suggested in the well-argued paper by Chopra and White (n 10).

good deal of complex further definition, since 'operator' is itself a vague term, and furthermore the owner of an AIEM may well not be the person in whose name the machine affects to act.[27]

A better characterisation, and the one we favour, would be to attach liability and rights to the person (or corporation) that fulfilled two criteria. First, they would have to be the person in whose name the machine operated or purported to contract. And secondly, they would have to be the person who 'made the arrangements', whether personally or through a human agent, for the machine to operate in that way.[28] That person could, we suggest, be christened the 'controller' (though the title is not important).

When would the controller be liable or entitled? The best way forward, it is suggested, would be a presumption that any act done by the machine in the controller's name would presumptively be treated in law as if it had been the act of an authorised human agent of the controller.[29] This presumption would be rebuttable, but only in limited circumstances: namely, by proof either that that the machine had malfunctioned through some external cause that could not have been foreseen or guarded against, or that the act had been caused deliberately and wrongfully by a third party.

Furthermore, even here it is suggested that there would be a need for a further control device. Where a third party had reasonably relied on the continued existence of the relationship between machine and controller and had had no reason to suspect such a malfunction, then in our view their rights against the controller should be unaffected.

b. Ascription of Knowledge

The above paragraphs refer to acts: archetypally these might involve entering into contracts, but they might also include other matters such as accepting payment on behalf of a controller. But the issue also arises of other matters, such as knowledge. What is to be done about information supplied to, or present on the storage of, an AIEM supposedly acting for a controller where that knowledge is not present to the mind of the latter? Issues arise very frequently of whether a person has knowledge or notice of a fact for the purposes of liability or determining civil

[27] If, for example, the machine is merely leased or provided for a fee by a software consultancy or an organisation like Amazon AWS, ascribing liability to the 'owner' would give the wrong result.

[28] The apparently abstruse term 'made the arrangements' is carefully chosen to be wide enough to catch various means of using an AIEM and narrow enough to avoid catching too many people. Compare the (admittedly distant) analogy applicable under copyright law where it is necessary to determine who has the copyright in a computer-generated literary, dramatic, musical or artistic work. This is the person 'by whom the arrangements necessary for the creation of the work are undertaken'. See Copyright, Designs and Patents Act 1988, s 9(3).

[29] This could be important. Sometimes a liability attaches as a result of something being done by an 'agent'. An example is s 109(4) of the Equality Act 2010 (liability for acts of an agent in the discrimination sphere). See too Law of Property (Miscellaneous Provisions) Act 1989, s 2(3) (contract signed by 'or on behalf of' a party to a land contract).

rights;[30] again, the law of mistake involves, normally, a belief present to the mind of a person which causes that person to act in a particular way.[31] In all these cases, the issue needs to be covered: how far should a person be affected by information on a computer controlled by them?

As regards information *simpliciter*, it might be argued that as against a third party, an AIEM should be regarded as if it were, and always had been, an agent authorised to receive and retain information from any source on behalf of the controller.[32] However, this would in our view be an over-simplified solution, since in some cases this could yield unfortunate results. (For example, for the tort of deceit, it is suggested elsewhere that we should not treat a representor as being fraudulent merely because of the presence of data on an AIEM they control.[33]) We therefore suggest a different solution, whereby there is no general rule attributing the 'knowledge' of AI to its controller, but in individual instances such attribution should apply where this is seen to be desirable.

There is, however, it is suggested, a need for specific provision about the relevance of electronic information to a cause of action or defence based on mistake. Imagine that a computer makes a payment on its controller's behalf which it would not have made but for inaccurate information available to it but not the controller, and that the controller wishes to recover that money: or imagine a contract made by the computer which the controller wishes to escape from on a similar basis. With increasing business done online, the present rule, which it seems would bar both claims,[34] is likely to become increasingly unreal. It is suggested that to deal with this, we need an enactment to the effect that for the purpose of any relief from the consequences of a mistake, inaccurate information supplied to an AIEM in the ordinary course of business – for example, to an AIEM set up to arrange insurance cover – was deemed to have been made to the controller.

The result of the above two suggestions would be, in effect, that any act of an AIEM would potentially be sufficient to create or modify a contractual liability in the controller, since all this requires is agreement by the latter. It would not, admittedly, give rise to an automatic liability in tort in so far as the relevant tort required a state of mind on the part of the agent, since a machine, unlike a human agent,

[30] For example, for the purposes of applying the rules of estoppel, or of deciding whether a person has been negligent, or has notice of an equitable interest in property, or has paid an assigned debt to the assignor knowing of the assignment. Knowledge of underwriter or assured for the purpose of insurance law, dealt with in extenso elsewhere in this book, is another example.

[31] The need for such a view to be present to the allegedly mistaken party's mind, or at least form the subject of a tacit assumption, appears from cases such as *Pitt v Holt* [2013] UKSC 26, [2013] 2 AC 108.

[32] This slightly cumbersome expression would be necessary to make it clear that the knowledge attributed to the controller includes: (1) knowledge previously 'acquired' by the computer; and (2) knowledge 'acquired' by the computer from others as well as from the particular third party concerned.

[33] For more detailed discussion see Chapter 4 above.

[34] On the basis of a combination of the reasoning of *Pitt v Holt* [2013] UKSC 26, [2013] 2 AC 108, requiring a belief to be at least present to the mind of the person seeking to invoke mistake, and *B2C2 Ltd v Quoine Pty Ltd* [2020] SGCA(I) 02, [2020] 2 SLR 20, saying that in the case of a computer contract that person is the physical person behind the computer and not the hard disk of the latter.

cannot have a mental state.[35] However, there would be the potential for tortious liability if the controller had the requisite mental state and in the relevant tort that could be combined with the action of the agent.

c. Ratification

Although we see serious difficulties in applying the doctrine of ratification to the acts of an AIEM under the law as it stands, our view is that this is not satisfactory. We see no reason why the idea behind ratification should not be extended, in at least some form, to the acts of AIEMs which have purported to act for particular controllers. Imagine, for example, that an AIEM purports to act on my behalf without my having set it up, either because of a malfunction or because of the act of some third party done without my agreement; and suppose that later, in knowledge of the facts, I say that I am happy to stand by what it has done. No injustice is done to me if I find myself bound as a result of my own subsequent agreement; conversely, if a third party was prepared to contract with me through the agency of the machine they get exactly what they bargained for if held to their agreement. Accordingly, we suggest legislation providing that where an AIEM acts in the name of a controller, any express or implied statement by the controller that they accepted the act should have the effect that the controller was liable for, and entitled under, the acts of the AIEM as if the latter had been the controller's agent.

III. Vicarious Liability

A. The Present Position

Vicarious liability, at least in practice, has a good deal in common with agency.[36] This goes too for the application of the doctrine to the activities of AIEMs, as will appear below.

As with agency, while there can clearly be no question of a machine being liable for the act of a human,[37] the acts of an AIEM can certainly engender liability in a human or corporate defendant. Imagine, for example, that a company replaces customer-facing staff with an online AI portal for enquiries about its products, and that the portal misleads customers. Just as the company would be liable for misadvice by a human employee, so too in many cases with machine-generated advice.[38]

[35] See our discussion on tort liability of AI in Chapter 4.

[36] Indeed, when it comes to negligent or fraudulent misrepresentation the two doctrines to all intents and purposes coalesce: see cases such as *Kooragang Investments Pty v Richardson & Wrench* [1982] AC 462 and *Armagas Ltd v Mundogas SA* [1986] AC 717, 779–83 (Lord Keith).

[37] See above, p 117.

[38] Compare the facts of the British Columbia small claims decision in *Moffatt v Air Canada*, 2024 BCCRT 149 (airline chatbot promising discount).

This also applies with an AIEM set up to run a piece of machinery or a production line. If it runs it dangerously and injures a worker, or for that matter a passer-by or consumer, liability will often follow.

However, again as happens with agency, a closer look shows that despite the factual similarity of the situations, the legal parallel with vicarious liability is distinctly problematical. While a controller can clearly be liable for their own fault (or intention, or malice, or whatever), the same does not go for vicarious liability, which is not dependent on any showing of personal fault.

One reason is theoretical and is tied in with the legal thinking that lies behind vicarious liability. The prevailing explanation of this head of liability is the 'servant's tort' theory. Under this a tort committed by the actor in the course of employment is a prerequisite of the employer's vicarious liability: the employer is added into the equation as someone jointly liable for that tort.[39] But applying this to an AIEM is impossible. As we say elsewhere,[40] a machine with neither personality nor patrimony is unable to commit a tort or be sued for it. Nor, for that matter, can it satisfy the requirements of liability for most torts dependent on intention or negligence, in any case; there is no such thing as a malicious or careless computer. From this it follows that if we apply the 'servant's tort' theory, there can never be vicarious liability for the acts of an AIEM.

Could we overcome this problem by applying the competing 'master's tort' theory, under which vicarious liability represents a personal duty in the employer to see that a job is properly done?[41] Unfortunately the answer is still no, for two further reasons.

The first of these other reasons has to do with the relationship that gives rise to vicarious liability. Under the law as it stands, vicarious liability can apply only where that relationship is one of employment or something like it.[42] Nothing short of this will do: in particular there cannot be vicarious liability for the acts of an independent contractor (or actor) working on their own account.[43] But this requirement only makes sense where both parties have legal personality and the ability to make a contract or enter into legal relations. With an AIEM this requirement becomes inoperable. In addition, the distinction between employers

[39] For statements of the theory, see in particular *Staveley Iron & Chemical Co Ltd v Jones* [1956] AC 627 and *ICI Ltd v Shatwell* [1965] AC 656, where the peculiarities of the cause of action for breach of statutory duty forced the House of Lords to choose between theories, and it chose the 'servant's tort' theory. See too *Clerk & Lindsell on Torts*, 24th edn, para 6-63.

[40] See in particular our discussion in Chapter 2.

[41] Although judicially discountenanced in large degree, this theory is not without backers even today. It is passionately supported in, for example, R Stevens, 'Vicarious Liability or Vicarious Action?' (2007) 123 *Law Quarterly Review* 30.

[42] There is no need, strictly speaking, for a contract of employment. A gratuitous service will do (eg *Ormrod v Crosville Motor Services Ltd* [1953] 1 WLR 1120), as will working for someone without being employed, as with someone working in a religious institution or an inmate in a prison kitchen (see *Various Claimants v Institute of the Brothers of the Christian Schools* [2012] UKSC 56, [2013] 2 AC 1 and *Cox v Ministry of Justice* [2016] UKSC 10, [2016] AC 660).

[43] A proposition put beyond doubt by the decision in *Barclays Bank plc v Various Claimants* [2020] UKSC 13, [2020] AC 973.

and independent contractors also stands firmly in the way. One can ask a person whether they are working on their own account or as part of someone else's business and get a sensible answer. Asking the same question about an AIEM, however smart it might be, is nonsensical.

Further, even if a machine could be an employee or in the position of one, the lack of any legal relation between it and its user would make it difficult, if not impossible, to satisfy the second inescapable requirement of vicarious liability: action within the course of employment.[44] Just as authority in the law of agency carries with it the idea of some kind of limited permission which may or may not be exceeded, the 'scope of employment' in vicarious liability does much the same, depending as it does on what function the employee has agreed to fulfil.[45] But a machine does not agree to do anything or fulfil any function: it simply works (or does not). In short, we reach a dead-end here too.

If the above argument is right, vicarious liability as we know it cannot work with AI. The nearest we can get to it is where some form of direct liability can be found, for example where personal negligence can be proved against the controller, or possibly where there is a duty to see that a task is carried out with due diligence.[46]

B. AI and Vicarious Liability: Should the Law be Changed?

This leads us on to the next question: is the present position the right one, or do we need to provide some sort of analogue to vicarious liability in the AI context? It is submitted that the answer is emphatically the latter. This is for two reasons.

First, the result of the present law is that we have fundamentally different regimes in tort according to whether the same function is performed by human staff or AI. Presumptively this looks wrong as a matter of horizontal equity.[47] Where a company replaces consumer-facing staff with an AI interface, for example, or human control of a production process with AI-based supervision, the misadvised or injured claimant immediately becomes worse off. Whereas previously all they had to prove was that an employee had been negligent, they now

[44] See *Clerk & Lindsell on Torts*, 24th edn, para 6-29 ff.

[45] See the previous note and, most recently, *Trustees of the Barry Congregation of Jehovah's Witnesses v BXB* [2023] UKSC 15, [2024] AC 567.

[46] See generally *Woodland v Swimming Teachers Association* [2013] UKSC 66, [2014] AC 537. It is just arguable that an AIEM used in such a situation would be seen as having not provided the necessary due diligence, and that this would be seen as engaging the liability of the entity that used it. But this is remarkably uncertain.

[47] This is essentially the point made in M Diamantis, 'Employed Algorithms: A Labor Model of Corporate Liability for AI' (2023) 72 *Duke Law Journal* 797.

have to show negligence by the company in setting up or supervising the AI, which is a much taller order.[48]

Secondly, even if the rules of vicarious liability itself do not readily transfer over to the AIEM scenario, the social arguments in favour of them most certainly do.[49] Many claimants relying on vicarious liability are less well-provided with advice and funding than the employer: it can be important to make available to claimants the deep pockets of the employer and the fact that the latter rightly tends to be the liability insurance carrier;[50] and as a matter of cost internalisation, making an employer (or, in the case of an AIEM, a user) liable without personal fault for damage caused by what is essentially their business helps make sure that the business bears the costs it should.[51]

How can this be done? In our view, there are two reforms that need to be introduced. The first, which we deal with in greater detail in Chapter 4 on tort, is to deal with the theoretical barrier of the negligent machine and the concomitant need to prove personal fault in the person making use of it. Strict liability for damage done by malfunctioning or defective AIMs would be a theoretical possibility. But this would raise difficulties in determining what counted as a malfunction or a defect and would also risk actually privileging the victims of AIM-caused harm over those of human negligence. A more straightforward solution, which we propose,[52] would be a provision requiring that, for the purposes of vicarious liability, an act by an AIM that would have created liability in negligence if done by a natural person be treated in the same way as if it had been a negligent human act giving rise to liability.[53]

Our second suggested change is aimed at enabling the carry-across of the existing rules of vicarious liability to cover AIEMs, in order to get over the problems described above of applying the criteria of 'employment' and the 'course of

[48] Furthermore, this is likely to become increasingly important. As AI improves its autonomous development potential, it will become more and more difficult to trace back a malfunction to any human act or default. See A Matthias, 'The Responsibility Gap: Ascribing Responsibility for the Actions of Learning Automata' (2004) 6 *Ethics & Information Technology* 175, 182; P Huberman, 'A Theory of Vicarious Liability for Autonomous-Machine-Caused Harm' (2021) 58 *Osgoode Hall Law Journal* 233, 236–37.

[49] *cf* Diamantis (n 47) 824 ff, where similar arguments to those appearing here are laid out at some length.

[50] Compare A Stern et al, 'AI Insurance: How Liability Insurance Can Drive the Responsible Adoption of Artificial Intelligence in Health Care' (2022) 4 *New England Journal of Medicine Catalyst* 3.

[51] On which, see generally eg A Honoré, 'The Morality of Tort Law' in D Owen (ed), *Philosophical Foundations of Tort Law* (Oxford, Clarendon Press, 1995) 85; H Sheinman, 'Tort Law and Distributive Justice' in J Oberdiek, *Philosophical Foundations of the Law of Torts* (Oxford, Oxford University Press, 2014); and Huberman (n 48) Part II.

[52] See p 61.

[53] Compare R Abbott, 'The Reasonable Computer: Disrupting the Paradigm of Tort Liability' (2018) 86 *George Washington Law Review* 1, esp 25. D Johnson, 'Computer Systems: Moral Entities, But Not Moral Agents' (2008) 8 *Ethics & IT* 195 provides an interesting analysis of why AIEMs deserve special treatment here: while incapable of acting for a reason as we do, they are nevertheless capable of non-deterministic action.

employment' to them. The best solution here, it is suggested, would be a partial import into tort from the agency reforms concerning 'controllers' advocated above.[54] Where a person P is proved to have been the 'controller' of an AIEM utilised other than for purely domestic purposes, two things should follow for the purposes of liability tort. One is that the acts of the machine should automatically fall to be treated as though they were the acts of an employee of P for whose acts P was responsible.[55] The other, reflecting the fact that 'course of employment' ceases to mean much where there is nothing resembling an agreement as to the job to be done, is that any act by the AIEM in the employer's name, or about the employer's business, should be treated for the purposes of vicarious liability as if it were an act in the course of employment. This could be subject to exceptions – for example, where it was shown that the machine's action was due to the deliberate and wrongful act of a third party – but these would need to be kept as narrow as possible. The general rule would be straightforward: anything done or omitted by an AIM would, save in exceptional circumstances, make its 'controller' liable in the same way as the negligence of an employee would make an employer liable.

It should also go without saying that any legislation introducing new liability of this sort should make it clear that it is without prejudice to any existing liability, for example where actual fault, or intentional wrongdoing, is proved against the person or corporation using the AIEM.

Such a solution would, it is suggested, come close to approximating the position of human staff and AIEMs. The requirement that the person to be made liable be a controller would go some way towards replicating the distinction between employees and independent contractors; it would, for example, exonerate a professional such as a lawyer who commissioned a one-off report, such as a survey report, that was prepared by an AIEM, since they would not have made the arrangements for its use. And similarly, the proposed exception would go a long way towards reproducing the need in vicarious liability proper for an act within the course of the employer's business.[56]

Furthermore, when combined with rules about, for example, attributing negligence to an AIEM if it acted in a way that would have been negligent if the actor had been a human being (which we advocate in Chapter 4), this would go a long way towards approximating the negligence liability of those making use of human and digital staff. It would mean, for example, that if an AIEM set up to supervise

[54] See p 59.

[55] It is possible that two 'employers' might share the services of one machine. If so, there would be no objection to joint liability where it was operating on behalf of both – just as at common law there can be joint vicarious liability for the same human servant (see eg *Viasystems (Tyneside) Ltd v Thermal Transfer (Northern) Ltd* [2005] EWCA Civ 1151, [2006] QB 510).

[56] It might be argued that the exception for acts not apparently part of the business would not go the whole way, and in particular would go against the cases holding employers liable for deliberate wrongdoing. But this may not be too significant. As we illustrated in Chapter 4 on tort, the idea of deliberate or malicious wrongdoing by AIEDs is problematical: the issue is one in practice of negligence, which this fits well.

some hazardous industrial process failed to act as a reasonable human in the same position would have acted, causing a disastrous fire, then there would be liability in the person making use of it. More prosaically, it would also mean that if a company replaced human telephone advisory staff with a chatbot which then negligently advised a customer or made some misrepresentation, the liability would remain the same.

This is not to say that there cannot also be cases of stricter liability. As it is, for example, the producer of a product is strictly liable for any harm due to a defect in it. Although at present it seems clear that AI is not within the definition of a 'product', this is largely for historical reasons: in 1985, when the Product Liability Directive was passed, AI was hardly on the horizon. There is a case for removing this anomaly and making the user of AI liable at least for any personal injury suffered as a result of a defect in it.[57]

IV. Company Law and Representation of Companies

The corporation, a purely legal creation without any of the other attributes of a natural person, is the most plausible analogy for those who support giving AI some sort of legal personality in its own right. We have already suggested above that arguments of this sort are ultimately unconvincing. Nevertheless, this does not mean that company law is itself free from AI problems. On the contrary, it raises at least two, both arising from the fact that a company can only act through others: company action, and company decision-making.[58]

A. Company Action

When we talk about the acts of a company, what we normally mean is acts attributed to the company under principles of agency or vicarious liability. In concluding an employment contract with a worker or contracting to sell products or buy stationery or raw materials, a corporation will normally act through an agent, such as someone in its human resources or its purchasing departments. In parallel to this, when we say a company is liable in tort this usually comports some form of wrongdoing by one of its workers (or exceptionally an independent contractor) in the course of their employment; and so on. To this extent, the comments in the previous sections on agency and vicarious liability apply just as much to company action through AIEMs as to anyone else's rights and obligations.

[57] As has occurred in the European Union: see our comments and observations in Chapter 1, where we set the scene for this study by referring to the existing rules and regulations.

[58] A third issue also arises: directors' duties, in so far as functions that would otherwise be deputed to members of the board, are performed instead by AI-enabled machines.

But this is not the whole story. By a legal fiction,[59] a company is in some cases regarded in law as acting personally rather than vicariously or through an agent. Historically, under the 'directing mind and will' doctrine,[60] where very senior management of a company, or those with specific responsibilities to direct action in its name, acted on its behalf those acts might, quite independently of any issues of agency, be regarded as the personal act of the company itself.

This can be important not only in the case of criminal law,[61] but also in a substantial number of private law liability issues. Some liabilities, for example, require the company, and not merely its agents, to be fixed with knowledge[62] or malice;[63] again, there may be cases where fraud bars a company's claim if it is the fraud of the company, but not if that of a mere employee.[64] In a few specialised cases, notably in shipping law, a company is liable for its own negligence, but not vicariously for that of its employees,[65] and in addition can limit liability for the deliberate act of its employees but not for its own deliberate act.[66] The fact that a person is a directing mind and will of a company may equally override the fact that

[59] It must be a fiction because a corporation as an abstract entity can actually do nothing. For the origins of this legal creation, it is worth considering the landmark case of *Salomon v Salomon & Co Ltd* [1897] AC 22.

[60] An expression coined by Viscount Haldane in *Lennard's Carrying Co Ltd v Asiatic Petroleum Co Ltd* [1915] AC 705, 713, a case concerning what was meant by the 'actual fault or privity' of a shipping company under now-repealed provisions of the Merchant Shipping Act 1894.

[61] For example, there may exist separate rules according to whether a company acts personally or through a mere employee: see, eg, *Tesco Supermarkets Ltd v Nattrass* [1972] AC 153 and *Seaboard Transport Ltd v Transport Secretary* [1993] 1 WLR 1025. See also *R v McDonnell* [1966] 1 QB 233 (director who effectively ran company not guilty of conspiring with it). But here the matter is somewhat cloudy and depends ultimately on the interpretation of the underlying penal statute: see generally *Meridian Global Funds Management Asia Ltd v Securities Commission* [1995] 2 AC 500.

[62] eg *Quilter Private Client Advisers Ltd v Falconer* [2022] IRLR 227 (QB) [310]–[316] (knowledge for purpose of inducing breach of contract). See also *El Ajou v Dollar Land Holdings plc* [1994] 2 All ER 685 (knowledge of directing mind and will adequate for purposes of knowing receipt in trust law, even though no knowledge of authorised agent). This may be laid down by statute: see eg Insurance Act 2015, s 4(3) (knowledge of insured's 'senior management'), and *cf* Financial Services and Markets Act 2000, s 90A (liability of company for fraudulent or reckless information provided by those discharging 'managerial responsibilities'). Note also *Jafari-Fini v Skillglass Ltd* [2007] EWCA Civ 261 (knowledge of making of bribe for purposes of triggering contractual right).

[63] eg *Willers v Joyce* [2018] EWHC 3424 (Ch), [194] (Rose J) (malice for malicious prosecution). See too *Re Odyssey Ltd* [2000] 1 Lloyd's Rep IR 1 (judgment obtained by fraud: fraud must be that of company itself). A number of examples are maritime: eg Art 4 of the Limitation Convention ('personal act or omission') and s 186(4) of the Merchant Shipping Act 1995.

[64] *Bilta (UK) Ltd v Nazir* [2015] UKSC 23, [2016] AC 1, [65] ff (per Lord Sumption); see too *Re Odyssey Ltd* [2000] 1 Lloyd's Rep IR 1 (judgment obtained by fraud). Conversely a company can, it seems, by contract exonerate itself from liability for the fraud of its employees but not for its own fraud: *HIH Casualty & General Insurance Ltd v Chase Manhattan Bank* [2001] EWCA Civ 1250, [2001] 2 Lloyd's Rep 483 (left open in the HL: [2003] UKHL 6, [2003] 2 Lloyd's Rep 61, [14]–[17] (per Lord Bingham), [76]–[82] (per Lord Hobhouse), [122] (per Lord Scott)). Contra, however, K Handley, 'Exclusion Clauses for Fraud' (2003) 119 *Law Quarterly Review* 537.

[65] Notably in shipping law, under Art IV.2(b) of the Hague-Visby Rules (liability for fire): *Glencore Energy UK Ltd v Freeport Holdings Ltd (The Lady M)* [2019] EWCA Civ 388, [2019] 2 Lloyd's Rep 109.

[66] See Art 4 of the Convention on Limitation of Liability for Maritime Claims 1976, taking away the right to limit liability in the case of '*personal* act or omission, committed with the intent to cause such loss, or recklessly and with knowledge that such loss would probably result' (emphasis added).

as a matter of agency law they have no authority from it, meaning that their acts – even though unauthorised – bind it.[67]

How does AI fit in here where it has been utilised by a company? This is a difficult question to answer, particularly since the response to the question whether in a particular situation the act of a given person within a company amounts to that of the company is itself notoriously context-dependent and fact-specific.[68] In most cases, however, it is suggested that just as an AIEM cannot in the nature of things be an agent or employee, the chances are vanishingly small of an AIEM being seen as acting as a company's directing mind. Even if the AIEM plays a large part in the direction of a company,[69] it is suggested that in the context of a human manager the essence of a 'directing mind' finding is that the human either: (a) used the company as their own tool to carry out their own purposes;[70] or (b) was authorised by the company to exercise wide-ranging discretionary control over all or part of its business.[71] This will not really fit an AIEM, for the reasons stated above. AIEMs may have the ability to do acts in a company's name but talk of the precise limits of their authority makes little sense. Furthermore, as we point out in greater detail in Chapter 4 on tort: talking about AI using a corporate vehicle to further its purposes also creates difficulty, given that in our view an AIEM, however smart, cannot have a purpose in any real sense.

B. Company Action: Should the Law be Changed?

We suggested earlier in this chapter that there was a case for changing the law to clarify the position of AI as regards agency and vicarious liability, and to some extent to bring the legal position of AIEMs closer to that of other legal persons. This then raises the question: should we do the same thing as regards direct representation of companies, by providing that at least in some cases AI can also be regarded as a company's 'directing mind and will'?

Although this solution may have some attraction in terms of legal tidiness, our view is that the answer is no. This is for two reasons. First, the suggestions made above already go some way beyond the strict rules of agency and vicarious liability. In recognition of the fact that the concepts of authority, employment and

[67] *Senex Holdings Ltd (in Liquidation) v National Westminster Bank plc* [2012] EWHC 131 (Comm); and see the earlier *London Intercontinental Trust Ltd v Barclays Bank Ltd* [1980] 1 Lloyd's Rep 214 (order given to bank to move account outside written mandate, but still valid because person giving it account-holder's directing mind and will).

[68] See *Meridian Global Funds Management Asia Ltd v Securities Commission* [1995] 2 AC 500, above; E Ferran, 'Corporate Attribution and the Directing Mind and Will' (2011) 127 *Law Quarterly Review* 239.

[69] Conceivable if the company is set up, for example, to engage in stock trading or currency speculation.

[70] As in cases such as *El Ajou v Dollar Land Holdings plc* [1994] 2 All ER 685 (company as fraudster's instrument).

[71] As in cases such as *The Lady Gwendolen* [1965] P 294.

course of employment are hard to apply to AIEMs, we have proposed what is in effect automatic liability (subject to a few exceptions) of a controller for acts of AI done in the controller's name, and also for acts and omissions by AI that would have amounted to negligence if done by a human. This will cover most cases of AI involved in management anyway. It is our view that to add to this a further liability for AI acting as if it were a 'directing mind and will,' even if it were possible to come up with an acceptable formulation (which is doubtful), would introduce unnecessary complexity for very little advantage.

Secondly, and more importantly, at least some of the justification for a separate category of direct corporate liability is ethical or moral. The thinking is, it is suggested, that in some cases it can be more appropriate to penalise a company, or hold it liable, where what it does is driven by top management or someone in substantial control of it than where it is merely a question of the actions of some employee or agent. But moral arguments of this sort are a little difficult to apply where the management or control is in the hands not of a human but of a machine. For this reason, too, it seems simpler to limit a company's liability to a statutory one for the acts of AI and draw no distinction between different statuses of AI.

V. Conclusions

As illustrated in this chapter, the traditional principles of agency law are likely to be both challenged and tested, particularly in cases where litigants seek to attribute liability for the actions of intelligent machines to individuals. The conclusions drawn from this analysis are as follows:

A. AIEMs and Agency

Under the present law there are as we see it almost insuperable difficulties in holding controllers liable for, and entitled under, arrangements entered into by AIEMs on their behalf in the same way as a principal in respect of their human or corporate agents. In our view this is unsatisfactory. We would urge a statutory reform.

First, a new category of person, a 'controller,' should be created, being defined as the person (or corporation) in whose name the machine operated or purported to contract and who in addition had 'made the arrangements', whether personally or otherwise, for the AIEM to operate in that way.

Secondly, there should be a statutory presumption that any act done by the AIEM in the controller's name would presumptively be treated in law as if it had been the act of an authorised human agent of the latter. This presumption would be rebuttable, but only in limited circumstances: namely, by proof either that that the machine had malfunctioned through some external cause that could not have been foreseen or guarded against, or that the act had been caused deliberately and wrongfully by a third party.

Thirdly, while in these circumstances the *acts and omissions* of the AIEM would be attributed to the controller, it should be enacted that – without more – there should be no attribution of *knowledge* available to an AIEM to the controller, save in one case: namely, where relief was sought by the latter from the consequences of a mistake.

Fourthly, we suggest that legislation should provide that where an AIEM acts in the name of a controller, any express or implied statement by the controller that they accepted or ratified the act should have the effect that the controller was liable for, and entitled under, the acts of the AIEM as if the latter had been the controller's agent and the controller had ratified the latter's unauthorised act.

Fifthly, it should be made clear that these rules were without prejudice to any other right or liability existing at law or in equity, or to the terms of any agreement between the parties.

B. Vicarious Liability

Just as agency is problematic in the case of an AIEM, so also (at least under the present law) is vicarious liability in tort. In our view this is unsatisfactory, and legislation should attempt as far as possible to assimilate the employer of human and algorithmic resources. In our view the legislation should provide three things.

First, for the purposes of vicarious liability, it should be enacted that an act by an AIEM that would have created liability in negligence if done by a natural person be treated in the same way as if it had been a negligent human act giving rise to liability.

Secondly, where a person P is proved to have been the 'controller' of an AIEM utilised other than for purely domestic purposes, two statutory consequences should follow for the purposes of the law of tort. One is that the acts of the machine should automatically fall to be treated as though they were the acts of an employee of P for whose acts P was responsible. The other, reflecting the fact that 'course of employment' ceases to mean much in the case of an AIEM without a contract of employment, is that – subject to a few exceptions – any act by the AIEM in the employer's name, or about the employer's business, should be treated for the purposes of vicarious liability as if it were an act in the course of employment.

Thirdly, the legislation should make it clear that it is without prejudice to any existing liability, for example where actual fault, or intentional wrongdoing, is proved against the person or corporation using the AIEM.

8

Intelligent Machines, AI and Insurance Law

The previous chapters in this book have covered general areas within the law of obligations and property. In this, the final substantive chapter, we have thought it important to change the emphasis and instead look closely at one specialised area of law and how its rules can be reconciled with the growth of AI. We have chosen for these purposes the law of insurance.

There is ample evidence that AI, having the capacity to analyse vast and abstract sources of data and information and detect patterns that might escape human cognition, is being increasingly utilised in insurance practice to carry out various functions traditionally performed by human agents.[1] For example, it can be used to identify critical documents and extract information among the huge datasets presented to underwriters by assureds or their brokers, and then feed the relevant information to the human agents within the underwriting organisation entrusted with decision-making. Similarly, AI can be utilised to assist in underwriting decisions by reinforcing classification methods already defined by the insurance organisation. It has, for example, been reported that Ping An, one of the China's biggest insurance companies, now uses facial recognition software to refine its health insurance coverage and premiums by analysing the risk a potential assured presents based on their facial features.[2]

It is also gradually becoming more feasible for AI to be utilised to make actual decisions on behalf of insurance organisations, rather than merely assisting in the decision-making process. This capability is more likely in areas of insurance practice where risks are more homogenous in nature (for example, motor and home insurance). In those areas, AI can be trusted to aggregate and interpret data and reach underwriting decisions by contextualising risk scoring independently.[3]

The purpose of this chapter is to evaluate in which areas of insurance practice AI could be used, either to assist or replace human agents, and identify whether

[1] See SCOR, *The Impact of Artificial Intelligence on the (Re)insurance Sector* (2018).

[2] A Lior, 'Insuring AI: The Role of Insurance in Artificial Intelligence Regulation' (2022) 35 *Harvard Journal of Law & Technology* 467, 477.

[3] See *Lewis v Allstate Ins Co*, 2016 WL 5408332 (D Ariz, 28 September 2016) where a plaintiff before the District of Arizona alleged that the insurance company was negligent by improperly using software to deprive the assured of coverage under a homeowner's policy.

the current legal framework is in a position to respond to the issues that might emerge as a result. We shall develop the debate by considering various AI applications that are currently used or likely to be used in the near future in insurance practice.

I. Use of AI in the Underwriting Process

AI is clearly capable of assisting underwriters in rating risks presented to them, and ultimately in making decisions whether to offer insurance and on what basis. Applications with this purpose could be used in any area of insurance: however, given that the legal framework that applies in consumer insurance is different from the one that governs business insurance contracts, the position in each will be evaluated separately. While it is beyond the scope of this book, it is worth mentioning that when it comes to consumer insurance, data protection legislation[4] could provide an additional level of protection for consumers, especially in cases where the personal data[5] of consumers has been harvested and used by insurers for risk assessment purposes.[6] The position is different in the field of business insurance, as any data processed by AI systems will not normally include personally identifying information[7] and thus will not raise personal data privacy issues.

A. Consumer Insurance Contracts

i. The Legal Framework

Pre-contractual information duties of consumers are governed by the Consumer Insurance (Disclosure and Representations) Act 2012 (CIDRA 2012).[8] For the purposes of this Act:

[4] The relevant legal framework in this context can be found in the UK General Data Protection Regulation (UK GDPR), which is based on the EU General Data Protection Regulation, Regulation (EU) 2016/679 and the Data Protection Act 2018, designed to supplement UK GDPR. These legislative measures impose several limitations on the manner in which insurers could use big data analytics and other forms of artificial intelligence for risk assessment purposes.

[5] UK GDPR, Art 4(1) defines 'personal data' as 'any information relating to an identified and identifiable natural person'.

[6] For a detailed analysis of the data protection issues that might arise in consumer insurance context, see B Soyer, 'Use of Big Data Analytics and Sensor Technology in Consumer Insurance Context: Legal and Practical Challenges' (2022) 81 *Cambridge Law Journal* 165, 174–75.

[7] One exception would be disclosure of previous criminal histories of those in control of a company seeking insurance but that is unlikely to raise issues concerning data protection legislation.

[8] This Act, which came into force on 6 April 2013, aims to codify the principles found in Financial Services Authority's new Insurance Conduct of Business Sourcebook (ICOBS), which came into force on 6 January 2008.

'consumer insurance contract' means a contract of insurance between –

(a) an individual who enters into the contract wholly or mainly for purposes unrelated to the individual's trade, business or profession, and
(b) a person who carries on the business of insurance and who becomes a party to the contract by way of that business (whether or not in accordance with permission for the purposes of the Financial Services and Markets Act 2000).[9]

The Act, therefore, applies essentially to natural persons acting wholly or mainly for non-business purposes. Where a policy covers some non-business and some business use, the Act will still apply if the main purpose of the insurance is non-business related.

ii. The Assured's Duty under CIDRA 2012 and the Role of AI

The main change that CIDRA 2012 introduced was to remove the traditional duty on consumers to disclose any facts or circumstances that a prudent underwriter would consider material.[10] Instead, under the CIDRA 2012 regime, potential assureds are expected to exercise reasonable care not to make a misrepresentation.[11] This change means that insurers now need to rely either on their ability to gather information on individuals themselves, or on the answers provided by the assureds in response to the questions put to them, in order to be rate the risks that they are asked to insure.

a. Insurers Gathering Information from Various Sources

In contemporary practice, insurers have at their disposal enormous datasets obtained from third parties or even from social media sites, which they can utilise with the aid of algorithms to identify patterns. Once a pattern emerges from the examination of datasets, it can be used as the basis for the operation of predictive analytics[12] that can hugely assist underwriters in rating risk. The only obstacle for insurers using such datasets, as mentioned above, is the data protection legislation. As the law currently stands, it does not prohibit insurers from obtaining personal data[13] relating to consumers seeking insurance cover directly or from third parties for the purpose of processing (for risk assessment purposes) as long as they obtain

[9] CIDRA 2012, s 1.

[10] The duty of disclosure at pre-contractual stage can be traced back to the Marine Insurance Act 1906 (MIA 1906), especially ss 17 and 18.

[11] CIDRA 2012, s 2. A similar approach has been adopted in Australia with regard to consumer insurance contracts. The Financial Sector Reform (Hayne Royal Commission Response) Act 2020 (Cth), Schedule 2, Pt 2, amending the Insurance Act 1984 (Cth), has replaced the assured's duty of disclosure by the assured's duty to take reasonable care not to make a misrepresentation to the insurer.

[12] Predictive analytics is a branch of analytics concerned with making predictions as to the risk and probabilities of future events. Insurers have been using the basic principles of predictive analytics for decades, but today it is mainly used to produce reliable reports, which accurately identify levels of risk and aid in underwriting and policymaking by using a wide variety of methods, including data mining, predictive modelling, statistics, machine learning and artificial intelligence.

[13] As described in Art 4(1) of the UK GDPR.

consent from those consumers.[14] In addition the UK GDPR[15] allows insurers to subject consumers to automated decision-making with their consent.[16] Therefore, as long as insurers make their consumers aware of the fact that they have ability to source and process personal data through big data analytics, there is no restriction on insurers in utilising AI tools in the process of making an informed underwriting decision.

b. Insurers Asking Questions to Potential Assureds

In determining whether the assured has exercised reasonable care in answering the questions posed by the insurer, section 3(2) of CIDRA 2012 identifies the clarity and precision of the insurer's questions as an important factor. Accordingly, the clearer and more direct the questions are, the greater the likelihood that an insurer could demonstrate that the assured has failed to present the risk correctly and hence made a false or misleading representation. It is at this juncture that the AI-driven analytics of big data could play a significant role in assisting insurers to shape the questions that they use in their standard products. AI could, therefore, be a vital tool for insurers in personalising the questions they use, by considering the type of product and the profile of the assured.

iii. Proving Qualifying Breach and Potential Remedies

The insurer can seek a remedy under the CIDRA 2012 regime, as long as it establishes that the assured when responding to its questions has made a misrepresentation and also that the misrepresentation is a qualifying one – that is, one committed either: (i) deliberately or recklessly;[17] or (ii) carelessly.[18]

If a qualifying breach is deliberate or reckless, the insurer may avoid the contract and refuse all claims, and the premiums need not be returned except to the extent that it would be unfair to the consumer to allow the insurer to retain them.[19] If the misrepresentation is merely careless, the insurer can avoid the contract and refuse to pay claims if they can demonstrate that they would not have entered into the contract if the correct state of affairs had been made known to them.[20] If

[14] Art 9(2) of UK GDPR.

[15] Regulation (EU) 2016/679 (General Data Protection Regulation), as amended (retained EU law since Brexit).

[16] It is very common today for insurance companies to require customers to sign consent forms giving them authority to undertake automated decision making with regard to pricing and underwriting.

[17] Pursuant to CIDRA 2012, s 5(2), a qualifying misrepresentation is 'deliberate or reckless' if the consumer: (a) knew that it was untrue or misleading, or did not care whether or not it was untrue or misleading; (b) knew that the matter to which the misrepresentation related was relevant to the insurer, or did not care whether or not it was relevant to the insurer.

[18] CIDRA 2012, s 5(1). It should be noted that an innocent misrepresentation is not a qualifying breach under the Act.

[19] CIDRA 2012, Schedule 1, para 2. See *Tesco Underwriting Ltd v Achunche* [2016] EWHC 3869 (QB).

[20] In this case, they must also return the premium (CIDRA 2012, Schedule 1, para 5).

they would have provided cover but on different terms (excluding terms relating to premium), the contract will be treated as if it had been entered into on those different terms if the insurer so requires.[21] If they would have granted cover but only at an enhanced premium and a loss has occurred, a system of proportionality applies.[22]

In cases where the insurer utilises AI to take underwriting decisions on its behalf, the provisions highlighted above would not present any obstacle, as they focus primarily on the state of mind of the assured. The matter could, however, prove problematic if the consumer relied on AI to assist them in construing the questions posed by the insurer as part of the underwriting process. What if, for example, the AI system, misconstruing the questions posed, prompted the consumer to give an answer which was not accurate? As long as the consumer was relying on the AI as an aid, we believe that they should be ultimately responsible for the accuracy of the answers presented to the insurer.[23] There might be difficulties for the insurer in proving that a consumer, who had allegedly relied on the AI system's construction of the questions posed, might have realised the error but nevertheless decided to follow the advice given, but this poses an evidential problem for the insurer rather than highlighting any problem with the statutory rules as they are currently formulated.

The analysis becomes more complex in cases where a consumer relies on AI to respond to insurer inquiries during the insurance application process, but without any direct personal involvement. This scenario raises significant challenges under the current legal framework, particularly when attempting to determine whether the provision of misleading information was deliberate or careless. Given that the burden of proving a qualifying breach as deliberate or reckless rests with the insurer, it would be extremely difficult – if not impossible – for the insurer to demonstrate that the AI had been programmed to intentionally or recklessly mislead it. Insurers typically lack access to the internal workings or programming of third-party AI systems, making such evidentiary burdens impractical. As a result, under the existing regime, insurers might well be limited to arguing that a qualifying breach was merely careless, while also proving that they would not have entered into the contract had the correct information been disclosed. While this may suffice in certain cases, it leaves a significant evidentiary and legal gap where AI is used autonomously on behalf of consumers in responding to questions at the formation stage. Although it remains unclear how frequently consumers currently rely solely on AI to answer underwriting questions, the increasing prevalence of such practices might call for legislative attention. A prospective solution may lie in statutory reform: for example, introducing a rebuttable presumption that any misleading information provided by AI on

[21] CIDRA 2012, Schedule 1, para 6.

[22] See CIDRA 2012, Schedule 1, paras 7 and 8.

[23] That said, there might always be a possibility of a recourse action against the manufacturer by the consumer, subject to various legal tort principles, but these have been discussed elsewhere in the book. See our discussion on tort-related issues in Chapter 4.

behalf of an assured is to be treated as a 'careless' misrepresentation for the purposes of CIDRA 2012. This would provide legal clarity while still allowing insurers to take action where there is genuine prejudice.

iv. Inducement

In order to be able to seek a remedy under the CIDRA 2012 regime, as discussed above, the insurer must establish on the balance of probabilities that had it known the true state of facts, it would not have entered into the contract at all or would have done so only on different terms.[24] This point reflects the position that common law arrived at in *Pan Atlantic Insurance Co Ltd v Pine Top Insurance Co Ltd*[25] and effectively introduces a test of inducement. Such an inquiry is a hypothetical one and depends on what the underwriter in question would have done had the risk been represented accurately.[26]

When the underwriter is a natural person, to establish inducement the relevant individual is often called to testify what they would have done if the misrepresentation had not been made,[27] it being adequate that the relevant misrepresentation is one of the causes inducing the insurer's conduct (it need not be the sole cause).[28] An interesting question arises as to how an insurer relying on AI to make underwriting decisions will be able to establish inducement. On paper, this presents a significant problem in the absence of clear evidence of what datasets the AI system consulted and how it functioned in reaching the underwriting decision. Machine learning plays a vital role in this process, and such a system relies on algorithms that can learn from examples and improve their performance with more data over time.[29] This is known as 'deep machine learning', which is a branch of machine learning relying on complex statistical models and algorithms with multiple layers of parallel processing that loosely model the way the biological brain works. Such systems are very complex, and there might be difficulties in establishing the nature of an AI model in handling large numbers of heterogenous features.[30] This challenge creates what is referred to in computer science an 'opacity problem'

[24] CIDRA 2012, s 4(1)(b).

[25] [1995] 1 AC 501, [1994] 2 Lloyd's Rep 42.

[26] See, for example, *Axa Versicherung AG v Arab Insurance Group* [2015] EWHC 1929 (Comm), [2016] Lloyd's Rep IR 1 and more recently *ABN Amro Bank NV v Royal and Sun Alliance Insurance plc* [2021] EWHC 442 (Comm), [2021] Lloyd's Rep IR 201.

[27] *Glencore International AG v Alpina Insurance Co* [2002] 2 Lloyd's Rep 591.

[28] *St Paul Fire & Marine Insurance Co (UK) Ltd v McConnell Dowell Contractors Ltd* [1995] 2 Lloyd's Rep 116, 124–25.

[29] See PwC, *Explainable AI: Driving Business Value through Greater Understanding* (2018) https://www.pwc.co.uk/audit-assurance/assets/explainable-ai.pdf.

[30] J Burrell, 'How the Machine "Thinks": Understanding Opacity in Machine Learning Algorithms' (2016) 2 *Big Data Society* 1 at 5. See also W Knight, 'The Dark Secret of the Heart of AI' (2017) 120 *MIT Technology Review* 54, 56 and the Geneva Association, *Promoting Responsible Artificial Intelligence in Insurance* (2020) https://www.genevaassociation.org/sites/default/files/research-topics-document-type/pdf_public/ai_in_insurance_web_0.pdf.

(also known as 'black box problem'), and it has been suggested that it might be impossible even for the programmer to work out why a particular decision was made.[31]

We do not believe, however, that the opacity issue creates an insurmountable problem here. Although a human underwriter could not give evidence about a non-human underwriter's decision process, experts could clearly testify on how they would expect a system of that nature to perform (considering especially the factors the system was programmed to take into account). Further, despite the subjective nature of the inducement test, the courts have recognised that in some instances an inference of inducement might be drawn.[32] It is therefore likely that courts, adopting a pragmatic stance on the matter, will allow an inference of inducement to be drawn relying on the expert evidence, unless of course a statutory amendment is made to recognise this possibility in cases where underwriting decisions are made solely by AI systems. Of course, rather than relying on the courts to adopt a pragmatic approach, a more effective and transparent solution would be to amend CIDRA 2012 to clarify that, in cases where underwriting decisions are made by AI systems, the element of inducement may be established through expert testimony. Such a statutory amendment would offer welcome clarity and align the law with evolving industry practices. However, even with such clarification, the increased reliance on AI in underwriting is likely to transform litigation over inducement into a contest between competing AI experts.

Needless to say, we do not expect any difficulty in terms of establishing inducement when final underwriting decisions are made by a partly automated underwriting system, given that in such a case human underwriters would still be in a position to give evidence in court.

v. Potential Role of the Insurer's Duty of Good Faith?

CIDRA 2012 is silent with regard to the pre-contractual duty of the insurers. Some commentators have argued that the general duty of good faith, which has been encapsulated in section 17 of the MIA 1906,[33] should be expanded to require insurers who rely on underwriting conducted through big data analytics and AI

[31] Burrell, ibid, 3–5.

[32] See, for example, *Aldridge v Liberty Mutual Insurance Europe Ltd* [2016] EWHC 3037 (Comm), [28]–[29]. In *Laker Vent Engineering Ltd v Templeton Insurance Co Ltd* [2008] EWHC B6 (QB), [142] HHJ Hegarty QC accepted that actual inducement could be made out by inference but indicated that he should be 'particularly cautious' before drawing such inference. See also *Cape plc v Iron Traders Employers Insurance Association Ltd* [1999] EWHC 840 (Comm), [2004] 2 Lloyd's Rep IR 75.

[33] In its amended version, this section stipulates: 'A contract of marine insurance is a contract based on utmost good faith.' Provisions of the MIA 1906 on good faith have historically been applied by courts to all types of insurance contracts, unless a particular issue is regulated specifically by specialist legislation (eg CIDRA 2012), through common law. See, for example, the comments of Lord Hobhouse in *Manifest Shipping Co Ltd v Uni Polaris Shipping Co Ltd* [2001] UKHL 1, [2003] 1 AC 469, [47].

to explain all risk-related information, to have an actuarial basis for the use of that information, and to identify which risk factors have a particular bearing on the price of a particular risk (essentially to explain to consumers how they have reached an underwriting decision and what information they hold in relation to them).[34] As attractive as this might sound, we do not believe that the good faith doctrine should have a role to play in this context. Several reasons could be put forward to support this stance.

First, as mentioned before, such AI systems are by nature very complex, making it difficult even for programmers to unravel them and explain how they have reached a particular underwriting decision. In fact, computer scientists warn that in most systems it is not usually possible to interpret and explain the role of the different variables.[35] That being the case, one might forcefully query how realistic it is to expect insurers to be able to explain to every assured the weight of the personal data used in the decision-making process. Secondly, expecting insurers to make full disclosure on how an AI system is developed and operated (assuming that this is technically possible) might pose risks to the security of such system by making it more vulnerable to a cyber-attack. Lastly, in our opinion, the task of ensuring that what is not understandable for consumers works fairly and is used in their best interest should be delegated to the supervisory authorities and is not a legitimate function of insurance contract law.

Another related question is whether the doctrine of good faith could be used as the basis of bringing an action against insurers who use for underwriting purposes an AI system which was sub-standard and might for that reason have a detrimental effect on consumers. Again, we see this as a matter that the supervisory bodies need to deal with. This risk can be reduced significantly if guidelines are produced by such bodies setting out what the minimum expectations of such systems are; in addition, regular audits could be carried out.[36] At this juncture, it should be mentioned that the Law Commissions did not envisage that the good faith doctrine would have such a role. In their view, the doctrine should continue

[34] B McGurk, *Data Profiling and Insurance Law* (Oxford, Hart Publishing, 2019) 158–64.

[35] See the Geneva Association, *Promoting Responsible Artificial Intelligence in Insurance* (2020) https://www.genevaassociation.org/sites/default/files/research-topics-document-type/pdf_public/ai_in_insurance_web_0.pdf.

[36] There is at the moment no regulatory mechanism in place that requires insurers utilising such systems to adhere to any particular standards. However, just like other retailers and financial institutions, insurers are expected to comply with a new consumer duty when selling new and existing products and services to their customers since 31 July 2023. This duty has been introduced by the Financial Conduct Authority (FCA) with an amendment to existing Principles for Business and intends to impose a higher standard of behaviour for firms interacting directly or indirectly with retail customers. This duty does not impose an obligation on the FCA to run audits on insurance companies using AI and algorithms as part of the risk-rating process, but it enables the FCA to investigate any allegation of breach and accordingly, in case of a complaint, inform the consumer that such an audit might be conducted. It should be noted that the duty does not provide consumers with a private right of action, but enables the FCA to issue fines against insurers and secure redress for consumers who have suffered harm through an insurer's breach of this duty.

as an interpretative principle but should not in itself give either party a cause of action.[37]

B. Business Insurance Contracts

i. The Legal Framework

This area of law has been reformed with the introduction of the Insurance Act 2015 in force since 12 August 2016 and applying to all contracts of insurance concluded on or after that date.[38] The Act retains some of the law originally encapsulated by sections 17–21 of the MIA 1906,[39] codifies some of the developments since the enactment of the 1906 Act and also introduces some novel concepts.[40] The terminology is also amended, the assured's pre-contractual duty of good faith being rechristened the 'duty to make a fair presentation'. The 2015 Act sets a default scheme for business assureds, but it is also possible to contract out of this regime by following transparency requirements stipulated in sections 16 and 17.

ii. The Duty of Disclosure – Future in Doubt in the Light of AI and Big Data?

Given insurers' ability to gather extensive information regarding any risk proposed through the big data resources at their disposal and to use AI to correlate such data and acquire a superior understanding of the likelihood of loss, some might question whether the traditional justification for the assured's duty of disclosure (information asymmetry)[41] still applies in modern times.[42] Nevertheless, under the Insurance Act 2015 regime, a would-be business assured (or its intermediaries)

[37] Law Commission and Scottish Law Commission, *Insurance Contract Law: Business Disclosure: Warranties, Insurer's Remedies for Fraudulent Claims; and Late Payment*, Cm 8898/2014, para 30.8.

[38] Insurance Act 2015, s 22.

[39] These provisions were largely a codification of common law principles relating to marine insurance. For example, s 17 is a reinstatement of the common law rule in *Carter v Boehm* (1766) 3 Burr 1905.

[40] The 2015 Act also reforms the traditional warranty regime and sets out remedies available when a fraudulent insurance claim is advanced. For a comprehensive analysis of the changes introduced by the Act, see M Clarke and B Soyer (eds), *The Insurance Act 2015 – A New Regime for Commercial and Marine Insurance Law* (Oxford, Informa Law, 2017).

[41] Famously, Lord Mansfield in *Carter v Boehm* (1766) 3 Burr 1905, 1907, said: 'Insurance is a contract based upon speculation. The special facts, upon which the contingent chance is to be computed, lie mostly in the knowledge of the insured only; the underwriter trusts to his representation and proceeds upon the confidence that he does not keep back and circumstance in his knowledge.'

[42] Some commentators do not believe that there is a need for the assured to make any disclosure to the insurer. For example, B McGurk, *Data Profiling and Insurance Law* (Oxford, Hart Publishing, 2019) 163, observes that, in the current global transacting environment, 'insurers are increasingly originators of risk related information about the assured' and accordingly, with ever increasing frequency are 'stepping into the shoes of the assured in identifying and modelling risk factors which they consider apply to the assured'.

is still required to disclose every material circumstance[43] which it knows or ought to know, or failing that to provide disclosure which gives the insurer sufficient information to put a prudent insurer on notice that it needs to make further enquiries.[44] The exceptions to the duty of disclosure under section 3(5) of the Insurance Act 2015 are broadly the same as the exceptions under the repealed section 18(3) of the MIA 1906.[45]

We do not believe that it would be wise to abolish the duty of disclosure in business insurance contracts even though it is undeniable that insurers in recent years have acquired tools, including AI, that enable them to capture and analyse vastly more data on the proposed risk. This is for several reasons. First, commercial risks (especially those that are introduced to the market from other jurisdictions) are more heterogenous. For example, in the context of marine insurance a shipowning company with its headquarters in one jurisdiction and a fleet involved primarily in the bulk trade might present a very different risk profile to another company with headquarters in a different jurisdiction and involved solely in the container trade. Similarly, despite the potentialities of AI, some business assureds will still present unusual or specialist risks which makes it impossible for insurers to lead the disclosure process in the way they are now expected to do as regards consumer assureds.

Secondly, owing to geographical, cultural and practical factors there remains a significant amount of data that is primarily in the domain of the assured and difficult for insurers to reach and comprehend despite advances in technology. And thirdly, although insurers might have access to an increased number of datasets, there might be serious constraints in utilising them in a meaningful way as part of the underwriting process owing to the presence of older, legacy information technology systems which are often not recorded in an easily interrogable form for consideration for future use.[46]

iii. Knowledge of the Insurer

Like its predecessor, the MIA 1906,[47] the Insurance Act 2015 introduces a limitation on the scope of disclosure that is expected of the assured at the pre-contractual stage. By virtue of section 3(5)(b)–(d) of the Act, the assured is not obliged to disclose material circumstances to the insurer if the insurer knows or

[43] Materiality in this context has been defined in s 7(3) of the Insurance Act 2015 in the following fashion: 'A circumstance or representation is material if it would influence the judgment of a prudent insurer in determining whether to take the risk and, if so on what terms.'

[44] Section 3(4) of the Insurance Act 2015.

[45] In the absence of inquiry, the duty of fair presentation does not require the assured to disclose circumstances if (a) it diminishes the risk; (b) the insurer knows it; (c) the insurer ought to know it; (d) the insurer is presumed to know it; or (e) if it is something as to which the insurer waives information.

[46] See *Artificial Intelligence Applications in Financial Services* (New York, Marsh & McLennen, 2019) 28.

[47] In the case of marine insurance. Other insurance was governed by the common law, but this largely reflected the position in the MIA 1906.

ought to know, or is presumed to know, the relevant circumstances. The key provision in the Act is section 5, which is designed to define the scope of the insurer's knowledge.[48] This section reads:

(1) For the purposes of section 3(5)(b), an insurer knows something only if it is known to one or more of the individuals who participate on behalf of the insurer in the decision whether to take the risk, and if so on what terms (whether the individual does so as the insurer's employee or agent, as an employee of the insurer's agent or in any other capacity).

(2) For the purposes of section 3(5)(c), an insurer ought to know something only if—

  (a) an employee or agent of the insurer knows it, and ought reasonably to have passed on the relevant information to an individual mentioned in subsection (1), or
  (b) the relevant information is held by the insurer and is readily available to an individual mentioned in subsection (1).

(3) For the purposes of section 3(5)(d), an insurer is presumed to know—

  (a) things which are common knowledge, and
  (b) things which an insurer offering insurance of the class in question to insureds in the field of activity in question would reasonably be expected to know in the ordinary course of business.

In a case where underwriting decisions are taken by AI with the system trawling through various databases and sources by making full use of big data analytics, to what extent can we assume that information that such systems has access to could be deemed to be information that is known – or ought to be known or is presumed to be known – by the insurer so that there is no need to disclose such information on the part of the assured? This is an intriguing question and the language of section 5 of the Insurance Act 2015 does not assist much.

If AI is taking underwriting decisions by using the information obtained from datasets and resources (as well as information provided by the assured), this could not, it seems, be deemed to be information that the insurer knows under section 5(1), given that this section refers to the knowledge of a human agent (ie an individual) regarding the proposed risk. In a case where no human agent participates in the decision-making process, it is very unlikely that the information that the system might have access to could be attributed to the insurer, as such information is not within the contemplation of any individual as required by that provision.

Alternatively, could the information that AI potentially has access to be deemed to be information that the insurer ought to know under section 5(2) of the Insurance Act 2015? This is also rather problematic considering the manner

[48] There is a significant difference between the Insurance Act 2015 and the MIA 1906 in this context. Under the 1906 Act, what ought to have been known to the insurer were matters that were known to him 'in the ordinary course of business' (s 19(3)(b)). Section 5 of the Insurance Act 2015, on the other hand, defines the insurer's constructive knowledge more simply by reference to the information held by the insurer.

in which the provision has been worded. It is clear that section 5(2)(a) would not respond in a positive fashion to such an inquiry, as the sub-section also assumes that underwriting decisions are taken by human agents; so the insurer is deemed to know circumstances only if a human agent in the possession of that information ought to have passed that information to another individual taking part in the underwriting process. In similar fashion, section 5(2)(b) would probably make no difference, as it refers to 'information held by the insurer' being readily available to an individual participating in the underwriting process on behalf of the insurer. Two difficulties would emerge if one attempted to apply this provision in the context of underwriting decisions taken by AI systems. The first problem is the fact that the relevant provision seems to refer to information that is held within the insurer's organisation, such as the insurer's electronic records. Therefore, if the AI system has the capacity to search more widely, for example by looking into external or public databases that it has access to, it would be very hard to sustain an argument that the information kept on those databases was information held by the insurer itself.[49] More fundamentally, section 5(2)(b) refers to information that is readily available to human agents who are in a position to take underwriting decisions. Therefore, this section also does not envisage a situation where underwriting decisions are taken by the AI system on behalf of the insurer. It would require a very creative judicial re-writing of this section to stretch its application to cases where underwriting decisions are taken by AI systems utilising the data provided and acquired from various sources.

The truth of the matter is that the prospect of non-human agents making underwriting decisions was not contemplated at the time when the rules about the insurer's actual and constructive knowledge were developed by the Law Commissions and incorporated as part of section 5 of what became the Insurance Act 2015. These rules were predominantly intended to require a relevant human underwriter to make a reasonable effort to search such information as was available to them within the insurer's organisation, such as information kept in in-house electronic records.[50] If this section is to apply in cases where underwriting decisions are taken by AI systems, one envisages several problems emerging, as almost in every case where non-disclosure of material circumstances is raised by the insurers, they are likely to face calls for disclosure of the information that AI systems had access to and potentially used in the underwriting process. This

[49] In a different context, it was held by Blair J in *Sea Glory Maritime Co v Al Sagr National Insurance Co (The Nancy)* [2013] EWHC 2116 (Comm), [2014] 1 Lloyd's Rep 14 that the insurer could not be deemed to know information on a database that it had access to unless there were reasons for the underwriter to search such sources. Therefore, the information that is available online does not necessarily give rise to a presumption of knowledge.

[50] See para 64 of the Explanatory Notes to the Insurance Act 2015. This provision was essentially intended to deal with situations where one arm of an insurer was not aware of what the other arm was doing, which raised significant problems in cases like: *London General Insurance Co v General Marine Underwriters' Association* [1921] 1 KB 104; *Malhi v Abbey Life Assurance Co Ltd* [1996] LRLR 237 and *Aldridge v Liberty Mutual Insurance Europe Ltd* [2016] EWHC 3037 (Comm).

requirement will pose significant technical issues not only due to the opacity problem such systems suffer from, as highlighted above,[51] but also it is unlikely that such a system will record all databases it has consulted in rating an individual risk. It is possible that the AI system might have known far more information than it records as knowing and using in rating a risk. The probable cause of this opacity is the system drawing inferences as a result of machine learning from the data it had access to.[52]

There are two plausible ways to deal with this problem and address the issue of constructive knowledge of the insurer when underwriting decisions are made by non-human agents. One would be explicitly to exclude the application of section 5 of the Insurance Act 2015 in such instances. Another would be to define how this provision should apply by introducing a statutory presumption that an insurer knows (or, as the case may be, ought to know) any information that an AI-equipped information system would reasonably be expected to gather, if such a system were used. Both options admittedly present significant challenges. The first option gives rise to legitimate concerns that it could grant insurers an unfair advantage, allowing them to leverage any available data in risk assessment without at the same time being deemed to have constructive knowledge of that information. Conversely, however, the second option is also problematic because AI systems have not yet matured sufficiently to enable clear specification of which information should be attributed to the insurer and which should not. At this stage, we believe the most appropriate approach is to assume that section 5 is unlikely to apply when underwriting decisions are made solely by AI systems, while reserving the right to revisit this debate as AI capabilities and solutions to opacity issues become better understood. Regardless of the path chosen, legislative intervention will be necessary to provide clarity and consistency.

iv. Materiality and Inducement

To establish breach of the duty of fair presentation of the risk, an insurer needs to establish that the circumstance or representation is material[53] and that it has been a factor inducing it to enter into the contract.

Materiality has been defined by the Insurance Act 2015 as referring to a circumstance or a representation that 'would influence the judgment of a prudent insurer in determining whether to take the risk, and, if so, on what

[51] It needs to be borne in mind that big data analytics adopt techniques and methods that involve processing data with high volume, velocity and variety. See R Kitchin, *Data Revolution: Big Data, Open Data, Data Infrastructure and Their Consequences* (London, Sage Publications, 2014) 68.

[52] JM Skopek, 'Big Data Epistemology and Its Implications for Precision Medicine and Privacy' in IG Chen et al (eds), *Big Data Health and Bioethics* (Cambridge, Cambridge University Press, 2008) 30; L Edwards and M Veale, 'Slave to the Algorithm? Why A "Right to Explanation" Is Probably Not the Remedy You Are Looking For?' (2017) 16 *Duke Law & Technology Review* 18, 25.

[53] See Insurance Act 2015, ss 3(4)(a), 7(5) and (6).

terms'.[54] Traditionally, the issue of materiality is tested by taking into account the actions of a hypothetical prudent insurer when assessing the risk,[55] the main task of the courts being to determine whether such an insurer would have liked to know the relevant circumstances or representation when evaluating a risk of that nature.[56] An interesting question arises as to how this can be applied to underwriting decisions taken by AI systems. In that case, would materiality be judged by taking into account what a prudent human underwriter in that situation would have liked to be informed of in assessing the risk, or should it now be considered from the perspective of the kind of cognitive technology that would normally and reasonably be used to evaluate a risk of that nature? The latter seems to be the logical position, although the inquiry will possibly also involve the views and perceptions of human agents on the risk concerned. There is nothing in the Insurance Act 2015 militating against this stance,[57] and the fact that the test is an objective one would allow courts to engage in a factual inquiry as to what factors an AI program of this nature would consider if engaged in deciding whether to underwrite a similar risk. There is no doubt that technical expertise would be essential as part of this process, and evidence would need to be provided by the insurer (possibly with the assistance of the developer of any AI program it used) as to how such systems were designed to function when undertaking risk assessment. Inevitably, reference would also need to be made to underwriting practices adopted in the sector, such as physical and moral hazards considered for that kind of risk, that would prompt a prudent programmer of an AI system to design their program to take into account when underwriting such insurance risks. Assuming that such systems will be programmed to take into account the risk considerations of human agents, it will be inevitable that the input of human agents would still be needed in any inquiry about the materiality of certain facts and representations.

While we have maintained that the issue of materiality could be addressed by the judiciary, there is considerable merit in contemplating the introduction of a statutory clarification stipulating that, where underwriting decisions are made by AI systems, due regard must be given to the information such systems would reasonably be expected to consider.

[54] Insurance Act 2015, s 7(3).

[55] *Pan Atlantic Insurance Co Ltd v Pine Top Insurance Co Ltd* [1995] 1 AC 501, [1994] 2 Lloyd's Rep 42. The circumstances not disclosed or the misrepresentation need not be decisive.

[56] In *Axa Versicherung AG v Arab Insurance Group* [2015] EWHC 1929 (Comm), [2016] Lloyd's Rep IR 1, Males J summarised the legal position in the following fashion, [115]: 'Whether a circumstance or a representation is material is a question of fact, the question is objective, in the sense that what matters is the judgment of a prudent insurer and not that of the particular insurer … Materiality therefore covers a wide spectrum, from matters which (if disclosed) would mean that no prudent insurer would under any circumstances have anything to do with the proffered risk to matters which the prudent insurer would wish to take into account but which would ultimately make no difference to what he would actually do.'

[57] The Act provides examples of matters that may be material in s 7(4) but these are for illustrative purposes.

When it comes to inducement, as discussed above,[58] the matter might be slightly more problematic owing to the subjective nature of the test, but there is nothing in law preventing a human agent from adducing evidence to demonstrate that the system was programmed to reject the risk and/or charge a higher premium for the policy or agree to other terms or conditions to the policy, had it been provided with the full or accurate information.

It needs to be stressed that when AI and big data analytics are utilised by insurers in rating risks, the insurers view these hard-headedly as useful tools designed to provide optimum risk assessment for them. Therefore, it is highly likely that such AI tools will aim to deliver the underwriting objectives of the insurance company utilising them. Hence, we still expect evidence on materiality and inducement to be provided by human agents explaining how they would expect an intelligent machine to behave in various circumstances.

v. The Insurer's Duty of Good Faith

Given that section 17 of the MIA 1906 was drafted broadly, indicating that both parties to an insurance contract are under a duty of good faith, it is worth examining whether this provision could play a role in protecting the interests of the assured when underwriting decisions are taken by AI systems. Prior to the reform introduced by the Insurance Act 2015, even though it was recognised that section 17 could potentially be relevant in this context,[59] the doctrine as far as it related to the pre-contractual stage was not fully developed, mainly because the statutory remedy of 'avoidance' was regarded as one-sided in any case, and not as really providing any tangible benefit for the assured.[60] However, now that the Insurance Act 2015 has removed the remedy of 'avoidance' from the equation, does this give a new lease of life to the doctrine at the pre-contractual stage?

One can see a role for the doctrine in some instances. Imagine, for example, an assured providing some important new information regarding the risk to the underwriter, or some information being obtained by sensor devices (eg telematics or health monitoring devices) utilised by the insurer which would have been in the policyholder's favour in rating the risk; and suppose further that the insurer's AI system fails to take that information into account at the renewal stage. In such instance, it could forcefully be argued that the insurer is in breach of the duty of good faith, taking into account the opinions expressed in *Drake Insurance plc v Provident Insurance plc*[61] to the effect that it is necessary to give wider effect to the

[58] See pp 138–139.

[59] Lord Mansfield in *Carter v Boehm* (1766) 3 Burr 1905, 1906, famously said: 'The policy would equally be void against the underwriter if he concealed, as, if he insured a ship on her voyage, which he privately knew to be arrived: and an action would lie to recover the premium.'

[60] See, for example, *Banque Financière de la Cité v Western Insurance Co Ltd* [1990] 1 QB 665 (CA); [1991] AC 249 (HL).

[61] [2003] EWCA Civ 1834, [2004] QB 601, [89] (per Rix LJ).

doctrine of good faith and recognise that its impact may demand that ultimately regard must be had to a concept of proportionality implicit in fair dealing.

That said, there would be two obstacles facing an assured who is in this predicament. The first problem is practical. It is hard to see how an assured who has been given a renewal or contract variation quote would ever know that the AI system had failed to take into account information that would have militated in their favour. And even assuming that somehow it found out, the next problem is what remedy this section provides in its favour. The Law Commissions, in their final Report on Insurance Contract Law published before the introduction of the Insurance Act 2015,[62] suggested that the concept of utmost good faith encapsulated by section 17 would serve a subsidiary principle of interpretation rather than create substantive rights and duties. However, this statement fails to take into account the fact that common law judges often have made available remedies in insurance law other than avoidance in cases of breach of the good faith doctrine, such as inability to exercise rights under the contract,[63] reduction of liability, or the loss of the right to rely on a limit of liability.[64] The removal of the remedy stipulated in the Act specifically does not alter this fact. Also, the judgment in *Banque Financière de la Cité v Western Insurance Co Ltd*,[65] which seems to have rebuffed an attempt to invoke a breach of the duty of utmost good faith as a breach of contract sounding in damages in a case where the assured deliberately failed to inform the underwriters, seems to be based on a misapprehension that the duty of good faith has origins in equity.[66] This is not the case.[67] That decision seems at best to suggest that damages are not available for breach of good faith where the breach lies in non-disclosure. To us, it does not rule out damages for breaches of other aspects of the duty of good faith, such as here when the AI system utilised by the insurer makes an error in assessing the risk appropriately.[68] It is, therefore, suggested that regardless of the comments the Law Commissions made regarding the role of the doctrine in insurance law, the removal of reference to any specific remedy, coupled with

[62] *Insurance Contract Law: Business Disclosure; Warranties; Insurer's Remedies for Fraudulent Claims and Late Payment*, Cm 8898/2014, para 30.22.

[63] *Groom v Crocker* [1939] 1 KB 194 and *Drake Insurance plc v Provident Insurance plc* [2003] EWCA Civ 1834, [2004] QB 601.

[64] *Gan Insurance Co Ltd v Tai Ping Insurance Co Ltd* [2001] EWCA Civ 1047, [2001] Lloyd's Rep IR 667.

[65] [1990] 1 QB 665.

[66] P Macdonald-Eggers, 'Remedies for the Failure to Observe the Utmost Good Faith' (2003) *Lloyd's Maritime & Commercial Law Quarterly* 249, 250 and B Soyer, *Marine Insurance Fraud* (Oxford, Informa Law, 2014) 126–27.

[67] Lord Bingham MR in *Cox v Bankside Members Agency Ltd* [1995] CLC 671, 680, commented as follows: 'I cannot for an instant accept [counsel's] suggestion that a breach of this duty [to act with good faith in conducting legal proceedings] by an insurer, once a policy is in force, gives the assured no right other than recession.'

[68] For a comprehensive analysis on the potential role of s 17 of the MIA 1906 in insurance context see B Soyer and A Tettenborn, 'Mapping (Utmost) Good Faith in Insurance Law – Future Conditional?' (2016) 132 *Law Quarterly Review* 618.

the reaffirmation of the underlying nature of insurance contracts as requiring utmost good faith, it is likely that courts will be willing to develop alternative remedies, as they did prior to the law reform. In this context, an assured who succeeds in showing that the AI system has failed to take into account certain conditions at renewal will be able to seek adjustment of the premium accordingly or reversal of the decision not to provide insurance cover.

A more difficult question is whether the duty of good faith would require the insurer to reveal facts it finds out as part of the risk assessment process, especially if the assured is not aware of them and they may be important to it in managing its business affairs. At first sight, one might be tempted to argue that this is an instance where the insurer's duty of good faith might intervene and require the insurer to reveal such matters to the assured.[69] However, how realistic would it be to expect an AI system to explain in a coherent manner the reasons behind an underwriting decision, let alone reveal other factors that it found out that it might deem relevant to the business affairs of the assured? Furthermore, would it be appropriate for the duty of good faith to impose an obligation on a party, in this case the insurer, to provide advice and support to its counterparty, the assured, in running its business affairs? It is our opinion that in the context of business insurance contracts, the doctrine should only intervene in extreme circumstances where one of the contracting parties clearly abuses its position or uses its contractual rights to the detriment of the other party.[70] This is not the case in this instance. However, there is another complication here. In a case where the risk is written by a human agent who notices that the potential assured is operating under a misapprehension as to the nature of the risk or recoverability under the contract of insurance, there are dicta suggesting that the duty of good faith requires the insurer to bring this to the attention of the assured.[71] Would this be the case if underwriting decisions are taken by non-human agents (AI systems)? We do not think so, mainly because it would be

[69] In *Banque Financière de la Cité v Western Insurance Co Ltd* [1990] 1 QB 665 (CA), Slade LJ indicated that insurers must disclose all facts known to them which are material either to the 'nature of the risk' or 'the recoverability of a claim under the policy' so that the policyholder can decide whether or not to enter into the policy. As such, his Lordship introduces a test of materiality in this context.

[70] It is worth noting that the duty of good faith has been used only in a handful of cases to imply a term into the contract of insurance, usually when a discretion is conferred upon one of the parties by the contract. See, for example, *Socimer Inter Bank Ltd v Standard Bank London Ltd* [2008] EWCA Civ 116, [2008] 1 Lloyd's Rep 550 and *Paragon Finance plc v Nash* [2021] EWCA Civ 116, [2008] 1 Lloyd's Rep 558.

[71] Parker LJ, in *Container Transport International Inc v Oceanus Mutual Underwriting Association (Bermuda) Ltd* [1984] 1 Lloyd's Rep 476, 512, said: '… it is necessary to mention at this stage that the duty imposed by s 17 goes, in my judgment, further than merely to require fulfilment of the duties under the succeeding sections. If, for example, the insurer shows interest in circumstances which are not material within s 18, s 17 requires the assured to disclose them fully and fairly. Again, if the assured or his broker realized in the course of negotiations that the insurer had made a serious arithmetical mistake or was proceeding upon a mistake of fact with regard to past experience he would, under s 17, be obliged to draw attention to the matter. It would, and this was accepted by the respondents, be the plainest breach of the duty under s 17 not to do so.'

unrealistic to expect a system that is programmed to look for correlations in the data that it has in its use to be able to have a cognitive appreciation of the mental state of the assured engaging with the system.

II. Use of AI in the Claims Context

One area that has attracted significant attention from the insurance sector is the potential to use AI and data analytics to detect fraud and manage the claims process,[72] leading several insurtech companies to work to develop such systems with a view to offering them to insurance companies. With regard to the former, AI-driven analytics of big data could give insights from textual and unstructured information, such as claims applications, assessor notes, social media searches and the like. This may help to detect anomalies and patterns of conduct indicative of fraud.[73] More sophisticated AI tools could employ machine learning to review claim datasets by engaging in predictive modelling. This kind of modelling has the capability to match the variables in every claim against the profiles of past claims that were fraudulent, the network of people that the claimant is associated with (as discerned from social media, credit reference agencies, etc) and partner agencies involved in the claim (eg vehicle repairers who may have, for example, been involved in previous exaggerated claims), so that a claim can be flagged up for further investigation. In terms of the claim management process, machine and deep learning techniques can be invoked to extract information from documents and pictures. For example, in motor insurance, insurers can use an artificial intelligence platform that utilises a Convolutional Neural Network (CNN)[74] to identify damage to a car based on videos and images. Once the model is trained for a particular jurisdiction, vehicle type, and features, it can accurately estimate the extent of the damage. Based on the image, the system can also validate whether or not the image is actually of the insured vehicle, thus further promoting fraud detection.[75]

In this section, we discuss whether the use of such tools might create unforeseen legal difficulties. As we understand it, at the moment the tools developed and

[72] For an illuminating analysis on how AI could transform the claims process see Insurance Institute, *AI and Big Data – Implications for the Insurance Industry in Canada* (2021) and The Geneva Association, *Big Data and Insurance: Implications for Innovation, Competition and Privacy* (2018).

[73] The use of such devices might create data protection issues, especially in the context of consumer insurance. Hence, such policies invariably contain consent clauses that give insurance companies the right to the collection, use, and analysis of personal data, including claims history, policy information, and relevant external data sources, for the purpose of detecting, investigating, and preventing insurance fraud.

[74] CNN is a deep learning algorithm which can take in an input image, assign importance (learnable weights and biases) to various aspects/objects in the image, and differentiate between them.

[75] See AR Saputro et al, 'Analysis of Deep Neural Networks for Automobile Insurance Claim Prediction' (2019) *Communications in Computer and Information Science* 114.

put into use aim to assist human agents in claims departments to make decisions. In other words, a fraudulent pattern is identified, a human agent is accordingly informed by the system, but the ultimate decision whether to reject the claim on that basis lies in the hands of the human agent. Thus here the insurer will be fully responsible for the decision taken, regardless of the fact that it is wholly or partly based on the advice provided by the AI system.

This immediately raises an important question: what is the legal position of an assured if a legitimate claim has been rejected due to the malfunction of the AI system (for example, a claim wrongly flagged as possibly fraudulent by an algorithm owing to the use of misleading and/or inaccurate proxies used by the system)? Would the assured have a claim against the insurer? Our view is that it is highly unlikely that the duty of good faith could be used as a vehicle to substantiate any claim for damages in this instance – not only because the Law Commissions, as discussed earlier, do not view the doctrine as being capable of substantiating any cause of action. However, there are other statutory provisions that might potentially be used here instead. To these we now turn.

First, section 13A of the Insurance Act 2015[76] implies a term into every insurance contract that if the assured makes a claim, the insurer must pay any sums due in respect of the claim within a reasonable time.[77] There can be very little doubt that an insurer by this provision is intended to be liable not only for its own unreasonable foot-dragging, but also for mishaps of algorithms or similar programs it engages in the claim management process, especially in cases where its insistence on relying on the decisions assisted by such systems without further evaluation is the reason for its failure to make timely payment. However, by virtue of section 13A(4), the insurer is not in breach of this implied term if it shows that there were reasonable grounds for disputing the claim and that at the relevant time the dispute was continuing.[78] Therefore, the reliability of the conclusions reached by the AI tool indetecting a fraudulent pattern will be critical in determining whether there were reasonable grounds for the insurance company to insist on not paying the claim.

This is encouraging, but one should not lose sight of the fact that general principles of contract law could potentially add further complications in this

[76] This section was inserted by the Enterprise Act 2016 (ss 28–30).

[77] What is reasonable will depend on all relevant circumstances, especially: (a) the type of insurance; (b) the size and complexity of the claim; (c) compliance with any statutory or regulatory rules or guidance; and (d) factors outside the insurer's control (s 13A(3)). Presumably, in assessing what constitutes a reasonable time for decision-making in the handling of insurance claims, due account should be taken of the insurer's ability to utilise AI or other automated technologies that could reasonably be expected to accelerate the process. Where such tools are available and routinely deployed in the industry, their use (or failure to use them) may be relevant in evaluating whether a delay is justifiable or unreasonable.

[78] These statutory guidelines have been considered recently in *Quadra Commodities SA v XL Insurance and Others* [2022] EWHC 431 (Comm), [2022] 2 Lloyd's Rep 541 and *Delos Shipholding SA v Allianz Global Corporate and Specialty SE (The Win Win)* [2024] EWHC 719 (Comm), [2024] 1 Lloyd's Rep 489.

context. First, the damages must be foreseeable at the time of the contract.[79] In the insurance context, this means what might have been envisaged as a plausible consequence of late payment of claims at the time the relevant policy was taken out. Whilst this might significantly limit claims for late payment under business insurance contracts, as the loss of particular business opportunities only becoming apparent during the currency of the policy is likely to be too remote even if shown to result from late payment, one envisages that in consumer insurance contracts it will be less problematic to show that many financial consequences that emerge from late payment are not too remote. For example, in a case where an insured house is damaged by fire, if delaying payment would mean that the consumer had to find alternative accommodation for longer than initially required for repairs, it is very likely that such expenses will not deemed to be too remote. A second, more difficult issue is whether the assured can be allowed to claim damages for distress caused by late payment. Unlike most Commonwealth jurisdictions, in England and Wales damages for distress resulting from breach of contract are not available on the basis of foreseeability, but only in contracts aimed wholly or partly at protecting peace of mind.[80] It is certainly open to argument that courts should categorise consumer insurance contracts as such, but the matter has not yet been given judicial airing. Thirdly, could it be a defence for insurers if losses are suffered partly because of late payment of insurance monies but partly also because of contributory negligence by the assured? The weight of legal authority indicates that this is irrelevant, as contributory negligence affects contractual duties that parallel tort duties, and it seems that the insurer's duty to pay on time is a purely contractual duty.[81] Nevertheless, this cannot be regarded as entirely beyond doubt in the light of a recent judgment which indicated that it is at least arguable that a contractual duty to pay money within a reasonable time may give rise to liability in tort in the event of negligent late payment.[82] Fourthly, it should be noted that third-party victims who are paid late will not be able to take advantage of section 13A to bring a claim against the insurer.

[79] *Hadley v Baxendale* (1854) 9 Ex 341. An important question arises as to the appropriate standard by which foreseeability should be assessed in the context of AI-assisted claims handling. Specifically, should it be judged from the perspective of a human decision-maker (or corporate entity), or from the internal logic and predictive capacity of the algorithm itself? Given that AI systems are currently used as tools or aids in the decision-making process – and not as autonomous legal actors – it is logical and legally coherent to judge foreseeability from the standpoint of a reasonable human or corporate entity deploying the system. The AI, while sophisticated, lacks agency, intention, and legal personality. As such, liability or accountability for any failure to foresee a particular outcome should rest with those who design, deploy, supervise, or rely upon the system, not the system itself.

[80] See *Johnson v Gore Wood & Co* [2002] 2 AC 1. Also see *Farley v Skinner (No 2)* [2001] UKHL 49, [2002] 2 AC 732, 746 (per Lord Steyn), 752–53 (per Lord Clyde), 757 (per Lord Hutton) and 767 (per Lord Scott).

[81] See *Forsikringsaktieselkapet Vesta v Butcher* [1989] AC 852.

[82] *Equitas Ltd v Walsham Bros & Co Ltd* [2013] EWHC 3264 (Comm), [2014] PNLR 8. It should be emphasised that this point was raised only in passing in the case and does not establish any binding or unassailable precedent on the issue.

Another statutory provision that might be utilised to form the legal basis for an action for damages is section 49 of the Consumer Rights Act 2015.[83] This section provides that every contract to supply a service is to be treated as including a term that the trader must perform the service with reasonable care and skill. There can be little doubt that this provision implies a term within any consumer insurance contract. On that premise, it can hardly be argued that any insurer who relies on the decisions made by a substandard algorithm with regard to claims put forward and fails to evaluate such claims further when irregularities are pointed out by the assured, is performing the service required of him under the contract with reasonable care and skill. However, any claim for damages under this section will also be subject to the limitations mentioned above imposed by the general principles of contract law.

What about instances where the AI system is authorised to manage claims and take decisions (ie to offer a level of indemnity based on the manner in which it assesses the loss emerging)? Imagine, for example, the AI system might be programmed in such a way that when receiving a legitimate claim, it offers to pay the lowest reasonable amount until it receives negative feedback about the offers it makes. It is possible that the system might learn to price claims at the lowest point possible to extract the most from policyholders without negative feedback. At first sight, this scenario looks problematic, but is this process any different than what insurers do when managing claims under traditional policies? A motor insurer who admits liability and makes an offer to the assured to settle the claim of total loss inevitably engages in a process of predicting the market value of the insured car and ultimately aims to settle the claim as cost effectively as possible from its perspective. Is it, therefore, a problem if an algorithm is designed to do the same thing? At the end of the day, the assured is not obliged to accept the settlement offer made and can engage in further negotiations, as most consumers do today under traditional motor insurance policies.

The analysis might differ slightly if in the future the AI tool is entrusted to make an assessment on its own to determine whether the claim submitted is legitimate or not with no involvement of a human agent. Would it be possible in such instance for the assured to claim that the AI tool has inaccurately classified a claim as fraudulent, leading to a delay in payment? We believe that an insurer who relies entirely on an AI tool to make such a finding will be responsible for the errors and/or negligence of the system that it uses.[84] On that basis, it might be open to the assured to claim damages for late payment of claims under section 13A of the Insurance Act 2015 subject to the caveats discussed above.

[83] This is obviously an option open only to those who come under the scope of this Act. This part of the Act applies where there is an agreement between a trader and a consumer for the trader to supply goods, digital content or services, if the agreement is a contract (s 1(1) of the Consumer Rights Act 2015).

[84] This matter has been discussed more comprehensively in Chapter 4 when considering tort law related issues.

III. Use of AI in Offering Dynamic Insurance Coverage

Sensor technology, by enabling continuous monitoring through the mobile network, provides opportunities for insurers to use various technological devices to obtain real-time data on the subject-matter of insurance. For example, the use of telematics devices enables insurers to gather dynamic information regarding the driving habits and style of the assured as well as determining with precision how much the insured vehicle is used and in what geographical limits. The AI tools, by using this dynamic information obtained, could adjust conditions of cover, including taking decisions to cancel the cover.[85] Such technology could be used as part of medical or life insurance products (eg wearables) that can provide dynamic information to the insurer as to the lifestyle and health of the assured. These devices could have a role to play in the context of commercial insurance as well, and there are plans to use them in the marine insurance sector so that the assured could be charged an additional premium automatically with the aid of an AI tool in a case where the insured vessel operates in certain geographical locations.

When sensor technology is used in this manner in the consumer insurance sector, data protection issues might emerge[86] but, more significantly, individuals might find it difficult to obtain insurance cover at an affordable premium if the data transmitted through such devices contribute to the relevant person being classified as a bad risk.[87] These issues are beyond the scope of this work but it will be briefly discussed in this section whether the use of terms in policies that

[85] See for example, Condition 8, Unacceptable Driving Behaviour, in HughesDrive, an insurance policy which reads: 'You and any additional drivers must observe the law at all times. Poor driving behaviour by any drivers (including driving at speeds which exceed the speed limit for the road on which the car is being driven) will affect your Driving Style Score. If the HughesDrive® App detects that your Driving Style Score is Red, a score less than zero, for any given week, you will receive notification. If, following this notification, you have a Red Driving Style Score for a further week, a final notice will be issued. Three consecutive weeks, or a total of five weekly scores which are Red during the life of your policy (including the week which prompted the original notification), will result in your policy being cancelled in accordance with the cancellation section of the private car policy booklet. In addition to this, we and/or the Insurer reserve the right at any time to provide you with seven days' notice and cancel your policy forthwith in the event that excess speed is detected. You have the right to appeal any decision made concerning your or any named driver's driving behaviour by contacting Hughes Insurance.' A copy of the terms can be found at https://www.hughesinsurance.co.uk/pdf/Telematics-Customer-Terms-Conditions.pdf.

[86] Art 20 of UK GDPR gives the data subject a right to request the data controller to provide him/her with a copy of his/her personal data in a structured, commonly used and machine readable format and also request the data controller to transfer this data to another controller. Therefore, insurers are under an obligation to provide data obtained from telematics devices or wearables with regard to the consumer in question to him/her or other insurance companies if requested by the consumer.

[87] For a detailed analysis on this matter see B Soyer, 'Going Beyond "Risk Solidarity" in Private Insurance: The Changing Function of in Modern Times' in B Soyer and O Gurses, *Insurability of Emerging Risks: Law Theory and Practice* (Oxford, Hart Publishing, 2025) 59.

enable the insurer to cancel the policy when there is a serious alteration of risk, or impose changes in the terms of the policy as a result of the data transmitted by such sensor technologies and processed by AI tools, would pose any difficulty under the current law.

In business insurance contracts, as long as such terms are written in plain language and transparent, it is difficult to see any reason why any restriction on their use could be imposed. Terms designed to prevent the assured from altering the risk have traditionally been incorporated into insurance contracts.[88] For example, in most marine insurance contracts there are warranties to the effect that the insured vessel will not operate in certain parts of the world. So why should things be different if a business assured today warrants that the insured vehicle would not be used at certain times of the day, but an incident occurs and the telematics device confirms that the vehicle was in use during those times?

Conversely, the validity of such terms could be challenged under consumer protection legislation or regulations put in place to regulate the conduct of business of insurers. However, it is highly unlikely that terms used in the market concerning telematics devices or wearables will fall foul of such statutory provisions. For example, a warranty in a telematics motor policy that requires the assured not to drive the insured vehicle when under the influence of alcohol or drugs is unlikely to be viewed as unreasonable under Rule 2.5.1 of ICOBS,[89] affording a consumer assured a right of action for damages for breach of statutory duty under section 138D of the Financial Services and Markets Act 2000. In *Parker v National Union Mutual Insurance Society*,[90] a term that required the assured to provide all written details and documents requested by the insurer was not deemed to be contrary to the rules stated in ICOBS, as it could not be said that such term could give rise to a significant imbalance in the rights of parties, given that the assured alone possessed the information which might be required by the insurer. By analogy, it can be said that a term that puts a restriction on the actions of the assured that are in his/her control is unlikely to give rise to a significant imbalance in the rights of parties. Even a term affording the right to the insurer to cancel the contract if the assured displays unacceptable driving behaviour as captured by a telematics device is unlikely to be viewed as 'unreasonable' given that such a right usually crystallises only after the assured engages in a very unacceptable form of driving, and under such terms it is common to give a notice of cancellation to the assured, and some time before cancellation becomes effective, so that s/he can make alternative insurance arrangements.[91]

[88] See, for example, *Sea Insurance Co v Blogg* [1898] 2 QB 398.

[89] This rule reads: 'A firm must not seek to exclude or restrict, or rely on any exclusion or restriction of, any duty or liability it may have to a customer or other policyholder unless it is reasonable for it to do so and the duty or liability arises other than under the regulatory system.'

[90] [2012] EWHC 2156 (Comm), [2013] Lloyd's Rep IR 253.

[91] For the sake of completeness, it should also be stressed that the authors do not believe that the Consumer Rights Act 2015 alters the position in favour of the assured, either. Even though s 62(1) of the 2015 Act provides that a term that is judged to be unfair will not be binding on consumers,

IV. Conclusions

The analysis carried out in this chapter illustrates that when AI systems are entrusted to take decisions on behalf of the insurers or they operate with other disruptive technologies (eg sensor technology) to broaden the scope of insurance coverage, from the perspective of insurance law some difficulties are likely to emerge. However, we do not think these difficulties are insurmountable, and several solutions have been offered throughout the chapter. Below is a summary of our main recommendations:

If underwriting decisions are taken by AI systems, both in consumer and business insurance, there is a need to clarify how 'inducement' could be established when the risk is not fairly presented to the insurer. We believe that the sensible way to do this is to allow expert evidence to be provided by human agents as to how the system is expected to function. Judicial pragmatism could solve this issue, but a statutory clarification is probably the best way forward.

Given the objective nature of the inquiry, in business insurance contracts we do not expect any difficulty in proving materiality in the way it is currently framed by the Insurance Act 2015.[92] However, there is a persuasive argument for legislative intervention to clarify that, where underwriting is conducted by or through AI-driven systems, the standard of reasonableness should reflect the types of information such systems ought, in the ordinary course, to be designed to process and evaluate.

In business insurance, when underwriting decisions are taken by AI systems, there will be a difficulty in establishing what the insurer knows or ought to know. This is significant, as such information and circumstances do not need to be disclosed by the assured and it is an undeniable fact that AI systems with the aid of

s 64(1) clearly states that a term of a consumer contract may not be assessed for fairness 'if it specifies the main subject matter of the contract, or if the assessment concerns the appropriateness of the price payable under the contract by comparison with the goods, digital content or services supplied under it' as long as this term is 'transparent and prominent to an average consumer'. When this section is read in conjunction with the explanatory notes that accompanied the EU legislation forming its origins (this section replaces relevant parts of the Unfair Terms in Consumer Contracts Regulations 1999, which were designed to implement the EEC Unfair Consumer Contract Terms Directive 93/13/EEC, into English law) and the reasoning of English courts on the matter (*Parker v National Union Mutual Insurance Society* [2012] EWHC 2156 (Comm), [2013] Lloyd's Rep IR 253), it is strongly arguable that any term in an insurance contract excluding or restricting the scope of the cover will not be subject to the fairness test referred to in s 62(1) of the Consumer Rights Act 2015 as long as it is transparent and brought to the attention of an average consumer. This will certainly be true for a term in a consumer insurance motor policy that affords a remedy for the insurer in a case where telematics devices confirm unacceptable (dangerous) driving practice demonstrated by the consumer for a sustained period of time. Ultimately, insurance cover here is offered on the basis that the risk will be retained at a particular level (ie the assured will not alter the risk by engaging in unacceptable and/or dangerous driving behaviour during the currency of the policy). If the assured acts contrary to this term, by virtue of the relevant term the process of cancellation commences. This is a very clear indication that the relevant clause is one that defines or circumscribes the insured risk and ultimately the liability of the insurer, so it is highly unlikely that it needs to be subjected to the 'fairness' test stipulated in s 62.

[92] It is worth noting that 'materiality' is no longer a requirement under CIDRA 2012.

big data analytics could go through a significant amount of data. As it is currently worded, the relevant statutory provision (section 5 of the Insurance Act 2015) is not capable of providing a satisfactory answer to this question. We believe that unless the relevant provision is altered, insurers could not be imputed with knowledge of the sheer amount of data that an AI system would go through in rating a risk proposed. This matter will need to be considered when we have better understanding of the capability of AI systems in data assessment and accuracy of reporting of the datasets they search. There may be a case to suggest that the duty of disclosure in business insurance might need to be reconsidered and perhaps removed in cases where underwriting decisions are left in the domain of AI systems.

It is our view that the duty of good faith might play a limited role here, but we do not envisage it requiring the insurer to disclose factors that the system has taken into consideration when rating insurance risks or other circumstances related to the business affairs of the assured that have been identified as part of this process. We also believe it would be realistic to expect the insurer using such a system for risk rating to be able to spot the potential assured operating under a misapprehension as to the nature of the risk or recoverability under the contract and be able to inform the assured accordingly.

If an AI system is used by an insurer in the claim management process and it wrongly identifies a legitimate claim as fraudulent, this might trigger the application of statutory remedies, such as breach of the implied term to pay claims within a reasonable time, but we do not think there is any need to reconsider any aspect of the current law. We also believe that the insurer itself is responsible for the actions of any AI systems it utilises in the claim management process.

Sensor technology coupled with AI systems is aiding insurers to offer new insurance products. Such products, when used in the consumer field, might create data protection or insurability questions, but we do not think there is any rule of law that will present difficulty to the development of such products as long as the language used in insurance policies is clear and unambiguous.

PART III

The Future

9

Some Conclusions: The Future Directions of Law

I. Our Approach

In the course of this book, we have examined some fundamental principles of English private law, both judge-made and statutory, with a view to picking out the challenges that may arise, and the changes that may need to be made, from the interaction between them and AI and intelligent machines. Our coverage has necessarily been selective: this is not meant to be a textbook on AI and the law generally or to supplant such works as already exist.[1] Our concentration has been particularly on provoking thought about how far rules predicated on human standards, beliefs, intentions and emotions may have to be modified, or understood differently, when AI comes into the picture.

It will be noticed that we have generally avoided advocating radical solutions such as the grant of personality to AI. This is partly because in our view such a grant would make little sense,[2] but also for another reason. This is that it would arguably have made this book redundant. The whole structure of our private (and public) law is based on the participants in it being moral beings (individuals), or bodies set up to achieve purposes set by such beings. It might be possible to have something like law for amoral, if thinking, beings, but it would be so far from any existing conception of private law as to render any attempt to adapt the latter futile.[3]

Our approach has accordingly been slightly eclectic. Some enormously specialised areas, such as intellectual property, we have left out, our feeling being

[1] See for example the excellent M Lavy and M Hervey, *The Law of Artificial Intelligence*, 2nd edn (London, ThomsonReuters, 2024).

[2] A similar point has been made forcefully by S Chesterman, 'Artificial Intelligence and the Limits of Legal Personality' (2020) (2020) 69(4) *International & Comparative Law Quarterly* 822. See also B Brozek and M Jakubiec, 'On the Legal Responsibility of Autonomous Machines' (2017) 25 *Artificial Intelligence and Law* 293, and RD Brown, 'Property Ownership and the Legal Personhood of Artificial Intelligence' (2021) 30 *Information & Communications Technology Law* 208.

[3] R Brownsword in *Technology, Humans and Discontent with Law* (Oxford, Routledge, 2024) expressed a similar sentiment by saying at 210: '… the regulatory approach that eases the way of recognising AI as a legal person represents a threat to human-centric view that treats the dignity of humans – in the sense of the human capacity and determination to do the right thing even when they have the opportunity to do the wrong thing – as being their distinctive characteristic'.

that – with the enormous degree of technicality involved – they are better left to experts in the field. Furthermore, we have concentrated on the areas where we think problems of principle are most likely to arise, such as contract law, agency, tort, unjust enrichment, and equity, rather than attempting to cover the entire legal field in the manner of a catalogue.

One such noticeable omission has been a chapter on commercial law. This is deliberate. True, with commercial law generally, digitisation is clearly of enormous importance: indeed, it is possibly the most important development in the last 30 years or so.[4] However, as regards the impact of AI, it is our view that the issues raised are likely to be fundamentally much the same as those arising in more general subjects like contract, tort, agency, equity and so on. Hence, it is our considered view that the discussions and analyses developed throughout this book may be effectively transposed to other areas of commercial law, as circumstances require.

Instead, what we have done is considered in some little detail the potential impact of AI on insurance law. In our view, this focus is justified for two principal reasons. First, AI is a specifically important feature of insurance law. The insurance sector has been at the forefront of adopting it, particularly – though not exclusively – in the underwriting and claims-processing fields. The gathering, transmission and processing of information, which readily lends itself to AI, is central to whole of insurance law; hence in this part of commercial law in particular it has the potential to affect fundamentally the rights and obligations of underwriter and assured.

Secondly, insurance law and the rights of parties under it are now governed by a relatively well-defined statutory framework, most notably the Consumer Insurance (Disclosure and Representations) Act 2012 and the Insurance Act 2015, both of which were introduced in relatively recent years. Inevitably, questions will arise regarding the effect of AI on the applicability and interpretation of this legislation. Put differently, we believe that the recent introduction of specialised statutory instruments in the field of insurance law provides a valuable opportunity to explore the extent to which these provisions are capable of accommodating the emerging challenges posed by AI. As demonstrated in the relevant chapter, we are of the view that further legislative refinement may, in due course, prove necessary to address the issues that the increasing use of AI – particularly within underwriting processes – could bring to light.

We see this book as very much a work in progress, aimed not only at offering tentative solutions but also at stimulating further discussion. AI, after all, is inherently unpredictable, and any attempt to regulate it must be grounded in a recognition that we should expect the unexpected. There is, therefore, no reason to assume that the ideas advanced here represent the final word on the subject. Nevertheless, we believe that the book establishes a solid foundation upon which

[4] For example, in matters such as payments, letters of credit, finance, commercial paper and forfaiting and carriage of goods, where (sometimes with the aid of legislation such as the Electronic Trade Documents Act 2023) paper has largely been replaced with digital documentation.

policymakers across common law jurisdictions may build when considering the legal reforms necessary to facilitate the smooth integration of AI into diverse commercial contexts. We are also of the view that several of our recommendations, particularly in the fields of contract and tort law, may serve as valuable points of reference for lawmakers in other legal systems. Despite differences in legal traditions, many of the challenges identified in this study are shared across jurisdictions. It should also be remembered that, in confronting the legal issues raised by the advent of AI, all jurisdictions find themselves at a comparable stage of development.

II. AI and the Law of Obligations – Where do We Go from Here?

It is unsurprising that the rapid introduction of intelligent machines into the commercial sphere has generated challenges. Some we have already seen, and it is reasonable to expect a considerable further increase in the number of such issues in the near future.

Our aim in writing this book has been to suggest, if necessary speculatively, how these challenges ought to be addressed. As we have noted, common law courts, consistent with their historical role in responding to novel developments, have demonstrated a capacity to develop solutions to emerging problems – and indeed at times have been compelled to do so. For example, in the absence of assistance from Parliament in the form of specialised legislation, they have had to grapple with the use of AI in contract formation,[5] addressing questions such as whether an AI machine learning program qualifies as a 'computer program'[6] (it does), and whether, for the purposes of intellectual property law, AI can be recognised as an 'inventor'[7] (it cannot).

At various points in this book, we have suggested that in many areas of private law, the impact of AI is something that existing judicial developments can, with a bit of flexibility, accommodate. Where such flexibility is possible, we have argued that courts should be allowed to develop the law organically, in the spirit of 'letting sleeping dogs lie', thereby permitting judicial innovation while preserving overall legal stability.[8] But we have been very aware of the limitations of relying too

[5] *Quoine Pte Ltd v B2C2 Ltd* [2020] SGCA(I) 2, [2020] 2 SLR 20.

[6] *Emotional Perception AI Ltd v Comptroller-General of Patents, Designs & Trade Marks* [2024] EWCA Civ 825, [2025] 1 All ER 790.

[7] *Thaler v Comptroller-General of Patents, Designs & Trade Marks* [2023] UKSC 49, [2024] 2 All ER 527.

[8] In recent years, several other authors have reached a similar conclusion when considering the common law's ability to deal with the emergence of AI and new technologies, See, in particular, SB Norum 'Changing All the Time: AI's Impact on Humanity's Role in Common Law Development and Interpretation' (2023) 103 *Boston University Law Review* 2215.

much on judicial ingenuity and on hopes that this will see us through. Judges are constrained, in a way that legislatures are not, by the need to maintain doctrinal coherence within the legal system; this can make it difficult at times to stretch or reinterpret established doctrines in a way that may be necessary to accommodate AI properly.[9]

Hence, we have also taken the view that leaving the matter to judicial development is not of itself likely to be enough. This is for two reasons. First, in some areas the influx of AI is likely to be so overwhelming, and its effects on some legal doctrines are so subversive, that legislation will be necessary to prevent the law taking a wrong turn. For example, we have suggested that the present stance of the law that there can be no such thing as a negligent machine,[10] and the apparent inapplicability of the doctrine of vicarious liability to AIEMs acting on behalf of human or corporate actors,[11] are inappropriate in the present state of AI development and likely to become more so. Realistically, these positions can only be changed by legislation.

Secondly, unless we can be fairly sure both of the answer likely to be reached, and that that answer is likely to emerge reasonably quickly, there is in our view an element of unfairness and short-sightedness in leaving the matter for subsequent judicial determination. Not only does the legal community have a right to know where it stands on important issues but more importantly, leaving the matter to be hammered out on the anvil of litigation exposes participants who end up on the losing side to big costs liabilities and may well inhibit the orderly development of the market.

We have, therefore, had no hesitation in recommending legislation, not only where we see it as necessary to change the law as we see it but also in some cases in order to confirm it. But this in turn raises a further issue. Should we aim for fairly comprehensive legislation on AI and private law generally, perhaps on the lines of the EU's Artificial Intelligence Act,[12] or even more extensive than that? Or should we engage in a more targeted, specifically problem-based approach equivalent to, say, the Electronic Commerce (EC Directive) Regulations 2002[13] on digitisation?

We would opt for the latter. This is for two reasons. First, as a rule technological innovation in AI progresses at a far greater pace than the rather cumbersome legislative process can keep up with. This creates a real risk that the work that goes into creating any rigid or supposedly comprehensive statutory framework will be wasted when it quickly becomes outdated, and that legislatures may lack the willingness to engage in the very large amount of work necessary for regular updating

[9] For a particularly illuminating analysis of the limits of judges in using existing doctrines to respond to challenges posed by new technologies, see R Brownsword, *The Future of Governance – A Radical Introduction to Law* (Oxford: Routledge, 2025), especially Chs 8 and 12.

[10] See Chapter 4.

[11] See Chapter 7.

[12] Regulation (EU) 2024/1689, in effect from 1 August 2024 and due to be in force from 2 August 2026.

[13] SI 2002/2013.

exercises.[14] Secondly, legislative bodies must, as a matter of practical politics, reconcile competing interests across diverse sectors, from finance to healthcare, while simultaneously contending with the rapid pace of technological evolution. If we were to opt for an AI code or general legislative attempt to cover the effect of AI on private law, this would lead to a risk either of a code that skated over important issues, or an illogical and uneven legislative scheme depending on the interests at stake.

We would, therefore, advocate a hybrid approach. Under this model, targeted legislation dealing with areas of particular difficulty would codify essential rules on (for example) agency, contractual capacity, and liability, providing clarity and uniformity where the law is most vulnerable to uncertainty. Simultaneously, common law doctrines would continue to evolve through judicial interpretation, allowing courts to address novel or unforeseen AI scenarios in a flexible and context-sensitive manner. This dual pathway balances the need for legal certainty and predictability with the adaptability required to accommodate rapidly evolving technologies, ensuring that English private law remains both principled and practically operable in an AI-driven environment.

Of course, determining the optimum point for legislative intervention is a difficult question. As several commentators have highlighted, premature intervention risks stifling innovation[15] and may result in statutory solutions that fail to address the legal challenges posed by increasingly sophisticated intelligent machines.[16] In our view, the European Union may have jumped the gun by attempting to legislate too early (and arguably too rigidly)[17] through the Artificial Intelligence Act 2024. By contrast, the United Kingdom has pursued a less interventionist approach at this stage, aiming to position itself as a leading AI innovation hub in Europe.[18] While this may be a sensible short-term strategy, offering potential political and

[14] History has repeatedly shown that legislative agility does not necessarily guarantee regulatory success. For example, the Computer Misuse Act 1990 was enacted in response to early hacking incidents during the 1980s. However, within only a few years, rapid developments in networking, data sharing, and cybercrime rendered many of its provisions outdated. The 1990 Act, for instance, failed to anticipate distributed attacks, botnets, and the use of malware for data theft – all of which have since become commonplace. Although the legislation has been amended several times, most notably in 2006 and 2015, these efforts have only partially addressed its shortcomings, and the Act remains widely criticised as technologically obsolete.

[15] See RA Epstein, 'Can Technological Innovation Survive Governmental Regulation' (2013) 36 *Harvard Journal of Law & Public Policy* 87 and AA Gikay, 'Risks, Innovation, and Adaptability in the UK's Incrementalism versus the European Union's Comprehensive Artificial Intelligence Regulation' (2024) 32 *International Journal of Law and Information Technology* 1. *Cf* A Bradford, 'The False Choice between Digital Regulation and Innovation' (2024) 118 *Northwestern Law Review* 377.

[16] See Brownsword (n 3) Ch 20, discussing the role of the law as a governance mechanism in a high-tech world.

[17] This is a view that several commentators also share. See, for example, M Almada and A Radu, 'The Brussels Side-Effect: How the AI Act Can Reduce the Global Reach of EU Policy' (2024) 25 *German Law Journal* 646 and N Sousa e Silva, 'The Artificial Intelligence Act: A Critical Overview' (2025) 16 *Journal of Intellectual Property, Information Technology and E-Commerce Law* 2.

[18] See Department for Science, Innovation and Technology, *Pro-Innovation Approach to AI Regulation* (Command Paper 813, 3 August 2023).

economic benefits, the growing volume of disputes reaching the courts across various areas of private law, coupled with AI's expanding role in commercial and everyday life, suggests that the time is ripe to begin deliberating on the legal solutions proposed in this book. AI is rapidly transforming commercial practices and the way we conduct business, and it is clear that relying solely on judges to stretch and reinvent legal principles and doctrines largely developed in the previous century will be insufficient to manage the legal complexities likely to arise in the 2030s.

BIBLIOGRAPHY

Books and Other Publications

Anson, R (ed), *Lindley & Banks on Partnership*, 21st edn (London, Sweet & Maxwell, 2024)

Arden, M et al (eds), *Buckley on the Companies Acts*, 15th edn (London, LexisNexis, 2000)

Beale, H (ed), *Chitty on Contracts*, 35th edn (London, Sweet & Maxwell, 2023)

Berry, M et al (eds), *Supervised and Unsupervised Learning for Data Science* (Cham, Springer, 2020)

Bostrom, N and Ćirković, MM (eds), *Global Catastrophic Risks* (Oxford, Oxford University Press, 2008)

Brindle, M and Cox, R, *Law of Bank Payments*, 5th edn (London, Sweet & Maxwell, 2017)

Brownsword, R, *The Future of Governance – A Radical Introduction to Law* (Abingdon, Routledge, 2025)

—— *Technology, Humans and Discontent with Law* (Abingdon, Routledge, 2024)

—— *Rethinking Law, Regulation and Technology* (Cheltenham, Edward Elgar, 2022)

—— *Law 3.0: Rules, Regulation, and Technology* (Abingdon, Routledge, 2020)

Burgess, P, *AI and the Rule of Law – The Necessary Evolution of A Concept* (Oxford, Hart Publishing, 2024)

Burrows, A, *Law of Restitution*, 3rd edn (Oxford, Oxford University Press, 2011)

Chen, IG et al (eds), *Big Data Health and Bioethics* (Cambridge, Cambridge University Press, 2008)

Clarke, M and Soyer, B (eds), *The Insurance Act 2015 – A New Regime for Commercial and Marine Insurance Law* (Oxford, Informa Law, 2017)

Department for Science, Innovation and Technology, *Pro-Innovation Approach to AI Regulation* (Cm 2023/813) (2023)

DiMatteo, L et al (eds), *The Cambridge Handbook of Smart Contracts, Blockchain Technology and Digital Platforms* (Cambridge, Cambridge University Press, 2019)

Donnelly-Lazarov, B (ed), *Neurolaw and Responsibility for Action* (Cambridge, Cambridge University Press, 2018)

Dworkin, R, *Taking Rights Seriously* (London, Duckworth, 1978)

Finn, PD, *Fiduciary Obligations* (Sydney, Law Book Co, 1977)

Goddard, D, *Making Laws That Work* (Oxford, Hart Publishing, 2022)

Hart, H, *Punishment and Responsibility – Essays in the Philosophy of Law* (New York, Oxford University Press, 1968)

Himmelreich, S et al (eds), *Oxford Handbook of AI Governance* (Oxford, Oxford University Press, 2024)

Holmes, OW *The Common Law* (Boston, Little, Brown & Co, 1881)

Insurance Institute, *AI and Big Data – Implications for the Insurance Industry in Canada* (2021)

Kitchin, R, *Data Revolution: Big Data, Open Data, Data Infrastructure and Their Consequences* (London, Sage Publications, 2014)

Księżak, P and Wojtczak, S, *Toward a Conceptual Network for the Private Law of Artificial Intelligence* (Cham, Springer, 2023)

Lavy, M and Hervey, M, *The Law of Artificial Intelligence*, 2nd edn (London, ThomsonReuters 2024)

Law Commission, *Artificial Intelligence and the Law* (discussion paper, July 2025)

—— *Smart Legal Contracts: Advice to Government* (Law Com CP 563)

—— *Electronic Execution of Documents* (Law Com No 386 (2019))

—— *Insurance Contract Law: Business Disclosure: Warranties, Insurer's Remedies for Fraudulent Claims; and Late Payment* (Law Com No 353 (2014))

Marsh Insurance Brokers, *Artificial Intelligence Applications in Financial Services* (2019) https://www.marsh.com/content/dam/marsh/Documents/PDF/UK-en/artificial-intelligence-applications-in-financial-services.pdf
McGurk, B, *Data Profiling and Insurance Law* (Oxford, Hart Publishing, 2019)
Martin-Bariteau, F and Scassa, T (eds), *Artificial Intelligence and the Law in Canada* (Toronto, LexisNexis, 2022)
Mitchell, C et al, *Goff & Jones the Law of Unjust Enrichment*, 10th edn (London, Sweet & Maxwell, 2022)
Nielsen, M, *Neural Networks and Deep Learning* (Determination Press, 2015)
Oakley, A (ed), *Trends in Contemporary Trust Law* (Oxford, Oxford University Press, 1997)
Oberdiek, J, *Philosophical Foundations of the Law of Torts* (Oxford, Oxford University Press, 2014)
Ord, T, *The Precipice: Existential Risk and the Future of Humanity* (New York, Hachette, 2020)
Owen, D (ed), *Philosophical Foundations of Tort Law* (Oxford, Clarendon Press, 1995)
Pearly, J and Mackenzie, D, *The Book of Why: The New Science of Cause and Effect* (New York, Basic Books, 2018)
Posner, R, *The Problematics of Moral and Legal Theory* (Cambridge, MA, Belknap Press, 2002)
Powell, J (ed), *Jackson & Powell on Professional Liability*, 9th edn (London, Sweet & Maxwell, 2021)
Reed, C, *AI Fairness and Beyond – Law, Regulation and Technology* (Oxford, Hart Publishing, 2024)
Reynolds, F and Watts, P (eds), *Bowstead & Reynolds on Agency*, 23rd edn (London, Sweet & Maxwell, 2023)
Ryle, G, *The Concept of Mind* (London, Hutchinson & Co, 1949)
SCOR, *The Impact of Artificial Intelligence on the (Re)insurance Sector* (2018)
Shanahan, M, *The Technological Singularity* (Cambridge, MA, MIT Press, 2015)
Soyer, B, *Marine Insurance Fraud* (Oxford, Informa Law, 2014)
Soyer, B and Gurses, O, *Insurability of Emerging Risks: Law Theory and Practice* (Oxford, Hart Publishing, 2025)
Tettenborn, A (ed), *Clerk & Lindsell on Torts*, 24th edn (London, Sweet & Maxwell, 2024)
Tucker, L et al (eds), *Lewin on Trusts*, 20th edn (London, Sweet & Maxwell, 2024)
Wiesmuller, S, *The Relational Governance of Artificial Intelligence* (Cham, Springer, 2023)
World Economic Forum, *Artificial Intelligence in Financial Services* (White Paper, 2025)
—— *Artificial Intelligence and Cyber Security: Balancing Risks and Awards* (White Paper, 2025)

Articles and Web Sources

Abbott, R, 'The Reasonable Computer: Disrupting the Paradigm of Tort Liability' (2018) 86 *George Washington Law Review* 1
Afghan, S, 'What Should Be Our Ethical, Legal and Regulatory Standards for AI in Financial Services? Part 1' (2022) 37 *Journal of International Banking Law & Regulation* 472
Almada, M and Radu, A, 'The Brussels Side-Effect: How the AI Act Can Reduce the Global Reach of EU Policy' (2024) 25 *German Law Journal* 646
Babu, VS and Banana, K, 'A Study on Narrow Artificial Intelligence' (2024) 24 *International Journal of Engineering Science & Advanced Technology* 210
Bajwa, J et al, 'Artificial Intelligence in Healthcare: Transforming the Practice of Medicine' (2021) 8(2) *Future Healthcare Journal* 188
Barocas, S and Selbst, AD, 'Big Data's Disparate Impact' (2016) 104 *California Law Review* 671
Bathaee, Y, 'The Artificial Black Box and the Failure of Intent and Causation' (2018) 31 *Harvard Journal of Law & Technology* 889
Bradford, A, 'The False Choice between Digital Regulation and Innovation' (2024) 118 *Northwestern Law Review* 377
Brown, L, 'Artificial Intelligence & Trusts and Trustees: A New Dawn of Investment Opportunities and Risks?' (2025) 31 *Trusts & Trustees* 210

Brown, R, 'Property Ownership and the Legal Personhood of Artificial Intelligence' (2021) 30 *Information & Communications Technology Law* 208
Brozek, B and Jakubiec, M, 'On the Legal Responsibility of Autonomous Machines' (2017) 25 *Artificial Intelligence and Law* 293
Burrell, J, 'How the Machine "Thinks": Understanding Opacity in Machine Learning Algorithms' (2016) 2 *Big Data Society* 1
Burrows, A, 'We Do This at Common Law but That in Equity' (2002) 22 *Oxford Journal of Legal Studies* 1
Cabral, T, 'Liability and Artificial Intelligence in the EU: Assessing the Adequacy of the Current Product Liability Directive' (2020) 27 *Maastricht Journal of European & Comparative Law* 615
Calo, R, 'Robotics and the Lessons of Cyber Law' (2015) 103 *California Law Review* 513
Capper, D, 'The Unconscionable Bargain in the Common Law World' (2010) 126 *Law Quarterly Review* 403
Chesterman, S, 'Artificial Intelligence and the Limits of Legal Personality' (2020) 69(4) *International & Comparative Law Quarterly* 819
Chopra, S and White, L, 'Artificial Agents and the Contracting Problem: A Solution via an Agency Analysis' (2009) *University of Illinois Journal of Law Technology & Policy* 363
Devenney, J, 'Developing Product Liability Networks for AI systems in the Medical Context' (2025) 76(1) *Northern Ireland Legal Quarterly* 118
Dheu, O and De Bruyne, J, 'Artificial Intelligence and Tort Law: A "Multi-faceted" Reality' (2023) 31 *European Review of Private Law* 261
Diamantis, M, 'Employed Algorithms: A Labor Model of Corporate Liability for AI' (2023) 72 *Duke Law Journal* 797
Doomen, J, 'Artificial Intelligence Entity as A Legal Person' (2023) 32 *Info & Communications Technology Law* 277
Edwards, L and Veale, M, 'Slave to the Algorithm? Why A "Right to Explanation" Is Probably Not the Remedy You Are Looking For?" (2017) 16 *Duke Law & Technology Review* 18
Epstein, R, 'Can Technological Innovation Survive Governmental Regulation' (2013) 36 *Harvard Journal of Law & Public Policy* 87
Ferran, E, 'Corporate Attribution and the Directing Mind and Will' (2011) 127 *Law Quarterly Review* 239
Forrest, KB, 'The Ethics and Challenges of Legal Personhood for AI' (2023) 133 *Yale Law Journal* 1175
Ftiti, Z et al, 'Insurance Fraud Detection: Evidence from Artificial Intelligence and Machine Learning' (2022) 62 *Research in International Business & Finance* 101744
Geneva Association, *Promoting Responsible Artificial Intelligence in Insurance* (2020) https://www.genevaassociation.org/sites/default/files/research-topics-document-type/pdf_public/
—— *Big Data and Insurance: Implications for Innovation, Competition and Privacy* (2018)
Gikay, A, 'Risks, Innovation, and Adaptability in the UK's Incrementalism versus the European Union's Comprehensive Artificial Intelligence Regulation' (2024) 32 *International Journal of Law and Information Technology* 1
Gray, K et al, 'Random Forest-Based Similarity Measures for Multi-Modal Classification of Alzheimer's Disease' (2013) 65 *NeuroImage* 167
Green, L, 'Positivism and the Inseparability of Law and Morals' (2008) 83 *New York University Law Review* 1035
Green, S, 'Smart Contracts, Interpretation and Rectification' (2018) *Lloyd's Maritime & Commercial Law Quarterly* 234
Gürses, O, 'The Supreme Court on Business Interruption Insurance and COVID-19: Financial Conduct Authority v. Arch Insurance (UK) Ltd' (2021) 32 *King's Law Journal* 71
Handley, K, 'Exclusion Clauses for Fraud' (2003) 119 *Law Quarterly Review* 537
Hart, H, 'Positivism and the Separation of Law and Morals' (1958) 71 *Harvard Law Review* 593
Hewitson, R, 'Electronic Signatures and Contracts for the Sale of Land' (2021) *Conveyancer* 120
Hildebrandt, M, 'Law as Information in the Era of Data-Driven Agency' (2016) 79 *Modern Law Review* 1

Hoffmann, L, 'Language and Lawyers' (2018) 134 *Law Quarterly Review* 553
Howarth, M, 'A Note on the Objective of Objectivity in Contract' (1987) 103 *Law Quarterly Review* 527
—— 'The Meaning of Objectivity in Contract' (1984) 100 *Law Quarterly Review* 265
Huberman, P, 'A Theory of Vicarious Liability for Autonomous-Machine-Caused Harm' (2021) 58 *Osgoode Hall Law Journal* 233
Johnson, D, 'Computer Systems: Moral Entities, But Not Moral Agents' (2008) 8 *Ethics & IT* 195
Kaushal, S and Kumar, S, 'Artificial Intelligence in Agriculture' (2023) *International Journal of Science and Research* 1682
Knight, W, 'The Dark Secret of the Heart of AI' (2017) 120 *MIT Technology Review* 54
Lior, A, 'Insuring AI: The Role of Insurance in Artificial Intelligence Regulation' (2022) 35 *Harvard Journal of Law & Technology* 467
Lowd, D and Rooshenas, A, 'Learning Markov Networks with Arithmetic Circuits' (2013) 21 *Artificial Intelligence & Statistics* 406
Lucy, W, 'The Death of Law: Another Obituary' (2022) 18(1) *Cambridge Law Journal* 109
McAuley, F, 'Mens Rea in the Brain: New Frontier or Dead End?' (2025) 141 *Law Quarterly Review* 437
Macdonald-Eggers, P, 'Remedies for the Failure to Observe the Utmost Good Faith' (2003) *Lloyd's Maritime and Commercial Law Quarterly* 249
McLaughlan, D, 'A Better Way of Making Sense of Contracts?' (2016) 132 *Law Quarterly Review* 577
Marrone, R et al, 'How Does Narrow AI Impact Human Creativity' (2024) *Creativity Research Journal* 1
Meggitt, G, 'Business Not as Usual – The Financial Conduct Authority v Arch and Others' (2022) 4 *Journal of Business Law* 257
Nikolinakos, N, 'Aligning Liability Rules with the Digital Age and Circular Economy: The Revised EU Product Liability Directive' (2025) 31 *Computer & Telecommunications Law Review* 126
Norum, S, 'Changing All the Time: AI's Impact on Humanity's Role in Common Law Development and Interpretation' (2023) 103 *Boston University Law Review* 2215
Novelli, C et al, 'A Conceptual Framework for Legal Personhood and Its Application to AI' (2022) 13 *Jurisprudence* 194
Ooi, V, 'Contracts Formed by Software: An Approach from the Law of Mistake' (2022) *Journal of Business Law* 97
O'Sullivan, D, 'Developing O'Brien' (2002) 118 *Law Quarterly Review* 337
Potts, K, 'A (t)test for the Traditional Deed? Examining the Scope of Electronic and Smart Deeds: Part 1' (2025) *Conveyancer* 69
Procopie, L, 'Are Smart Contracts Actually Contracts? How Smart Contracts Can Work Globally" (2021) 36 *Journal of International Banking and Regulation* 25
PwC, *Explainable AI: Driving Business Value through Greater Understanding* (2018) https://www.pwc.co.uk/audit-assurance/assets/explainable-ai.pdf
Quest, D, 'Robo-advice and Artificial Intelligence: Legal Risks and Issues' (2019) 34 *British Journal of International Banking & Finance Law* 6
Sage, N, 'Reconciling Contract Law's Objective and Subjective Standards' (2023) 86 *Modern Law Review* 1422
Saputro, AR et al, 'Analysis of Deep Neural Networks for Automobile Insurance Claim Prediction' (2019) *Communications in Computer and Information Science* 114
Scholz, L, 'Algorithmic Contracts' (2017) 20 *Stanford Tech Law Review* 128
Schönberger, S, 'Artificial Intelligence in Healthcare: A Critical Analysis of the Legal and Ethical Implications' (2019) 27 *International Journal of Law & Information Technology* 171
Sousa e Silva, N, 'The Artificial Intelligence Act: Critical Overview' (2025) 16 *Journal of Intellectual Property, Information Technology and E-Commerce Law* 2
Soyer, B, 'Use of Big Data Analytics and Sensor Technology in Consumer Insurance Context: Legal and Practical Challenges' (2022) 81 *Cambridge Law Journal* 165

Soyer, B and Tettenborn, A, 'Artificial Intelligence and Civil Liability – Do We Need A New Regime?' (2023) 30 *International Journal of Law & Information Technology* 385

——'Mapping (Utmost) Good Faith in Insurance Law – Future Conditional?' (2016) 132 *Law Quarterly Review* 618

Sprankling, J, 'Trade Secrets in the Artificial Intelligence Era' (2024) 76 *South Carolina Law Review* 181

Stevens, R, 'Vicarious Liability or Vicarious Action?' (2007) 123 *Law Quarterly Review* 30

Waldron, J, 'Ego-Bloated Hovel' (2000) 94 *Northwestern University Law Review* 587

Watcher, S et al, 'Counterfactual Explanations without Opening the Black Box: Automated Decisions and the GDPR' (2018) 31 *Harvard Journal of Law & Technology* 841

Whayman, D, 'The Rectification (and Construction) of Computer-Generated Documents' (2019) 30 *King's Law Journal* 489

INDEX

www.ingramcontent.com/pod-product-compliance
Ingram Content Group UK Ltd.
Pitfield, Milton Keynes, MK11 3LW, UK
UKHW020817290926
15470UKWH00003B/1217

9 781509 990580